Rethinking International Relations

Rethinking International Relations

Fred Halliday

MACMILLAN

First published 1994 by
MACMILLAN PRESS LTD
Houndmills, Basingstoke, Hampshire RG21 2XS
and London
Companies and representatives
throughout the world

ISBN 0–333–58904–1 hardcover
ISBN 0–333–58905–X paperback

A catalogue record for this book is available
from the British Library.

10 9 8 7 6 5 4 3
03 02 01 00 99 98 97 96

Printed in Hong Kong

Contents

Acknowledgements

The author and publishers are grateful to the following for permission to reproduce copyright material: Routledge Journals and the editors of *Economy and Society*; the editors of *Millennium, The Journal of International Studies*; Cambridge University Press; the editors of *New Left Review*; Blackwell Publishers and the editors of *Political Studies*; and the editors of the *Review of International Studies*.

Preface

The chapters in this book are elements of a double response – to developments in political and social theory and in the academic study of International Relations, and to changes in the international system itself over the past years, most particularly the collapse of the Soviet bloc. In this sense, and in what may be a reversal of conventional practice, the general, and in part theoretical, reflections follow from a number of more concrete studies of the international system and of the central conflicts within it which I have already published, most specifically *The Making of the Second Cold War* (1983) and *Cold War, Third World* (1989) and a number of third world case studies. In so doing, I hope not merely to extend these reflections on International Relations, but also to draw out assumptions and questions which were, to a greater or lesser extent, present within them. International Relations, like all branches of knowledge, faces two dangers – that of factual accounts devoid of theoretical reflection, explanatory or ethical, and that of theorising unanchored in, or tested by, the analysis of history itself. My hope is that these essays, as responses to ideas and to events, will find a passage between these two dangers. While making some general observations on the nature of the international system and of where analysis of it may proceed, I have also examined some more particular issues. My intention is to follow this overview of the subject with two further theoretical and historical volumes, one on the role of revolutions in the international system, the other on the ethical tension between nationalism and internationalism.

In preparing these essays I have benefited from the stimulation and criticism of many friends and colleagues over the past decade. In particular I would like to thank my colleagues and students in the International Relations (IR) Department at the London School of Economics (LSE) who have, through individual contacts and through the General Seminar in IR, provided many a challenge and stimulus. Martina Langer of the International Relations Department was ever helpful and speedy in assisting preparation of the text. I would also like to thank the members of the '1990s' International Relations discussion group, and of the Transnational Institute, for providing congenial intellectual contexts for the working through of many of these ideas. My greatest thanks are to my partner, Maxine Molyneux, whose support and ideas have been as enriching as they have been indispensable.

While the chapters of this book have been updated and considerably developed, many of the ideas and arguments contained in this book draw on a set of articles and essays published over the last few years: in particular parts of Chapters 1 and 2 have appeared in *Political Studies* (vol. 38, no. 3, September 1990), *Economy and Society* (vol. 18, no. 3 August 1989) and *Millennium* (vol. 22, no. 2, summer 1993); an earlier version of Chapter 4 was published in *Millennium* (vol. 16, no. 2, 1987); of Chapter 5 in *Millennium* (vol. 21, no. 3, winter 1992); of Chapter 6 in *Review of International Studies* (vol. 16, no. 3, summer 1990); of Chapter 7 in *Millennium* (vol. 17, no. 3, winter 1988); of Chapter 8 in Mike Bowker and Robin Brown (eds.) *From Cold War to Collapse: Theory and World Politics in the 1980s* (Cambridge University Press, 1993); of Chapter 9 in *Contention* (no. 2, winter 1992). Chapters 10 and 11 include material from *New Left Review* (no. 193, May–June 1992) and from the Barclay Enterprise Lecture, given at LSE, 17 May 1993, 'Sleep-Walking Through History: The New World and its Discontents', later published by the London School of Economics Centre for the Study of Global Governance.

London   FRED HALLIDAY

1

Introduction: The Pertinence of the 'International'

The purposes of this chapter are two-fold: first, to examine what is meant by the term 'international' and the confusion it occasions, and secondly, to provide a brief account of the growth in the discipline, and the factors underlying this development. International Relations (IR) has occupied an uneasy, often marginal, place in the study and teaching of the social sciences. Yet its subject matter is, in the simplest terms, clear enough, comprising three forms of interaction – relations between states, non-state or 'transnational' relations across frontiers, and the operations of the system as a whole, within which states and societies are the main components. While they may vary in the stress they lay on each of these forms of interaction, all theories of the 'international' propose some explanation of each: indeed the major debates within IR revolve, to a greater or lesser extent, around these three dimensions and the primacy of one or the other.

The 'International' in Perspective

Theoretical diversity is a strength, not a weakness of International Relations.[1] The difficulties it has experienced lie not in any theoretical uniformity or stasis, but above all in its methodological and historical bases. Unduly defensive about its own methodological and disciplinary strengths, IR has, in the main, been treated as an appendix to other, more established, subjects. National politics, economics and sociology have been the main

1

focus of these disciplines: the 'international' has for long been a supernumerary element, an option for students, a penultimate chapter for the scholar.

The dramatic change in the status of the 'international' in the past decade or two has only compounded this. Now that it has become fashionable to stress the pervasiveness of the 'international', and the displacement of national specificity by 'globalisation', this once neglected dimension has become the property of all: banishment has given way to promiscuity. Yet in the process, the degree of internationalisation has been distorted – overstated for the current world, and located far too simplistically in changes since 1945 or the 1960s. This historical foreshortening takes several forms, such as an unqualified assertion of the outdatedness of the nation-state or of the role of force, in the case of the literature on transnationalism, or the invocation of a new age of 'post-modernity'. The continued adaptation of the global and the particular – in politics, culture, economics – is understated, and the much longer histories of international processes, many of them going back to the workings of the international system in the sixteenth century, are obscured.

These two approaches – denial and exaggeration – are but two sides of the same coin, in that the the proponents of the latter make their point by contrasting the contemporary world with a period when, supposedly, states, nations, societies were separate and insulated from each other. 'Internationalisation' did not, however, begin with a world financial market or Cable News Network and its world-wide broadcasts. Nationalism itself, despite its apparently individual and discrete evolution and character, and its celebration of the specific, is an international process, a product of intellectual, social and economic change shared by societies and stimulated by their interaction over the past two centuries.[2] One can indeed argue that far from the 'international' arising from the national, and from a gradual expansion of links between discrete entities, the real process has been the other way around: the history of the modern system is one both of internationalisation and of the breakdown of pre-existing flows of peoples, religion, trade into separate entities; the precondition for the formation of the modern nation-state was the development of an international economy and culture within which these distinct states then coalesced.

Writers in Britain and the USA make much of the ways in which, over the past twenty or thirty years, forms of political control and sovereignty have been eroded by transnational processes: but this is a gigantic historical conceit, born of the particular, and very exceptional, national histories of these states. Of the 190 or so sovereign states in the world today, only half a dozen have escaped foreign occupation in the past two centuries. Even in the case of Britain, for example, a country where insular consciousness is greater than in most, and one of that half-dozen countries to escape foreign occupation, there is no purely national history: from Julius Caesar, St Augustine, the Anglo-Saxon invasions, through 1066, the Reformation, the emergence of the modern state in conflict with European neighbours, to the time of empire and world war, the national and the international have always interacted. The United States of America has escaped foreign occupation since independence in 1783: but its whole development has been one of interaction with the international – the acquisition by force and purchase of most of its territory from other states and peoples, the mass influx of populations from other countries, the expansion from around 1890 of US financial and industrial power across the world, the shaping of its economy and political system by international conflict.

In both countries the myth of national insulation compounds the other constitutive myth of their political development, that of non-violent evolution: while they have subsequently been able to acquire legitimacy through the gradual spread of democracy, both the United Kingdom and the United States were states created, and, on more than one occasion, maintained by force. What is more, even the briefest of comparative surveys will show, if only by implication, that the spread of democratic forms, and the arrival of universal suffrage was itself an international process, a result both of changing international norms, and of the impact on different societies of international processes: industrialisation and the arrival of mass society on the one hand, the political pressures born of the two world wars on the other. The same applies to the history of national economies: trade, and state intervention, shaped by the needs of inter-state competition, have determined this process, from the planting of oaks and the building of roads, to the promotion of industry, technology and education. Equally, a process such as the demise of slavery, preserved in particularist and ethical terms, reflects broad changes in international trade and production.[3]

What is lived, and usually studied, as something that happened 'within' countries, turns out to be part of a much broader international process of political and economic change. Throughout 'national' histories, international competition, influence and example all play central formative roles. Taxation for military purposes, and the levying of taxes on trade, lie at the heart of the modern state: the British Customs and Excise department enjoys wide-ranging autonomy from government ministries because it has existed longer than any ministry. There can, therefore, be no purely national history of any state; equally there can be no theory of the economy, the state, or social relations, that denies the formative, not just residual or recent, impact of the international. Thus neither of the conventional approaches – denial and over-statement – do justice to a question that is common to all social scientists but which is, within its particular disciplinary optic, the constitutive concern of IR, namely the interaction of the national and international, the internal and the external.

Formative Influences

The subject of International Relations is, like all academic disciplines, located in more than one dimension. All the social sciences owe their origins, and development, to an interaction with the outside world: economics arose as a response to trade and industrialisation in the eighteenth and nineteenth centuries, sociology to the evolution of urban society, anthropology to the colonial encounter and so forth. Yet each also has its own agenda as a subject taught at university: a need to resist the fashions of the moment and the pressures of power in order to look with detachment at its subject-matter; a mission to use its substance and methods as a means of sharpening and training the minds of its students; and its own set of enduring disciplinary concerns.

These enduring concerns of International Relations, as evidenced by the usual range of courses offered, have two distinct aspects: one is broadly analytic – the role of the state in international relations, the problem of order in the absence of a supreme authority, the relationship between power and security, the interaction of economic with military strength, the causes of conflict and the bases of cooperation. The other is normative – the question of when and to what degree it is legitimate to use force, the obligations we owe the state and those not from our state, the place of morality in international relations, the rights and wrongs of intervention.

International Relations is, however, equally located in another dimension, that of the 'real', or perhaps accurately 'non-reflective', world. Nowhere in the broad spectrum of human activity does the mythical and the imagined play such a role in everyday discourse as in the field of the international. One has only got to think of the strengths of national identification and antipathy, the almost universal incidence of conspiracy theory and suspicion about 'foreigners', the extraordinary ignorance, even among the better educated, about other countries, and the ease with which those whose business it is to arouse public passions can do so by resort to misrepresentation of the foreign, the alien, the 'other'.

Of all the students of a social science taught in universities, those concerned with IR probably encounter the greatest degree of misunderstanding and ignorance, and engage in more ground-clearing, conceptual, ethical and factual, than any other. This alone, of course, gives the subject a definite relevance, even if it lends to the clarification of international issues a certain Sisyphean character. When apparently highly educated and experienced people can include in their discussions of the future international orientation of other countries such primitive stereotypes as 'the German mind', 'the Japanese psyche', then we are all reminded just how far we still have to go. The best that International Relations can do may be – in the sphere of its activity, to apply Freud's famous dictum on the purpose of psychoanalysis – to reduce neurosis to everyday common misery.

The relationship of the academic study of international relations to the outside world is of course shaped, and stimulatingly so, by other concerns. Some are evident, and some are not. The most obvious is that people feel that the international is important: it is a source of threat, most obviously military, it is an arena where great economic benefits and losses may be incurred, it is apparently more and more intrusive into everyday lives. The academic study of international relations began as an attempt to study the causes of the greatest international intrusion of all, namely war, and to develop means of reducing its incidence in the future. It has since gone on to encompass a broader agenda – of international economic activity in particular. As the world changes, so do the questions posed for the academic study of the international. The difficulty is that the very pressure of international issues, and the demand for analysis and commentary on them, can act not only as a stimulant and a corrective of academic thinking, but also as a warp; the result is that not only the curiosity of the outside world, but the very work undertaken in universities is shaped by what funders and policy-makers read in the morning papers. To determine the academic agenda of International Relations by such concerns is, however, dangerous, not only for the loss of independence but also for the loss of perspective, historical and conceptual. Economists are happy to comment on, and be consulted about, the future of the stock exchange or the rate of inflation, just as political scientists can proffer a view on the outcome of the next election: this is not, any more than it should be in the case of International Relations, the basis of what they teach in a university.

The pressure on International Relations is, however, all the greater because of another, less evident, factor, and that is what may be termed its theoretical invisibility. Except for those who make it their business to teach and study it at a university, the subject does not have a clear definition at all, beyond sage commentary on yesterday's news, or the odd flash of comparative and contemporary international history. Part of this arises from an everyday confusion about the word 'international'. The term itself, invented by Jeremy Bentham in 1780 to denote legal links between states, is a misnomer in terms of the subsequent meaning of the term 'nation', since the least of its concerns has been relations between nations in the sense that we use the term today. Nations and states may or may not coincide, but even when they do those relations that are conventionally called 'international' refer to what passes between the *governments* of those countries, not that which occurs between the respective national populations. Moreover, for most users of the term, the word 'international affairs' covers two quite different things, namely what in newspapers is included in the foreign pages: i.e. internal affairs, the domestic politics of other countries, and international affairs in the strict sense, namely relations between states and societies themselves.

The former is, in academic terms, the purview of regional and comparative politics: the latter alone is what forms the basis of the academic study, International Relations.

To this is added, however, a final and curious twist. Most people interested in a general way in the social sciences are aware of theoretical work in a range of fields, even if they cannot spell out what these theories actually say. Thus the average reader of the more serious newspapers or of the *New York Review of Books* will have heard of theorists of economics, Keynes or Friedman, and may well be aware of debates in philosophy, between Rawls and Nosick and their followers, or of the general ideas of Foucault and 'post-modernism'. In the case of International Relations this is certainly not the case: very few outside the subject are aware of any of those engaged in theoretical work in International Relations, let alone the issues involved. It is assumed that a brisk combination of current affairs and common sense, with the odd historical reference thrown in, can do the trick. The preservation of an adequate and creative balance between the two dimensions of International Relations, the academic and the policy-related, is therefore all the more difficult. Yet precisely because of the pull of the present, this is the more important to get right, or as right as possible.

The Emergence of Theory

In the remainder of this chapter, I shall try to provide a brief sketch of how theorisation of the international has proceeded. The development of IR, like that of all social sciences, is in fact a product not just of two, but of three concentric circles of influence: change and debate within the subject itself, the impact of developments in the world, but also the influence of new ideas within other areas of social science. While straightforward academic genealogies are common, these latter two influences receive less attention. IR has a very limited 'self-knowledge', let alone an adequate account of the extra-disciplinary factors acting on it. Yet in both forms these are evident enough: the major events of twentieth-century history (the First and Second World Wars, the Cold War and its aftermath) have shaped its focuses at least as much as inter-paradigm disputes. Like other social sciences IR has, however, tended to obscure some of these connections, for fear of loss of intellectual prestige. Thus the enlisting of 'realism' by the Cold War, or the role of the Vietnam War in promoting awareness of 'interdependence', are neglected. Equally, national differences, of history and society, have shaped analysis and research: what in the USA is a study of decision-making may become in Germany the analysis of the relation between democracy and foreign policy;[4] third world countries are concerned with foreign domination, developed ones with integration. More generally, the very 'historicity' of its concepts, their generation in particular contexts and, in analytic terms, their relevance to specific periods, is denied.

The linkage of intellectual history to history in general remains intermittent and obscure, as does, in a more restricted vein, the relation between IR and other trends in the social sciences. Issues of international theory and analysis have been present throughout much of classical political thought.[5] Thucydides on the causes of war, Machiavelli and Hobbes on the nature of power, Grotius on international law, Kant and Marx on preconditions for cosmopolitanism are but some of the most obvious antecedents. These considerations were, however, part of a broader theoretical endeavour – of history, law, philosophy, political theory – and only rarely emerged as reflections upon a distinctive analytic subject-matter, the 'international'.

As a separate academic discipline, International Relations is less than a century old. The study of international relations began in the aftermath of the First World War, focusing on the factors precipitating war and the means to prevent its recurrence. It was in that period that the first British university chairs and departments were established – at Aberystwyth, LSE and Oxford – while in the non-academic realm the Royal Institute of International Affairs was set up to guide public policy. Contemporaneously and for similar reasons, academic departments and the Council on Foreign Relations were established in the US.

The three constituent elements of IR – the inter-state, the transnational and the systemic – allow of many specialisations and varying theoretical approaches. IR today comprises as sub-fields, in addition to international theory as such (that is, the theorisation of these three elements), strategic studies, conflict and peace studies, foreign policy analysis, international political economy, international organisation, and a group of normative issues pertaining to war: obligation, sovereignty, rights. To these analytically distinct sub-fields must be added the range of regional specialisms where theoretical approaches are applied to, and refract, the study of individual states and groups of states. These may not involve different theoretical approaches but vary considerably in the relative emphasis they give to issues of, say, ideology or law, economics or military power. In the 1980s alone a range of new international issues were incorporated into the analytic compass of the subject and taught as distinct courses: sea-use and ocean politics, women and the international arena, the international relations of the third world, ecological questions, international dimensions of communication, to name but some.

The growth and variation in subject-matter within IR, already alluded to, parallel an evolution in theoretical approaches.[6] In its initial phase, IR sought to distinguish itself from those disciplines out of which it had emerged: thus it was distinct from international, that is, diplomatic, history in its comparative and theoretical approach; over time it separated itself from international law in adopting a positivist rather than normative approach and in analysing dimensions of international interaction beyond the legal. It was distinguished from political science as such in seeking to combine the political with the economic and military and in taking as its object of analysis not the internal political system of any one country, but the international system itself, one distinguished above all by the lack of sovereign authority and the greater salience of violence within it. Its theoretical evolution has none the less involved continued interaction with, and borrowing from, these disciplines as well as a growing interaction with other social sciences, notably economics. Two disciplines with which it might have been thought cognate, but with which it had very little relationship, were sociology and geography: while, as we shall see in Chapters 4 and 5, it utilised certain ideas from sociology, notably 'society', and while in its early period it intersected with the concerns of geopolitics, neither discipline had a major impact on IR. The result has been, amongst other things, that subsequent theoretical developments in these subjects have often not been recognised within IR. It is only recently, as it has overcome its early 'protectionist' phase, that IR has again begun openly to learn from and contribute to other areas of social science. The recent interest of historical sociology in the dominance of strategic and 'war-making' concerns within state formation, and of the degree to which international rather than endogenous factors have shaped state development, is one pertinent example of this latter process.

If IR had a parental discipline it was not so much history or political science as international law. In continental Europe, this pattern prevails in many departments. In its initial phase, after the First World War, IR adopted a predominantly legal approach, today erroneously presented as 'utopianism' or 'idealism'. This school, of 'peace through law', arose in part out of the liberalism of Woodrow Wilson and sought to limit or prevent war by international treaty, negotiation procedures and the growth of international organisations, notably the League of Nations. Academic critics of this approach often refer to it as 'utopianism', but this is, in three ways, a misleading categorisation: first, it confuses an attempt to regulate or improve international relations, a perfectly down-to-earth project, with the pursuit of an ideal, a 'utopia'; secondly, it ignores what was for Wilson a central precondition for the effectiveness of peace through law, namely the general spread of liberal democracy, something he was wrong in anticipating after the First World War, but which does have, as we shall see in Chapter 10, considerable implications for the international;[7] and, thirdly, in disparaging the 'utopians', these critics derogate from the concept and analysis of utopia itself, a valid and long-standing part of social and political theory.

Realism and Behaviouralism

With the crises of the 1930s, 'idealism' gave way to 'realism', initially in the work of E. H. Carr and later in the work of a range of US-based writers, including Hans Morgenthau, Henry Kissinger and Kenneth Waltz.[8] They took as their starting point states' pursuit of power, the centrality of military strength within that power, and the enduring inevitability of conflict in a world of multiple sovereignty. While not denying entirely a role for morality, law and diplomacy, realists laid greatest stress on armed might as an instrument of maintaining peace. They believed that the central mechanism for regulating conflict was the balance of power, through which undue strength of one state would be compensated for by increased strength or expanded alliances on the part of others: this was something inherent in the system but also capable of conscious promotion.

In a parallel development, a group of realists on the European side of the Atlantic developed what came to be known as the 'English School': Charles Manning, Martin Wight, Hedley Bull and Fred Northedge emphasised the degree to which the international system was 'anarchical', that is, without a central ruler.[9] They saw it not as straightforward chaos but as in a certain sense a 'society': that is, a group of states that interacted according to certain conventions. These included diplomacy, international law, the balance of power, the role of the great powers and, most controversially, war itself. This school has continued to produce work of consistent orientation and quality, evident in the writings of Alan James, Michael Donelan, James Mayall, Adam Watson and others.[10]

Realism became the dominant, if not sole, approach to the subject with the growth in academic study of international relations after the Second World War. It possessed a powerful and comprehensive explanation of international relations and conflict. It accorded with common sense the terms in which international affairs were discussed in much public debate. It had received a powerful, apparently incontrovertible, affirmation from the events of the 1930s and their consequences. Normally presumed as an evolution *within* the English-speaking world, realism came to articulate criticisms of the League of Nations that had, from the 1920s, been voiced by the German right.[11] Indeed, many of the central themes of realism appear as (domesticated) descendents of the militaristic and racist Social Darwinism of the late nineteenth and early twentieth centuries. At the same time, it would seem probable that the increased concern of political science in the 1930s with 'power' and the processes by which it is allocated, as distinct from formal constitutional procedures compounded this 'power politics' trend within the academic field of International Relations.[12]

The dominance of realism began to be challenged in the 1960s and has remained under pressure ever since.[13] From the early 1960s onwards, behaviouralism constituted an alternative to orthodox IR as it did to other branches of the social sciences at both the methodological and conceptual levels. Thus the new 'scientific' school of IR, almost wholly based in the US, sought to get away from the traditionalists' use of history and orthodox political terms such as 'state' to a new, quantifiable, study of what could be observed, i.e. 'behaviour', in this case international processes and interactions. Karl Deutsch studied the growth of international communications; James Rosenau focused on informal interactions, 'transnational linkages' between societies that bypassed orthodox state-to-state relations; Morton Kaplan developed more 'scientific' theorisations of the international systems.[14] A wide-ranging and often acerbic debate between 'traditionalists' and 'behaviouralists' in IR took place, mirroring in substance and tone many of the themes raised in the parallel discussions within political science. The strictures of Bernard Crick – the analyst of politics – on US political science found their parallel in IR. In this exchange, in which both sides rather overreached their philosophical and methodological competencies, the 'English' school stood firm, positing history and 'judgement' against what was seen as the vulgar and mistakenly 'scientific' approach of American political science.[15] To this we shall return in Chapter 2.

The overall attempt by the behaviouralists to supplant 'traditional' IR failed in three key respects. First, realism, and its later variant 'neo-realism', remained the dominant approach within the academic and policy-related study of international relations.[16] Secondly, the very theoretical challenge posed by behaviouralism, to supplant the pre-scientific study of the 'state' and other conventional, historical concepts with a new scientific theorisation was not taken far enough, above all because it failed to provide an alternative theorisation of the state itself. Thirdly, its theoretical – and fund-raising – promise, to come up with major new conclusions on the strength of data collection, was never fulfilled. In the end behaviouralism became an adjunct, rather than an alternative to, the orthodox state-centred approach. None the less, out of the behaviouralist challenge and later theorisations of 'transnational' and systemic factors, a number of major new sub-fields developed within the discipline, three of which merit special attention: foreign policy analysis, interdependence and international political economy. Thus, if realism and neo-realism remained predominant, they no longer had an intellectual or institutional monopoly within the subject. Offshoots of the behavioural approach, foreign policy analysis, interdependence and international political economy, were to achieve a permanent place in the overall discussion.

Foreign policy analysis, the study of the factors determining foreign policy outcomes and decisions in particular, was an ambitious and in many respects successful attempt to challenge the core tenets of realism.[17] In seeking to analyse how foreign policy is made, it rejected some of the central premises of realism: that the state can be treated as a unitary actor; that it can be deemed to act rationally, to maximise power or defend a national interest; that the internal character and influences of a country can be treated as not relevant to the study of its foreign policy – this latter a favourite claim of Waltz's in particular. Instead, foreign policy analysis examined the composition of the foreign-policy-making process – first in terms of bureaucratic and individual fragmentation and rivalry within the state itself, then in terms of the input of broader elements within the polity, including legislatures, the press, public opinion and ideology.

This approach opened up the possibility of something that had been precluded by realism's denial of the relevance of internal factors, and which brought it into fruitful interaction with work in political science, namely the comparative study of foreign policy making and of the ways in which different constitutional, historical and social endowments affect the formulation and implementation of foreign policy. The conclusion reached on this route, in international as much as in more domestic investigations, was that the premise of 'rationality' had to yield, in the face of bureaucratic infighting, unintended consequences, individual and group delusions, 'group think' and so forth. The presupposition that states could be treated as rational power-maximisers and calculators of a national interest was shown to be an inadequate, and often diversionary, basis for analysing foreign policies.

The most important challenge of foreign policy analysis was, however, to realism's claim that states could be treated uniquely as units in an environment, without reference to their internal structures and changes therein. What foreign policy analysis sought to show was not only that its approach, incorporating domestic factors, could provide a more persuasive account of the making of foreign policy, and of its irrationalities, but also that it was necessary to identify the ways in which the domestic environments and processes of countries were affected by external factors, whether or not the state was involved in this interaction. This was evidently the case with economic processes – changes in the world price of oil had effects on countries, whatever governments chose to do – and also with a range of ideological and political ones. Societies were interacting in ways that were 'transnational' rather than inter-state and these 'linkages' were in turn having an impact on foreign policy. Faced with such external challenges and influences, states acted to accommodate or pre-empt, depending on circumstances.

Foreign policy analysis, born out of the behaviouralist rejection of 'institutional' concepts, did not develop the theory of the state itself. It had other limitations too: a narrow, fetished, concern with decisions and a sociologically naive concept of the internal 'environment'. It therefore failed to take the opportunity which later, historical sociological, literature was to benefit from, of a comprehensive, combined, analysis of the internal and external roles of state. Yet it was foreign policy analysis's achievement to have opened this question up and made it possible to examine the internal–external relationship in a new light.

It was in this context that there emerged the distinct approach based on 'interdependence', a concept used to focus on how societies and states were becoming increasingly interlinked and what the consequences of this process were. The development of the literature on interdependence illustrates well the opportunities, and pitfalls, of recognising the domestic–international connection: while it provides a context for examining this link, it has often led to a simplification of the relationship and a facile assertion that all is now 'interdependent'.

'Interdependence' is a term that has been intermittently in vogue for over a century. In contemporary usage it originated as a concept in economics, where it had a comparatively clear meaning, according to which two economies were interdependent when there was a rough equality of power between them and when their mutual interaction was such as to make each significantly vulnerable to actions by the other. Interconnection produced vulnerability and hence acted to restrain what others might do. In its classical form, this was indeed the idea that increasing trade between nations would strengthen peace, an idea common prior to the First World War but often heard since. Its re-emergence in the 1970s was a response both to economic events – the decline of the dollar, the OPEC (Oil Producing and Exporting Countries) price rises – and to the political impact within the USA of the Vietnam War. In its 1970s formulation, and especially in the work of Robert Keohane and Joseph Nye, it rested on three propositions: that the state was losing its dominant position in international relations to 'non-state' actors and forces, such as multinational corporations; that there was no longer a hierarchy of international issues, with military and strategic affairs, 'high politics', at the top and economic and welfare issues, 'low politics', further down; and that military power was losing its salience in international relations.[18] Even if the realist view of a state-centric strategy-orientated world had been true of an earlier epoch, this was no longer the case, as old barriers broke down and economic and political forces paid less and less attention to the state.

Interdependence theory was criticised from a number of perspectives. Waltz argued that it was historically misconceived, since interdependence had in many respects been greater in earlier periods than in the present.[19] Waltz and others saw increased interaction as a stimulant of conflict: 'good fences make good neighbours' they intoned. Northedge and Bull contested the view that it was either true or desirable for states to lose control over populations, or to cede responsibility for managing international affairs: for all the talk of 'global issues' and the universal 'commons', it was states who, for better or worse, remained responsible for resolving these questions, of peace, famine, ecology. Individuals identified as much as ever with the state and looked to it to perform security, representation and welfare functions. Marxists pointed out that interdependence applied, at best, to a small group of developed Western countries and that its application to North–South relations concealed asymmetries of power and wealth that the imperialist system was compounding.

The idea of interdependence was also dented by the deterioration in international relations in the latter part of the 1970s and early 1980s. It appeared less evident, in both East–West and third world contexts, that military power had lost its salience; international relations seemed to be concentrated once again and in a rather traditional manner on states in general, and great powers in particular; the supersession or circumvention of the state appeared in many cases to take a malign form, rather than the benign one that liberal exponents of interdependence theory had implied –

whether in situations of civil war (Lebanon, Sri Lanka), or in the growth of transnational processes that were unwelcome – terrorism, pollution and capital flight amongst them. 'Non-state actors', like new social movements, were not all benign: just as the former included fanatical religious sects and racist youth movements, in addition to Oxfam, Bandaid and Amnesty International, the latter category included the Mafia and the Medellin Cartel.

International Relations since the 1970s

The challenges to realism of behaviouralism, interdependence and international political economy eroded the former's monopoly on the subject and produced a more diverse and competitive discipline. This in its turn encouraged a variety of other approaches to emerge, both in vindication of realism and in further rejection of it.

The reaffirmation of realism, 'neo-realism', to which I shall return in Chapter 2, has engaged with the concerns of international political economy but sought to re-establish the primacy of states, and politico-military concerns, within the overall analysis. Thus Stephen Krasner ascribed the failure of third world states to gain acceptance for their New International Economic Order not to their economic weakness as such, but rather to their weakness as states and their espousal of principles that clashed with those of the dominant states in the international system.[20] Robert Tucker stressed the continued role of Great Powers and military force in maintaining the international system and ascribed the poverty of third world states to endogenous political and economic factors.[21] The central tenets of neo-realism were, however, most clearly laid out in two major works of the late 1970s – Hedley Bull's *The Anarchical Society* and Kenneth Waltz's *Theory of International Relations*: their arguments are reviewed critically in, respectively, Chapters 5 and 2.[22] Both recognised, and sought to refute, the criticisms of the past two decades. Thus they stressed the primacy of states in the international system, and the subordinate power and role of 'non-state' actors. At the same time, they argued that economic processes, like other transnational activities, required states to provide the security and regulation needed for their continuation. They were sceptical of claims that interdependence was on the increase and they stressed the continued importance of the great powers in managing international relations, for better or worse.

If 'neo-realism' responded to criticism of realism by reasserting traditional tenets, others took the analysis of IR even further away from established orthodoxy. In a radical extension of behaviourism, John Burton in his *World Society* and other works developed a theory of international relations based upon individual needs and the system of issue-related linkages established by such needs.[23] The international system was, therefore, in Burton's view, a cobweb of issue-defined interactions, within which the specific structures of military and state power played a distinct but not exclusive or predominant role. With a special emphasis upon the resolution of conflict through small-group and individual mediation, Burton's work broke flamboyantly with the state-centric view of international relations by introducing not only an alternative analysis but also an alternative approach to policy. In a parallel development, the World Order Modelling Project, Richard Falk developed a theory of alternatives and oppositions to state power at the international level based again on human needs and transnational, non-state, interactions.

The growing relationship of Marxism to IR constituted another, unorthodox, development in the 1970s and 1980s, which will be discussed at greater length in Chapter 3. As already indicated, Marxism's point of entry into IR was on the issue of underdevelopment, and in many ways remained confined to this area. Not only was the alternative, more classical, Marxist view on development downplayed, according to which it was in capitalism's interest to develop the third world, but Marxist concepts with more relevance to the central concerns of IR – on the causes of war, role of classes, character of ideology – were not applied to international analysis in the same way. In arguing for the primacy of an alternative agenda – North–South relations and international structures of exploitation – Marxism left the main terrain of International Relations relatively unscathed. This insulation of IR from Marxist influence, to a degree perhaps greater than in any other area of the social sciences, was of course compounded by the predominance of American writing on the subject, reflecting an intellectual climate from which Marxism was largely absent.

Only in the 1980s did this situation began to change. Within the

writing on international political economy, there was an application of Marxist concepts to analyse the causes and consequences of
an increasingly internationalised market and the new forms it was
taking. Within the writing on foreign policy analysis, it became
possible to examine not only how bureaucratic and constitutional
factors affect policy outcomes but also how these are themselves
shaped by broader historical social and economic factors, including
class factors, within the country concerned.[24] The role of military
production sectors in promoting international confrontation and
alarm is one obvious, and not negligible, example of this.

The growth of a historical sociological literature around issues of
international competition and state formation, itself engaging
critically with Marxism, provides a particularly fruitful opportunity
for new work on exogenous–endogenous relations and on the ways
in which states interact with the world system.[25] This literature has
made it possible, more than ever before, to discuss perhaps the
most deeply embedded and neglected element in realism, namely
the legal-territorial conception of the state which it uses, a subject
to which I shall return in Chapter 4. Much of the debate between
realism and Marxism has revolved around the question of the
state, yet it has too rarely been recognised that this involves two
quite distinct conceptions of 'state': the legal-territorial concept,
borrowed by IR from law and traditional political science, enables
one set of questions to be addressed and theorised; the alternative
concept, however, borrowed from Marxism and Weberian
sociology, in which the state is seen as an administrative-coercive
entity, an apparatus within a country or society rather than that
country as a whole, allows a very different set of questions to be
analysed. These include the vexed issues of how the international
and the domestic interact, and how changing relations of states to
peoples are affected by international factors, be these the role of
states in warfare, or shifting international standards of what does
and does not constitute legitimate government.

An even more recent critical current to emerge within IR has
been that influenced by feminism, the subject of Chapter 7 of this
book. Until the mid-1980s, IR appeared to be more indifferent to
issues of gender than any other area of the social sciences, a
situation compounded by widespread acceptance of the distinction
between a conventionally 'male' area of high politics, international
security and statecraft, and a 'female' one of domesticity,

interpersonal relations and locality. This mutual indifference has, however, given way in the face of two converging processes. One comes from the realm of policy: in a range of international policy areas, issues of gender have come to prominence in recent years. These include questions of women in development processes, issues in international law and EC policy pertaining to women, and the varying impacts on men and women of international socio-economic processes, among them migration and 'structural adjustment' policies. The widespread involvement of women in movements against war and nuclear weapons has made this another point of gender-specific intersection. In a quite different area, feminist writing has begun to engage with some of the core concepts of IR theory and to question how far a gender-neutral view of them is justified. These include the concepts of 'national interest', security, power and human rights. All are presented in the mainstream literature as gender-neutral concepts; yet, as feminist re-examination has shown, each has implicit gender significance. Above all, feminism, in common with other theories emphasising individual and social rights, questions the very core of conventional international relations practice, namely the supreme value of sovereignty. For example, the establishment of independent states has in many countries led to a deterioration in women's position *vis-à-vis* men, while assertions of sovereignty and nationalist identity have been used to deny the legitimacy of raising these issues: there is, therefore, room for considerable engagement by feminism, in practice and theory, with the claims of nationalism and with its correlate, the presumed authority of the sovereign state.

The Parameters of 'Rethinking'

This chapter has argued that the 'international' is not an additional, or recent, component of social and political reality but an enduring, constitutive, element in it. Equally it has argued for the location of IR in its broader intellectual and historical context. The relationship of IR to other social sciences can above all be defined by the joint approach which it, and other disciplines, could make to issues that are both domestic and international: in regard to specific issues or events it is possible to analyse how far the international does and does not play a determinant role.[26] Three groups of interrelated topics suggest themselves. The first are issues of political theory in the older, normative, sense of the term: of obligation, whether to family, state, or cosmopolitan community; of justice, its implementation at the national and international levels, and its conflict with rival values, notably security; of the legitimacy of force and coercion, within and between states; of the right to resist sovereign states.[27] There are, secondly, a set of theoretical issues in the more contemporary, analytic sense: the analysis of power; the relation between political, economic and ideological structures; the relevance of rational choice models to social and political action, by states, institutions and individuals within them.[28]

Finally, there is the focus of this book, the explanation of social and political systems in the light of both domestic and international determinants. Each level, the national and the international, has its own partial autonomy, yet, as indicated above, the insulation of the two levels of study, as with political science and IR, has done violence to explanation and analysis. As already argued, it is not possible to explain the politics of individual states without reference to a range of international factors, historical and current. The 'international' is not something 'out there', an area of policy that occasionally intrudes, in the form of bombs or higher oil prices but which can conventionally be ignored. The international predates, plays a formative role in shaping, the emergence of the state and the political system. States operate simultaneously at the domestic and international level and seek to maximise benefits in one domain to enhance their positions in the other. The requirements of inter-state competition explain much of the development of the modern state, while the mobilisation of domestic resources and the internal constraints account for much of states' successes in this competition. Disciplines such as political science and sociology, on the one hand, and International Relations, on the other, are looking at two dimensions of the same process: without undue intrusion or denial of the specificity of the other, this might suggest a stable and fruitful interrelationship.

This relationship can, however, only be realised if the discipline itself becomes more aware of each of the three circles of influence upon it, and in particular of the external factors affecting it – if, in effect, it evolves an acceptance of its own sociology of knowledge. A body of thought can relate to the 'real' world in an effective and critical way not by suppressing these connections, but by establishing a distance from them, in both the priorities set and the consciousness of how external factors have affected it. The history of IR provides many examples of how this external constraint was not adequately recognised, as does the history of social science in general, and indeed that of natural science. The priorities of the subject have, in the main, been the priorities of elites and of states, when not directly framed by the demands of state-related funding agencies. This is true, however, not just for the explicit content of work itself, but also for two other dimensions of this work: the issues avoided and not discussed, and the underlying, apparently neutral, methodologies used. The power of determining outcomes depends as much on determining what questions are *not* raised, and on excluding 'unacceptable' methods, as on imposing a particular analysis. The extraordinary misrepresentation by IR of the dominant conflict of the latter half of the twentieth century, the Cold War, a subject discussed in Chapters 8 to 10, is a remarkable case of ideological occlusion, the erection of a body of knowledge serving not to illumine but to obscure a historical process.

Equally, the dominance of inflatedly 'scientistic' methodologies, or of their conventional opposite, ahistorical concepts of the international 'system', have served to preclude other forms of discussions within the discipline, notably on the role of values, and on the linkage between domestic and international politics. As Chapter 4 indicates, the flight from what is, in both domestic and international politics, *the* central actor and concept, the state, serves analogous ideological functions. If the recovery of IR's history involves recuperation on all three levels – discipline, social science, history itself – a reconstitution or rethinking of the subject will simultaneously have to be aware of its significance in all three of these dimensions.

The chapters that follow are one attempt to 'rethink' International Relations along these lines. The next chapter is an attempt to provide a critique of four major trends in the literature from within the first circle, that of the discipline itself; the five chapters that follow seek to broaden the discussion to relate

International Relations to a broader conception of social science, while the final four locate the subject in the context of history itself, and the responses of International Relations specialists to it. The test of any such 'rethinking' will, however, consist as much in the research and analyses of histories, states and societies that it proposes and encourages, as in any strictly 'disciplinary' or methodological engagement.

2

Theories in Contention

Chapter 1 aimed to provide a summary account of the problems facing International Relations and of the difficulties it confronts. In the face of these challenges the discipline of International Relations has, in recent years, been riven by a series of methodological debates the declared aim of which has been to resolve its underlying uncertainties and establish a more rigorous relationship with the real world beyond. Yet what resulted was, in too many cases, not a clarification of method nor a more measured interaction with history, but – in the case of established approaches – a restatement of verities or – in the case of new theories – a flight into confusion, a meandering compounded by academic introversion, and a denial of both the significance and the challenges of history. On one side, invocation of history as a cult of facts served to deny historicity, i.e. political and intellectual change or context; on the other 'meta-theory', solemnly announced, i.e. debates on *how* to write theory, became detached from substantive analysis.

The point is not to argue against academic specialisation or theoretical development: both are, as already made clear, essential. But there is good specialisation and futile self-isolation; there is theoretical work that is rigorous, as clear as possible, and which has explanatory potential, and there is theory that is none of these, 'theoreticist' in the sense of theory for the sake of it, often covering old philosophic ground while pretending to say something new, pretentious where substance is lacking, and confused, even lazy, where alternative formulation is possible.

Two methodological guidelines above all are important in this respect. One is that while writing in IR needs to be methodologically aware and explicit, IR itself is not methodologically specific in social sciences. The problems it has – of fact and value, of rationality and interpretation – are those of other social sciences: the international has no epistemological or other privilege.[1] This was, above all, the abiding error of the 'third debate' that arose in IR in the latter part of the 1980s.[2] The attempt to resolve these issues through discussion of the international alone, or to write of IR in isolation from discussions in other social sciences, is a conceit.

Secondly, given that IR is applied to a subject-matter, be this the 'real', the 'concrete in history' or whatever, the test of its theory is its explanatory power, not its methodological remoteness. Abstraction may be necessary, but as a route to explanation. The alternative to bad theory is not empiricism, but good theory, in both its conceptual and explanatory dimensions: the discipline of IR has seen too much of the former, and, in recent years most of all, too much theorising unanchored in historical explanation.

Taking these guidelines as its starting point, this chapter looks at four of the more substantial approaches that have, at various points in the past decades, been propounded as solutions to the challenges facing International Relations. These are: traditional empiricism, 'scientific' empiricism, neo-realism, post-modernism.

Traditional Empiricism: History and the English School

All social sciences face, from within and without their particular disciplines, the argument that the 'facts' are enough, and that theories, concepts, specialist language are unnecessary, examples of 'jargon' and of academic pretension. This is particularly true of International Relations: as a result of its 'invisibility' most of those concerned with international issues, or having an opinion on them, seem unaware that any specialist, conceptually specific, literature on the subject exists. From within the discipline too, there are pressures in this direction: the diplomatic historians for one have long been wary of concepts and models and are quick to point to what they regard as aberrations in this regard; robust and practical dismissal of the need for such work recurs again and again in the literature.[3] For students, coming to the subject for the first time, the idea that there needs to be theoretical work often comes as a surprise: Surely the facts are sufficient? And knowledge of the international consists in knowing as many facts as possible?[4] Yet facts are not, in IR or anywhere else, enough.

The arguments against empiricism have been cogently and frequently stated elsewhere, especially in debates on sociology: these criticisms apply to the study of the international as much as to other social sciences.[5] First, there needs to be some preconception of which facts are significant and which not. The facts are myriad and do not speak for themselves. For anyone, academic or not, there need to be criteria of significance. Secondly, any one set of facts, even if accepted as true and as significant, can yield different interpretations: the debate on the 'lessons of the 1930s' is not about what happened in the 1930s, but about how these events are to be interpreted. The same applies to the end of the Cold War in the 1980s. Thirdly, no human agent, again whether academic or not, can rest content with facts alone: all social activity involves moral questions, of right and wrong, and these can, by definition, not be decided by facts. In the international domain such ethical issues are pervasive: the question of legitimacy and loyalty – should one obey the nation, a broader community (even the world, the cosmopolis), or some smaller sub-national group; the issue of intervention – whether sovereignty is a supreme value or whether other states or agents can intervene in the internal affairs of states; the question of human rights and their definition and universality.

In the field of IR, the initial facts/theory dividing line was drawn between the historical approach to the international, based on diplomatic history, and the first attempts to engage in 'International Relations' itself, comparative and theoretical work on the international. In several respects this division has been overcome, in a range of work which uses conceptual developments in IR to elucidate particular phases or episodes of international history.[6] Elsewhere a silly and futile argument continues as to where the historical dividing line between IR and international history exists: this misses the point that the issue is not 'history without archives', or 'international analysis without concepts', but a differing approach, the one factual and specific, the other comparative and theoretical.

One concerted attempt to move beyond traditional history and into a new theoretical domain, while still retaining a conventional empiricist perspective and method, was that represented by the

'English School', a body of writers who began to produce work in the 1950s and 1960s and who retain an influential following in British universities today. The strengths of the 'English School' are evident: a strong resistance to the fashions of 'presentism', a resolute insistence on the endurance of constraint and necessity in the international realm, an emphasis on the recurrence of concepts and values in the study of international relations, and, by no means least, a solid grounding in history itself. There is far more of explanatory substance, and of theoretical challenge, in their works than in most of the supposedly more 'scientific' or theoretically contemporary literature that has sought to displace them.

Two of the central concepts of the 'English School' – 'State' and 'Society' – are the focus of subsequent chapters. Beyond the difficulties raised by these terms, the 'English School', as reflected in the work of Martin Wight remained, in some respects, constrained by its origins, arrested by its concern to demonstrate equality with the diplomatic historians, and equally by the conceptual under-pinnings that IR brought with it from international history.[7]

In the first place, the concept of 'history' with which Wight operated was a curiously limited one: kings and queens, congresses and battles, treaties and laws. In remaining engaged with the historians, it failed to keep pace with changes in the concept of history itself: the economic and the social remained alien to it. What is most striking about reading Martin Wight, is that the use of history in his work, brilliant and erudite as it is, is one that historians themselves had in large measure ceased to practice. Equally, while Wight and his associates insisted on the importance of philosophic issues, and had their own conceptual schema (notably 'international society'), their concept of political philo-sophy was equally dated, consisting in the examination and re-examination of a set of recurring themes, favourably grouped by Wight into three transhistorical categories of rationalism, realism and revolutionism. As an antidote to 'presentism' and as a means of eliciting the conceptual issues, analytic and ethical, underlying discussion of international relations, this was fruitful: but it failed to recognise how far political philosophy itself had evolved and how it offered the possibility of very different, and in some ways more cogent, forms of political, including 'international', theory.

It was in some respects the misfortune of the English School that their 'philosophic' investigations, i.e. their eliciting of theoretical underpinnings within the international, should have been constituted just prior to the great revival of political theory of the 1970s and 1980s.[8] Wight's famous essay – 'Why is There no International Theory?' – presupposes a particular concept of theory, i.e. substantive classical philosophy – that was to be overtaken by other writing almost as soon as it was published.[9]

To these general limitations must be added the use of concepts themselves: as will be explored at greater length in subsequent chapters, the core terms used by Wight and Bull – 'society', 'state' – are not given adequate, or even explicit, conceptual elaboration. Definitions are introduced, or implied, in a way that suits the overall argument, but, in so doing, they preclude other possibilities of explanation and conceptual elaboration. The most obvious issue of all, derived from the still unchallenged assumptions of diplomatic history, is about what constitutes the international system itself. A definition in terms of the growth of relations between states is one, valid, definition: but, in addition to presupposing that somehow the 'international' is made up of the links between the national, or individual state, it also locates international history at the level of the diplomatic and the inter-state. Alternative histories and concepts of the international can be written by taking the starting point as being the economic and the social, within which the political, and the military, play an important role. The works of Hobsbawm, Wallerstein, Krippendorf, Wolf and more recently Rosenberg are all examples of such an alternative: the least that can be said is that these provide a very different history of the international system, and imply a variant set of ethical responses to the orthodox version of its growth, 'the expansion of international society'.[10]

'Scientific Empiricism': the Siren of Behaviouralism

One self-proclaimed alternative to the empiricist, factually based, approach came in the 1950s and 1960s from the 'scientific revolution' within the social sciences, and the rise of behaviouralism as an alternative to historical and empiricist accounts. This school announced the possibility of a new quantitative, ahistorical, and rigorous social science, in the field of the international as in other areas; at the same time, it involved a critique of the pre-existing schools as unfounded and outmoded. Yet the debate that ensued, between Hedley Bull and Fred Northedge on the traditional side, and James Rosenau and Morton Kaplan on the behaviouralist side, was, in both cases, misguided.[11]

In the first place, this debate, formally about methodology, acquired the character of a clash between two 'national' traditions, an 'English' and an 'American' approach. This misrepresentation, beyond obscuring the philosophic issues involved, served to present international relations as somehow grouped into two, implicitly monolithic, national camps, and in so doing obscured the diversity in both camps, such as the rise of international political economy in the British case, and the great range of theoretical and political approaches in the American one. In other words it served to reinforce both orthodoxy and polemic. The latter was particularly evident in the way in which non-American writers in critical traditions treated 'American' international relations as a single, at times 'imperialist', whole, something that was far from being the case: politically misguided, and analytically imprecise, this practice has continued, with enduringly negative results. Historical and regional differences do shape IR writing, but not necessarily in a homogeneous way. The conceits of North American behaviouralism have, rather too easily, found their counterpart in the complacencies of their opponents – whether English historiography or 'anti-imperialist' defiance.[12]

Secondly, while the critique of empiricism has much to recommend it, the alternative offered by such writers as James Rosenau or J. D. Singer[13] was itself spurious. The goal of a scientific, quantitative-based international relations or social science in general, is a chimera, one that, as already noted, ignores the necessary unpredictability of human behaviour, the impossibility of analysis without criteria of significance, the role of ethical issues in human affairs. Moreover, despite its claims to scientism, behaviouralism operates with a spurious concept of science: if it has been said that politicians operate with the conceptions of long-dead economists, many social scientists, and not a few in IR, operate with the prejudices of very long-dead philosophers of science (such as John Stuart Mill, 1806–73). In many areas of natural science, prediction is not a criterion of validity. Equally, the natural sciences also operate with many concepts that cannot be quantified or rendered very precise. Ironically for the positivists, natural science often operates with a concept of analysis rather akin to the 'judgement' that they so excoriated the traditionalists for employing. Indeed, it was ironic that at the very moment when behaviouralism, with its naive claim to 'science' was at its peak, Kuhn should have published his *Structure of Scientific Revolutions* showing how extraneous, 'institutional', factors shape specific agendas.[14] Why the USA, in other respects a modern society, should have made such a fuss about outdated methodologies is a curiosity in itself, rather like the lack of a national banking system.

To these methodological failings must be added the meagre record of such positivism itself: as in other social sciences, grand structures of quantification and algebra too often produced banality or obscurity, or both; in the rush to avoid supposedly outdated institutional categories such as the 'state' or 'war' scholars resorted to confused interactions or taxonomic excess; in the rejection of history, the behaviouralists produced conclusions that were often ignorant of historical analogy, and which exaggerated the contemporary specificity of phenomena (e.g. globalisation).

The results of behaviouralism in IR were, therefore, poor; the 'behavioural revolution' served as a massive intellectual and disciplinary detour, through feckless accumulation of data and meaningless transhistorical comparisons. However, beyond a welcome shaking up of the debate on methodology, some fruitful consequences followed. As already discussed in Chapter 1, there emerged, on the one hand, a wide-ranging exploration of the process of foreign policy making, known as 'foreign policy analysis'. The second positive consequence was the exploration of the new forms of international interaction, subsumed under the term 'interdependence'.

If these were significant achievements of the 'scientific' turn in IR, they were achieved as much in spite of as because of the theoretical reorientation of the discipline. For elsewhere many of the worst features of this inflated 'revolution' were to be seen: crazed pursuit of an elusive precision and prediction; increasing absorption of the discipline in a language both trivial and private, laboured and inflamed statements of the obvious. One example of this approach was the attempt to provide an empirically precise basis to theories of the causes of war.[15] Another was the assertion, without conceptual or historical depth, of the supersession of the state by 'transnational' development. Even those who did not fall into the methodological spirals of the more committed behaviouralists tended to counterpose their own, novel, approach to a supposedly outmoded concern with the state: this, despite his insights, was the enduring flaw in the work of James Rosenau. The result was in the end the failure to break from the theoretical premises of the dominant realist school, and its concept of the state. Many of those who, in the 1960s, had begun to announce the supersession of the state by new transnational phenomena, ended up by accepting the continuing relevance, theoretical and actual, of the state, and offering ameliorative modifications of the realist approach.

An important example of this was Robert Keohane, one of the originators of the transnationalism approach, and one of the most innovative, and widely read, of those working in the field of international relations theory. His 1970s work on transnationalism was amongst the best, and least dogmatically 'scientific' of the writing influenced by behaviouralism. His *After Hegemony*, published in 1984, marked an important turning point in the debate with transnationalism, since it addressed one of the central claims of the realists, namely that there could be no order without great powers, and without an element of direction and authority, termed 'hegemony', in the system.[16]

Important as it was in challenging this premise of realism, Keohane's work nevertheless contained a number of debatable assumptions. On the one hand, perhaps in order to establish a congenial historical context, it both overstated the degree of decline of US influence in the world, and, on the other, inflated the role of the supposedly successor transnational institutions, in this case the International Energy Agency. On the other, it proceeded by including some questionable theoretical assumptions: its historical account of US 'decline' established too abrupt a division between military and economic power, and failed to recognise the ways in which US military predominance and leadership, something that has continued after the Cold War, had economic and other 'seigniorial' benefits. Its account of power relations in the contemporary world was specific to those between developed countries, and did not include those between less and more developed states: hence as a general account, it understated hierarchies and oligarchic benefits, which are more openly recognised in theories of imperialism, on the one hand, and of realism on the other.

Keohane also used only the realist definition of the state, against which he sought to define his own transnationalist theory and so to distance himself from both realism and Marxism, seen in this light as sharing a common position. The result was that while not hostile to Marxism, and willing to take its arguments seriously (at one point he terms himself a Kautskyite),[17] Keohane declined to see that within Marxism the 'state' could mean something very different from what it meant in realist theory, and that this concept is incorporated into a theory of power that embraces many of the economic, social and ideological factors he subsumed within the theory of interdependence.

Neo-Realism: 'Systems' without Content

In the face of these challenges, and of the rising importance of economic issues on the international agenda, the school of realists previously confined to historical and philosophic reflection generated a new body of work, 'neo-realism'. The work of Krasner and Tucker, already mentioned in Chapter 1, was important here. If the 'neo-' served in some measure to conceal the reassertion of traditional themes – on state, power, conflict – it also reflected two important revisions of the earlier agenda: on the one hand, a much greater attention to the role of the economic in inter-state relations, not in terms of transnational or interdependent approaches, but as an instrument, mercantilist and competitive, of state power; on the other hand, a theoretical revision, in an attempt to make the theory more rigorous and to exempt it from the methodological assaults to which the previous generation had been subjected. Perhaps the most influential of these statements of neo-realism was Kenneth Waltz's *Theory of International Politics*.[18]

Waltz's reputation in the field of international relations was established with the publication of *Man, the State and War* in 1959, a work in which he compared three 'images' of the origins of war – the nature of man, the domestic constitution of states, and the international system: he concluded that it was the third image which provided the basis for a theory of the causes of war. One of the central themes to emerge from this study, and repeated in his later work, is the idea that the internal character of states is to be excluded from the study of international relations.

Yet *Man, the State and War*, a lucid statement of the realist position, achieved its apparently inexorable conclusions at the expense of two issues. First, its distribution of interpretations of conflict between three, apparently separate, compartments did violence to the way in which many provided explanations that straddled Waltz's divide: thus most theories based on image one, human nature, provided a 'nurture', i.e. socialisation, account of human personality and behaviour; more importantly, Waltz's theories based on image two, liberalism and Marxism, both contained an international dimension as an essential part of their explanation. Liberalism asserted a close relation of democracy and peace, not just as the first determining the second, but as an interactive process. Lenin's theory of imperialism could only be forced into the mould of the 'second image' by doing violence to its detailed examination of how imperialism, far from being the creation of an internal process, was the result of inter-state economic *and* military competition. Secondly, as in his 1979 work, Waltz contrasts what he terms 'reductionist' with 'systemic' theories, i.e. those which explain international relations in terms of the internal as opposed to those who look only at the international system. The argument he adduces to support this is that there is a regularity of outcomes in international relations that persists despite changes in the character of actors.[19] The consequence Waltz draws is, therefore, that it is no more necessary to study the character of states in international relations that it is necessary, when analysing markets, to study the internal workings of firms. As will be discussed below, this is a questionable conclusion.

Theory of International Politics begins with an assertion of the need for, and possibility of, theory in the study of international relations, and of the importance of analysing the structures of inter-state relations. By structure he means 'a set of constraining conditions'[20] and he exemplifies this in the international realm by reference to two processes: socialisation (i.e. the acceptance by states of certain behaviour) and competition.

The structure of the international political system is in Waltz's view characterised by three features above all: by the fact that it is anarchic, in the sense of their being no higher authority; that there is no differentiation of function between different units, i.e. all states perform roughly the same functions; and by an unequal distribution of capacities, i.e. the distinction between great and small powers. From these general propositions he derives a number of other conclusions: that the central mechanism of the international political system is the balance of power, and that the nature of an inter-state system at any one time is given by the character and number of its great powers. The world since 1945 had been constituted by relations between two great powers and is therefore one of bipolarity, in contrast to the multipolarity of the eighteenth and nineteenth centuries.

Waltz takes the opportunity of his restatement of realism to apply his theory to a number of contemporary issues in international relations. Thus he criticises the enthusiasts of inter-dependence theory for a lack of historical perspective – inter-dependence was, he claims, in some ways greater before 1914 than it is today – and for neglecting the dangers which excess interaction between states can produce. In contrast to those who argue, as part of the interdependence position, that military power is less useful than in earlier epochs, he claims that it retains its purposes in the bipolar world. For Waltz, the post-1945 bipolar system was desirable, since it reduced the risks of conflict. In the international system, he claims, small is better. Turning to the question of managing international relations, Waltz argues, against those stressing international institutions or diffusion of power, that the key lies in constructive management of international relations by the great powers.

There are two major problems with Waltz's analysis that become immediately evident on reading his exposition and that of most of his critics. The first is that it is ahistorical, in the sense that it takes as transhistorical, or permanent, features of the system that are the product of, and hence specific to, distinct phases of international relations. The words of Goran Therborn have as much relevance to IR theory as to other branches of social science: 'Even the most abstract theoretical discourses and scientific endeavours are the product of particular societies in a particular historical period.'[21] In invoking Thucydides and examples from a range of historical cases, Waltz argues that the structures of the international system have remained the same for thousands of years.[22] We are therefore dealing with a theory that abstracts from the contemporary states system and its formation, and from other historical processes that have intervened between the Greece of the fourth century BC and the post-1945 epoch. The assumption that he, and many other writers on international relations, make is that there was an 'international system' before modern states, or nations, or the international market emerged. This is, however, a questionable claim, much as if one was to study pricing policy in ancient Rome and contemporary America, or voting behaviour in the Greek *agora* and modern elections. Some very general statements can be made that apply to both systems, but these may be of such banality as to render them of marginal importance.

Indeed, elsewhere in the text, Waltz himself makes statements that would only hold for a much more limited historical scale. Thus in discussing the durability of states in the contemporary world he observes: 'The death rate among states is remarkably low'.[23] If by 'states' is meant independent states in the modern era, then Waltz is certainly right. If, however, his 'states' is set against the historical record of the last two thousand years, or even the last one hundred and fifty, then it becomes a nonsense: the number of plausibly distinct political entities in Europe and the third world that have been overwhelmed and wiped out by various form of conquest, not least the assaults of imperialism, must run into thousands. If Waltz's statement about the low death of states is taken as characteristic of the structure he is discussing, then that structure is a very recent creation indeed, post-dating not only the emergence of an international system in Europe in the seventeenth century, but also the end of colonialism.

This ahistorical perspective is reinforced by the absence of any history of the system itself, and in particular of the origins of the contemporary state system in the post-mediaeval period, and its relation to the rise of capitalism. Since Waltz aspires to a strictly 'political' analysis of international relations, and has a corresponding 'national-territorial' concept of the state, there is no room in his view for the concept of capitalism and for a study of the relationship of the rise of distinct states to the international spread of capitalism.

Indeed, for all its concern with international process, and, more recently with international economic processes, the literature on international relations seems remarkably shy of using the term 'capitalism' at all. One of the consequences of this neglect is that realist theory, and the history it implies, has a distinctive account of how states and the international system interrelate. According to this myth, states emerged as individual entities and then began, gradually, to have relations with each other. Thus Waltz: 'Structures emerge from the coexistence of states'.[24] This ignores one of the central lessons of historical sociology and its account of the development of states, which is that states, in the sense of administrative-coercive entities, develop as a result of international processes, and not the other way around. Military competition and the expansion of a market, together with the existence of a shared culture, were not the results of, but the preconditions for, the emergence of the state system. The orthodox view that states arose first and then began to interrelate to constitute an international system bears about as much relation to reality as the myth of the social contract, or the stork.

The confusion about the history and definition of states is evident in the second major difficulty with Waltz's analysis, namely the claim that international relations can and should be studied at a purely systemic level. The arguments Waltz advances for this are rudimentary: that there is sufficient regularity in inter-state relations to enable us to dispense with examinations of the internal workings of states, and the, more general, claim that 'elegance' of theory is desirable. Waltz's formulations on this are, again, revealing. His argument that systemic factors must be taken into account in analysing international relations, i.e. that states are not simply free to do what they want and are constrained by the system as a whole, is unexceptionable. Thus he plausibly states: 'It is not possible to understand world politics *simply by looking inside of states*' (my italics).[25] This is, however, quite different from arguing that the internal processes of states can be excluded altogether from a theorisation of international relations: the move from saying international relations cannot be studied 'simply' by looking at the internal workings of states to saying that the internal workings can be ignored is an important, and invalid, one.

Perhaps under the influence of other uses of the term 'structure', such as those in anthropology or linguistics, Waltz is drawn to a usage that is deterministic and denies the relevance of differences between individual units: but, in so doing, he conflates objects of analysis where internal workings may well be irrelevant to the workings of structure, such as linguistics can be, with ones in which the external and internal do interrelate to a greater degree. States are not analogous to morphemes, planets or kinship structures. Waltz is, of course, helped in this denial of the relevance of 'internal workings' by the standard International Relations confusion about what the word 'state' means: in the first, legal-political, sense of state it is strictly speaking impossible to ask about their internal workings, given the fact that all that is internal is comprised by definition in the concept of state. Instead, however, of taking this as a good reason for abandoning this conventional and confusing concept of the state, Waltz takes the national-territorial concept to its logical conclusion and produces an unbalanced theory of international relations.

In his reply to critics, at the end of *Neo-Realism*, Waltz seems willing to give some ground on this point, but not to the extent of abandoning his preference for a strictly 'systemic', as opposed to 'reductionist', theory.[26] In so doing, however, he provides an example which is at least as open to interpretation by 'reductionist' as by 'systemic' theory: France and Germany, he says, are no longer at all likely to go to war, because of their changed situation in the international system, i.e. they are no longer great powers.[27] But there are plenty of medium and small powers in the world that can and do go to war: Iran and Iraq, or India and Pakistan, are hardly greater powers than France or Germany. What determines their option is not structural position as such, but the combination of this with internal factors – the kind of historic experience they have had in the twentieth century (not least two world wars), the kind of political and socio-economic regimes they maintain, and the consequent alliances they have developed. On the basis of this example, one could well argue the opposite of Waltz's case: that international relations cannot be understood *simply by looking at relations between states*.

The alternative Waltz poses – either a reductionist or a systemic theory – is not necessary: what is needed, as several contributors to *Neo-Realism and its Critics* suggest, is a theory that combines the internal and external levels. As Ruggie points out, the emergence of the modern state system rested upon quite distinct kinds of state–society relation that had considerable impact on the workings of international relations.[28]

It is similarly evident that a study of the international dimensions of revolution can show both how international factors affect the internal workings of states and how these internal changes then, as a result of revolutions, have effects on the international system. Waltz, in common with most realists, seeks to underplay the international effects of revolutions and takes pleasure in telling the story of how the Bolshevik Revolution had, by 1922, come to accept the norms of international behaviour: had, in other words, been 'socialised' by the structure. As will be argued in Chapter 6, the fact that Chicherin wore a top hat and tails, and signed a secret treaty with Germany at Rapallo, did not, by any means, signify that the underlying ideological conflict between the Russian revolution and the capitalist West had been ended. Socialisation, in the sense of accepting the prevailing norms of the system and the legitimacy of other major actors within it, had certainly not occurred, any more than it had when Chou En-lai arrived in Geneva in 1954 and had tea with Anthony Eden. After the Bolshevik Revolution, a long-run conflict, one that acquired new life during and after the Second World War, had begun: it could not be explained merely by resort to balance-of-power theory and the abstractions of realism, but involved an incompatibility of social and political systems. To explain how and why that conflict developed requires examination of the internal workings of, respectively, the USSR and its Western adversaries, something that realist theory precludes us from doing.

The Tallest Story: Post-modernism and the International

The entry of post-modernism into the field of IR can be dated from the latter part of the 1980s, following upon its development in other areas of the academic domain, first aesthetics and the humanities, and later sociology, history and politics.[29] It thus formed part of what has been termed the 'third debate' in IR, actually the 'fourth' if the introduction of structuralism and Marxism is taken as the third. This 'third' debate covered very different challenges, two of which, feminism and historical materialism, will be considered later. In simplest term, the claims of post-modernism are two: first, that there is no single rationality, or historical narrative, in terms of which one can make sense of history or any particular branch of the social sciences; secondly, that the apparently discrete and unitary categories of social science and other forms of interpretation conceal a diversity of meanings and identities that make the subjects of political life much more complex and indeterminate than the more rational approaches would suggest. Strongly influenced, in concept and style, by French post-structuralist writing, but influenced by the earlier conceptual and moral indeterminacy of Nietzsche, post-modernism came in the 1980s to be the major new challenge within much of the social sciences.

Post-modernism's emphasis upon the role of 'discourse' in the widest sense – words, meanings, symbols, identities, forms of communication – in the constitution of society and of power has significant implications for international relations, not least in the very way in which states have sought to appropriate and project their legitimacy. In a world where communication and media images have an important role there is much to examine here: the work of Robertson and Featherstone, for example, examining the spread of various 'scapes' in the world, demonstrates the potential of such analysis.[30] At the same time, the assertion of a multiplicity of identities open to every human subject, and the denial of necessary contradictions (e.g. between 'national' and 'international'), has both explanatory and ethical import.

The advent of post-modernism in IR has, however, been accompanied by a number of more debatable contributions that have, far from advancing the subject, done much to confuse and divert. In the first place, the introduction and debate of post-modernism in IR has been conducted in almost complete separation from the broader debate on this trend within the social sciences: those advocating it in the late 1980s have given scant regard, or reply, to the many criticisms of the approach developed over the previous decade or more.[31] In summary form these criticisms highlight: the underlying amoralism of post-modernism, with its denial of any generally applicable moral principles; its inability to provide substantive explanation of historical events or periods; its overstatement of the role of 'discursive' or ideological factors in society; and neglect of the relation of these to other more material processes of production, social relations and indeed everyday life.[32]

To these general criticisms can be added two further ones, evident in the writing within IR. The first is the reliance of the whole approach on something termed 'post-modernity', a claim of questionable validity that in some sense the world has entered a new historical phase. Often of loose historical application, and based on some contingent observations about space, time, risk, perception, this invocation of a 'post-modern' world serves as a fetish rather than as an explanation. It suffers, moreover, from many other claims about the new and its methodological implications: for if the philosophical or epistemological claims of 'post-modernism' are valid, about the failings of enlightenment thought, identity, the fact-value distinction, categories and so forth, then they were always true, as much in the fifteenth, or fifth, centuries, as in the modern epoch. The strength of Foucault's work on madness or incarceration is that it applies across the historical span, of several centuries, that he examines; the conceit of his epigones is that they can conflate a historical turn with a revolution in ideas.

Beyond these substantive problems there is one further aspect of the post-modernist literature that merits criticism, and indeed invites it: namely its tone and style. Post-modernists make much of their concern for the dominated, the marginal, the subaltern: yet this is accompanied by prescriptive vacuity and a conceit that they are the first or only people to exhibit such a commitment. Time and again the writers of this tendency resort to stylistic devices, of mannered tentativeness and the hanging apodictic, when substantive analysis, of history or concepts, seems to fail. As in the writings of Islamic clergy, repetition, rambling and conceptual menace are too easily used, not to reinforce argument, but to compensate for the lack of it. Words such as 'meditation' are indicative of a contrived piety, that is part of this style, as is the use of fragments of literary and historical writing on the history of science, deployed for ornamental purposes, much as realists like to flavour their narrative with episodes from Thucydides or quotes from Cicero. Der Derian's *On Diplomacy* is a choice example of this genre. The temptations of *surenchère parisienne*, evident in earlier Anglo-Saxon schools derivative of French writing (notably that of Sartre and Althusser) is here reproduced in not always felicitous forms. The word 'continental' is used to give spurious cachet to these ideas and style, rather as the term 'imported beer' was pioneered in the 1970s: that an idea is 'continental', or 'insular', Parisian or Los Angelino, tells one nothing about its validity or explanatory scope.

Within this tone, the treatment of questions of 'epistemology' or, more mundanely, the philosophy of social science, plays an important part, yet it is handled in a precious, and often banal and incompetent, manner. Whatever else this strand of theory has represented, it is not an informal awareness of developments in the philosophy of science or of social science. These authors take great delight in announcing new forms of epistemology, hermeneutics, dialectics, closure and so forth: but in so doing they neither resolve questions of philosophy of science in general, nor contribute to the theorisation of IR. Their work is, in this field, pretentious, derivative and vacuous, an Anglo-Saxon mimesis of what was already, in its Parisian form, a confused and second-rate debate. The following from a pioneering collection of such texts, captures the tone:

> By no means a single school or unitary approach, the several practices known under the 'postmodern' or 'poststructuralist' rubric – deconstruction, semiotics, genealogy, feminist psychoanalytic theory, intertextualism, and their variants – despite their differences share several common themes. Above all, they address the questions of how knowledge, truth, and meaning are constituted. In the broadest sense, their works offer an explanation for their dissatisfaction with what the constitution Enlightenment project has brought about. Philosophical in its origin and practice, poststructuralism challenges the intellectual suppositions upon which Western rationalism and positivism are based. These turn out to be suppositions that found modern science and its adoring foster child, the social sciences.
>
> Poststructural critiques of rationalism by French philosophers turned out to be immensely attractive to other fields. For reasons that no one has adequately explained, the first enthusiastic interpreters were American literary theorists. Poststructuralist analyses pose a radical challenge to both the fact/value distinction and our concept of facticity generally, a concept that poststructuralists claim is conventional and culturally constructed rather than founded in nature. It is their specific focus on the workings of language that lets them reveal,

often quite persuasively, those conventions that found a 'fact's' convincing appearance. Discourses harnessed to powerful social forces have, in the name of scientific objectivity, come to constitute 'regimes of truth'. Poststructuralist methods of analysis purport to offer new means to critique such condominia of power and knowledge, methods potentially helpful for assessing social scientific theories as well.

One possible reason why poststructuralism found such a welcoming home among literary theorists is that these groups' necessary tolerance for plurality in interpretation had taught them something important about how meanings get constituted as well. Unsurprisingly enough, in the hands of literary theorists, such methods as deconstruction or genealogy tend to be adapted as finely honed tools for doing some intricate textual analysis.[33]

Here it all is: the mannered invocation of the Parisian; the confused salad of theoretical approaches; the ingenuously declared naivety about the difference between the domains of literary criticism and social science.

A representative example of this approach, in both its strengths and weaknesses, is the work of Robert Walker, *Inside/Outside: International Relations and Political Theory*.[34] One of the strongest aspects of Walker's critique is that he locates the main areas of disagreement not in the field of the international at all, but in political theory in general. The conceit of disciplinary autarchy has long compounded that of the international as a separate domain of the real, and of the ethical: his re-evaluation of the tradition sets IR theory firmly back into its broader intellectual and academic context. He has little time for the major alternatives propounded in recent years: if classical realism represents 'the careless embrace of acute ontological antagonisms', 'scientific' approaches are but 'kitsch Kantianism', neo-realism is just reheated reification, rational choice theories are 'utilitarian stories', political economy remains trapped in spatio-temporal eternalisation.

For Walker, broadly influenced by post-modernist and post-structuralist thinking, IR theory has three major weaknesses, all derived from political theory as such: it treats as eternal and given categories and contrasts which are historically produced, and hence liable to change; it fails to register the degree to which the political world, national and international, is changing, with the transformations of the 'post-modern world'; it therefore excludes and proscribes, by silence, the evolution of alternative theories and practices, that might enable an improvement in the human condition at national, international or local levels. If Martin Wight had to label Walker he would be a revolutionist, but a revolutionist sceptical of the categories of either Kant or Marx; they would, in Walker's view, be themselves the bearers of their own reifications.

Walker uses post-modernism to provide a critique of eternal categories, and in particular of a set of opposites which he sees as underpinning IR theory, in its utopian/idealist as much as in its realist forms: identity and difference, inside and outside, space and time, community and anarchy. He identifies the constitutive role of categories of time and space, concretised in the concept of state sovereignty, within international relations.

In his critique of these reifications, Walker cites the French philosopher of science, Gaston Bachelard, to the effect that the words 'here' and 'there' 'have been promoted to the rank of an absolutism according to which these unfortunate adverbs of place are endowed with unsupervised powers of ontological determination'.[35] The categories of 'inside' and 'outside' proclaimed in the title refer in the first instance to the argument of some radical difference between the characters of domestic and international politics, and of a chasm between the practices appropriate to, or possible in, each. They are also seen as providing a geometric and therefore apparently immutable foundation for two contrasting conceptions of sovereignty, one potentially democratic and responsive, operating within, the other necessarily competitive and antagonistic, operating without. In one of his most suggestive leitmotifs, he traces the evolution of this binary conception of sovereignty through Hobbes to a figure often ignored in the history of IR theory, but central to modern conceptions of the state and the grim inevitability of inter-state conflict, Max Weber.[36]

Even for those unconvinced by the theoretical underpinnings of Walker's argument there is much here that is cogent: the location of IR theory in a broader context of political theory and socially embodied power is a great improvement on the official genealogies of 'X read Y', or, even worse, 'B was the student of A'; the assertion of the historically constituted, and contingent, character of theories of sovereignty is equally welcome.

For those of other critical traditions, there is therefore plenty to welcome, with the caveat that much of this has been said before, and it has in recent years been taken further within the categories of these critical traditions, and with fewer claims to theoretical rebirth: historical sociology (as in Charles Tilly, Michael Mann, John Hall, Theda Skocpol), and Marxist historiography of the state (as in Perry Anderson, Ellen Wood, more recently Justin Rosenberg) have all explored the historicity of our conceptions of state and sovereignty. In these writings critical reassessment of IR's central political categories, of at least equal range, is matched by an engagement with historical processes and facts that post-modernists, rushing to the next acceleration, textual density or spillage, seem incapable of matching.

The question of novelty aside, the difficulties with Walker's theory arise precisely where he, in his own critique of IR theory, has located the problem: first, in the broader assumptions about historical change invoked to sustain his argument; secondly, in the positing of an alternative, of political or ethical pertinence, to existing eternalities. The first, as in so much 'alternative' thinking and modelling, remains elusive, indeed vapid – a benign invocation of the local, the cosmopolitan, the deconstructed, without anchorage in either social reality or ethical and historical necessity: indeed at one point Walker admits as much, summarising the argument to date as 'a web of barely theorised possibilities and tentative struggles'. One pertinent reading, central to his argument, is that of Kant as a statist: *Perpetual Peace*, not *Universal History*, is discussed. This, one can only suspect, is a symptomatic theoretical move, serving to repress the argument that, in terms of positing a transcendent theoretical and historical process, the Professor of Konigsberg had arrived two centuries ago and with greater intellectual vigour where his post-modernist counterparts have now beached.

Walker reproduces the general problem with the argument about 'post-modernity': it involves an argument about how the world is actually changing, and reads very like a variant on the enthusiasms of transnationalism – Rosenau crossed with Giddens and Derrida. The argument on 'post-modernity' as a global phenomenon rests upon the concept of a new phase in history, marked by a greater acceleration of change, and a disappearance of categories that we have inherited from another age. Walker, like Giddens and others, repeats the view that identities are no longer clear and that, in general, indeterminacy predominates where once clarity prevailed. Like many another post-modernist he is too quick to accept the claims of transnationalism, and ignores the many criticisms thereof. He is also happy to recruit Marx's phrase to the effect that 'All that is solid melts into air'. Yet all that is solid does not melt into air, and certainly not just because sociologists and alternative thinkers would have us believe it so: indeed they omit the second half of Marx's sentence which conveys a very different, rational, and teleological message: '. . . and man is at last compelled to face with sober senses, his real conditions of life, and his relations with his kind'.[37] For post-modernists, there can be no concept of the real, or indeed of the sober.

The social sciences are rather too full of people telling us about 'post-modernity' but it may, on closer examination, be just another apocalyptic fad, along with the end of ideology, the death of the novel, the new world order, the supersession of the state and so on.[38] Most of the claims about a new spatial and temporal world are at best metaphorical, at worst waffle, and often highly class- and place-bound – ethnocentric indeed! The argument on uncertainty of identity can be countered, if this is what post-modernists want, with evidence on how identity has, if anything become more important than ever before, as has indeed the oft-vaporised state: in the war in former Yugoslavia, what was striking was not the onrush of new forms of identity and political ideology but the vitality of old ones.

Beyond the assertion of some large-scale, but pretty obvious, changes in the world, it is dubious what empirical or ethical force can be attached to the concept 'post-modernity' at all: as already suggested, most of those who have used it have precious little qualifications, or inclination, to talk about the real. Witty incantations about alterity, dissolution and freeze-frames, and exaggerated claims about what has indeed changed in the world, are no substitute for a substantive engagement with history or a plausible conceptualisation of the alternatives for political and theoretical change. Rather too inebriated with its own phrases, post-modernism runs the risk of becoming the new banality, a set of assertions as unlocated and useless as the vacuous generalities, be they of balance of power or progressivist teleology, that they seek to displace, and equally lacking in any conception, of analytic or normative import, of how anything can be changed, of the question of agency. No wonder, as in Walker's case, there is a marked affinity with Machiavelli whose ethical scepticism, and historical randomness, presaged the Parisian fashions of our time. He, of course, was also very much a 'post-' man as well.

Yet it is precisely here, in the discussion of agency, that Walker's book is suggestive of an important new set of considerations, focused not on the abandonment of the nation-state but on providing it with a new, more democratic and polyvalent, content. And it is here too that one of the more substantive insights of post-modernism, namely that all individuals and political institutions have not one exclusive, but several overlapping identities, may be most helpful. Chapter 7 of Walker's book, on democracy, broaches these topics in a way that is not ethically indeterminate and which, in its suggestive vein, is compatible with earlier traditions of thought, at the domestic and international levels, of how democracy can advance: it is, in this way, eminently Kantian. This may suggest a conclusion that behind post-modernist excess there lurks a more substantive, rigorous and rational, modernist argument. Political thought has, in the past, moved forward by removing the rational kernel from the mystical and mystifying shell: this may be another case where such a transformation, or incursion, is appropriate.

To realise this potential would involve, however, going beyond the very general invocations of 'new' social movements that post-modernists and many others indulge in. The literature on the 'new' movements evolved in the 1970s in response, on the one hand, to the crisis of the old form of (mainly communist) political parties, and on the other to the evident growth of a range of movements that were not tied to particular parties or based on class identities: movements of gender, race, ecology, disarmament were the evident categories.[39] Yet, as often occurs with academic debate, the academic literature remained stuck in this regard, or clung to comforting assertions, such as that the peace movement had ended the Cold War.[40] Here a left-critical discourse ran alongside the more orthodox claims of transnationalism about non-state actors. What this literature overlooked were several less welcome considerations: first, that the role of these movements was far less than often claimed, and that they were, as often or not, riven by their own dissensions and factionalisms as much as any party of the old sort; secondly, that while some movements were of a benign and emancipatory kind, many others were not – mass movements of a racist kind, in Germany and France, for example, Hindu and Islamic fundamentalism, or the multiple expressions of the US right, were just as much 'social movements' as the left and green trends invoked by post-modernists. Their ability to meet two of the main challenges they claimed to confront – explanation and identification of an emancipatory subject – was, therefore, rather limited: like the behaviouralists before them, they issued many a promissory note.

Conclusion: Another Path

What kind of method is, therefore, appropriate for the study of International Relations? The chapters that follow are one attempt to contribute to such an endeavour, and to meet some broad criteria for theoretical work in this field. First they develop an approach that is anti-empiricist, conceptual, and where relevant, critical, in relation to existing 'facts' and 'reality'. Secondly, they seek to meet the criterion that is central to the social sciences, namely explanation, and through explanation, the generation of research agendas, i.e. programmes of work that remain to be explained. The discussions of the Cold War, in particular, are attempts to combine a set of theoretical concerns with historical explanation. Too many of the theoretical approaches of the 'second' and 'third' debates, lack such a capability. Thirdly, they are historical, not in the sense of seeking answers from history or narrative alone, but in examining historically, i.e. locating issues and concepts in their historical context. If realism seeks to make concepts ahistorical in applying them to all of history, behaviouralism denies the relevance of history at all, and post-modernism asserts a historical rupture between 'modern' and 'post-modern'. By contrast the chapters that follow seek both to recognise the continuities in history and to identify, where relevant, the specificities and contingencies of idea and event.

3

A Necessary Encounter: Historical Materialism and International Relations

A Challenge Evaded

The fate of Marxism within the social sciences has, throughout the past century, been profoundly uncertain, an ambivalence that has in some respects been accentuated by the collapse of the communist movements, and of communist regimes, since the late 1980s. On the one hand, the challenge of Marxism to established patterns of thought, and to the existing state system, has led to its exclusion from the academic domain, an exclusion compounded by the dogmatisms, polemics and simplifications of Marxists seeking or holding political power. On the other hand, Marxism, itself part of the radical liberal tradition inherited from the Enlightenment, and a response, along with the recognisable academic disciplines of sociology and economics, to the rise of industrial society, has shared many areas of common ground with more strictly academic concerns and has in a variety of ways influenced their evolution. If in some areas this has led to the emergence of an identifiable 'Marxist' current within the social sciences, it has a broader influence, one of diffusion, so that approaches originally associated with Marxism have become more generally accepted. In this sense, in Gramsci's phrase, Marxism has become 'the common sense of our epoch'.

If the ambivalence was accentuated by the communist challenge and the Cold War, it was certainly made all the greater by the end of that conflict and of the official challenge that communism posed. It is now easy to say that Marxism has been discredited and, in some respects to be examined in greater detail later in this chapter and in this book, this is so: any theory based on an implicit historical teleology, and an associated consequentialist ethic, or on the supposition that some radically different society can be created on this earth, has been discredited. Yet to recognise this is not to conclude that in its broader sense the approach crystallised in historical materialism has no relevance: it may indeed constitute an important contribution to interpreting, and, where both possible and desirable, prescribing for the contemporary world.

If realism can detach itself from its cousins – social Darwinism, racism and *Machtpolitik* – so can an interpretive Marxism be distinguished from its instrumental companion. Such a distinction involves above all an examination of what Marx and Engels themselves wrote, and of the work of independent Marxists who, throughout the Leninist and orthodox communist domination of the subject, sought to provide an alternative interpretation to that of the dogmatists.[1] Just as in sociology, history and other social sciences this independent, broadly 'Western', Marxist current has been able to establish a recognised and analytically fruitful body of work, so there exists the potential for it to do so in the realm of IR. It is this claim which the following chapter seeks to explore, with regard to a potential interaction of International Relations and the Marxist tradition.

Despite many decades of potential interaction, the establishment of a relationship between historical materialism and the discipline of international relations is still at an initial stage. At various stages in the history of the discipline, there have been surveys of the implications of Marxism for International Relations in which already constituted points of contact have been identified.[2] Since the 1970s a number of writers have advocated further theoretical work, be it the elaboration of a general Marxist approach to International Relations, or the development of domains in which the International Relations discipline, as presently constituted, can strengthen its analytic endeavours by drawing on specific elements within historical materialism.[3] In an innovative and judicious study, Andrew Linklater has examined the implications for IR of 'critical' Marxism, while stressing the constraints which the international system imposes on any emancipatory project.[4]

However, in contrast to such other areas of the social sciences as sociology, economics or history, historical materialism has never occupied a secure place within International Relations; there are many who seek to limit its application, be this explicitly, as was the case with those who denied its relevance, such as Martin Wight and Hans Morgenthau, or implicitly, by relegating it to a minor place, or by presenting it in a selective interpretation, such that its pertinence is constricted.[5] This is achieved above all by blocking out the main theoretical questions of Marxism. The fact that IR is almost wholly silent on what for Marxism is the central category of modern social analysis, namely capitalism, is itself indicative. Equally, as discussed in Chapter 8, the degree to which the Cold War embodied not just competing strategic interests, but different socio-economic ones, has been ignored in most IR literature.

The sources of this failure lie on both sides of the relationship. International Relations as a discipline has arisen primarily within British and American universities, and as a theoretical derivative of other disciplines in the social sciences. Neither institutional context, nor theoretical influence, have been ones in which Marxism has had a prominent or generally recognised place.

On the other hand, historical materialism has not itself developed the theoretical focus needed for a comprehensive and generally intelligible contribution to International Relations. Much of what was produced in the name of Marxism, by communist regimes or those following them, was vulgar polemic, a repetition of certain standard, formulaic, readings of Marxism itself and concentrated around a justification of political interests. The confining of Marxist discussion of the international to the question of 'imperialism', and a one-sided and banal interpretation of the phenomenon at that, was as much the responsibility of those espousing Marxism as of those opposed to it.[6] Those who, within the independent currents of historical materialism, have sought to elaborate a Marxist approach to International Relations have laboured under the theoretical difficulties that confront those who seek to analyse politics, and ideological factors, within the confines of specific states themselves.

At the same time, Marxism's stress upon economic factors at the international level has weakened any attempt to explain the political, ideological and security issues that international relations sees as quintessentially its domain. The very concept of the 'international' itself poses problems for Marxists, in that the implicit contrast with the 'national' is not one that they readily accept: from the cosmopolitan assertion of the *Communist Manifesto* onwards, as fine a statement of liberal transnationalism as one would want to find with its invocations of 'interdependence' Marxism has seen world affairs confidently in terms of a single world process: the result was that the very need for a study of inter-state and international relations might appear to be irrelevant, a diversion from analysis of the real, universal, forces shaping world politics. Marx's view of nationalism, while less hostile than later critics have suggested, was also one that denied any necessary contrast or contradiction between the formation of nations and the growing interlocking of states and societies, the former being but a precursor to the latter, and part of a broader, teleological, historical process.[7]

Marxism and IR's Three 'Great Debates'

This general lack of contact between the two intellectual bodies is compounded by a number of specific difficulties involved in such a theoretical exploration. As outlined in Chapter 1, in the seventy-odd years of its existence as an academic discipline, International Relations has gone through three major theoretical debates. These have tended to define the literature and the terms of further study. Yet Marxism fits uneasily into each of these three.

The first was that between the 'utopian' and 'realist' approaches. These were themselves factitious terms but served to constitute an ideological polarity. In this framework, Marxism shares elements of both: if it is 'utopian' in its postulation of another, alternative, way of ordering politics, and in the introduction of a set of ethical concerns into political analysis, it is 'realist' in its emphasis upon the material interests underlying human action, and its emphasis upon the hypocrisy, mendacity and cynicism of much political life. While there are striking parallels in the idealist projects each initiated after the First World War – the Communist International and the League of Nations – Leninism was resolutely distinct in the utopia it proposes as a counter to Wilsonian idealism.

A similar problem arises with the second general debate, that between traditionalists and behaviouralists. Marxism, enthusiastic about the scientific methodologies of the nineteenth century and imbued with the influence of classical British economics, certainly emphasises the scientific potential of social analysis: quantification, and the establishment of 'laws', lie at the heart of Marx's approach in *Capital*. As with much nineteenth-century radical thought, an earlier progressivism was given spurious scientific validity by Darwinian theories of evolution.[8] Yet Marxism also retains much of another approach: it is not just materialism – that was the domain of the philosopher Feuerbach – but *historical* materialism: history in the sense of events is as important in Marxist analysis as to any traditionalist student of International Relations, but is even more so in a different sense, that of identifying the historicity, or conditions of origin and reproduction, of a society or idea. Marxism is also intensely ethical, both in the language of its judgements and in the emphasis upon prescription, upon the injunction to act. That indeed was the fundamental difference between Feuerbach and Marx, the latter emphasising the need to *change* the world.[9]

The third fundamental debate within international relations, that between state-centred and world system approaches, can bracket Marxism with little more success. For sure, Marxism emphasises that capitalism creates a world market, and with it class forces that operate on a world scale. In *The German Ideology* Marx argued that the proletariat could only exist 'world-historically' i.e. both as the result of a world-historical economic process, the spread of capitalism, and as an agent acting on the world scale.[10] *Weltklasse, Weltpartei, Weltrevolution* – the very programme of the Comintern – sums up this view, as the earlier *Manifesto* had done.

Yet Marxism has devoted much of its theoretical energy, in the last century as in this, to theoretical and practical work upon the state: analysing its strength and tenacity, and the class interests embodied in it.[11] As discussed in Chapter 4, the conceptualisation of what the state is, and how it relates to to other forces in society, has been the subject of debate within and without the Marxist tradition. Yet the premise of this whole literature is that the state, far from disappearing or being transcended, remains a central factor in politics, subject to both internal and international pressures. Marxism recognises the importance both of the state as an object of political control, and of the nation-state as a fundamental organising principle, whether in the struggle of nationalist movements for power, or in the consolidation of revolutionary regimes in an otherwise hostile world. Most Marxists would be highly sceptical about contemporary liberal and transnationalist claims that the state, as the locus of class power, was being eroded as an element in international politics, or about the claim that force and coercion had been displaced as central, or at the very least reserve, instruments of class rule.

From the 1970s this apparent lack of communication began to erode: the academic IR literature did concede a certain place to Marxism. But with the exception of Linklater and a few others, the very manner of this concession posed difficult problems. In essence, it was argued that a theoretical approach, a 'paradigm' derived from Marxism could be used to explain International Relations, and that this paradigm, generally called 'structuralism', could yield significant results.[12] It seemed, at least, that historical materialism had found a place within International Relations.

But this equation of historical materialism, as a theoretical approach, with 'structuralism', as a paradigm constituted within the discipline, was uncertain. First, the very concept of structuralism, derived from linguistics and anthropology, differs in major respects from historical materialism. It is a form of determinism, in the sense of denying freedom of action, or agency, to the elements in the structure. Yet Marxism, for all its stress upon the 'iron laws' of history, and the determinations of the socio-economic context, contains an element of freedom, of will, of the possibility – indeed the necessity – of voluntarism: Marx, in the midst of the lengthy elaboration of the laws of the mode of production in *Capital*, asserts that, at a certain point in the conflict between owner and exploiter, the workers will rise up.[13] The *Manifesto* is an injunction to action.

The subsequent history of political Marxism, in the hands of such revolutionary leaders as Lenin and Mao, hardly confirms the image of man as a Prometheus chained to the ground by the structures of his social being. Equally, within the independent 'Western' Marxist tradition there has been no unanimity on this: while some theorists, notably Louis Althusser, did stress a determinism, others identified an ability of individuals and political forces to pursue emancipation defiant of objective constraints, and to challenge, through conscious action, the constraints that have been identified in society.

This has, indeed, occasioned the other major introduction of Marxism into IR, through the 'critical theory' associated with the Frankfurt School: in this perspective, exemplified by the work of Robert Cox, the emphasis is precisely on the emancipatory potential of groups and individuals and on the possibility of an appropriate theoretical response. One of the great contributions of Habermas's work has been his distinction between the three forms of knowledge – positivist, hermeneutic and critical, the last being the basis for an emancipatory project.[14]

Structuralism is misleading too since, in its conventional usage, it suggests a multiplicity of relations affecting any one element in the system: historical materialism, on the other hand, while recognising a multiplicity of influences, and the diverse determinations of class, nation, gender, place, culture and historical context, also stresses the primacy of one of the levels of determination. It postulates what Althusser has termed a 'structure in dominance'. This dominance is given by the material, socio-economic, level: in contrast to the contingency of conventional structuralism, Marxism is a theory of socio-economic determination.

Examples of contingent determination within the IR literature are Susan Strange's theory of the four 'structures' of international relations, and Galtung's 'structural' theory of imperialism.[15] Michael Mann's conceptualisation of four forms of power has a similar indeterminacy. All recognise the importance of forms of determination focused on by historical materialism, production and economic exploitation respectively, but these are equal candidates along with other forms of constraint. Structure in dominance is displaced by a randomness of determination.

The conventional IR image of 'structuralism' also entails another difficulty, that of limitation of scope. For, as a survey of textbooks will show, the association of the 'structuralist' paradigm is one with specific topics within International Relations, namely North–South relations. If it provides one general theory of these relations, it also asserts that they are central to international relations in a manner not previously recognised. There are, however, two significant limitations to this approach.

In the first place, the very theory subsumed under the name 'structuralism' provides a partial account even of what has been written on the subject within historial materialism: while much of the literature has indeed stressed the exploiting, dominating character of imperialism, another strand, and arguably one more true to Marx's initial perceptions, has argued a more complex case: this is that imperialism, a product of the global spread of capitalism, has a two-sided impact, both destroying and creating, both disrupting established forms of economic and social activity and forging new ones. This perspective is present in Marx's work itself where, while condemning the suffering visited on humanity by the spread of capitalism, including what was to become the colonial world, and the moralising hypocrisy associated with it, he also saw that it had positive economic and social effects. Neither Marx nor Lenin, in his earlier work on Russia, in any way sentimentalised the pre-capitalist societies of the world. It was only later, and particularly with the rise of the anti-colonial reading of Marx and of the theory of dependency, that Marxism came to be dominated by the view that imperialism had an unambiguously negative impact. Yet from the late 1970s onwards, and under the impact of evident successes in industrialisation and political change in a range of third world states, this older tendency within Marxism came to be more evident.[16]

Beyond this, selective, interpretation of the historical material-ism position, there was a further problem with this identification of Marxism with 'structuralism', namely its limitation of issues deemed relevant: while any paradigm seeks to make part of its impact by redefining the hierarchy of issues – the agenda – of the discipline, it is inescapable that this very focus on 'structuralism' weakened the scope of the paradigm. However important economic relations between North and South become, they cannot be seen as providing the key, as constituting (in the Kantian sense) world politics. The emphasis upon this dimension therefore restricts, indeed inhibits, as it also purports to legitimate, the scope of historical materialism. Relations between the countries of the North themselves, i.e. developed capitalist states, those between countries of the South themselves, war and related matters, as well as the role of specific national histories and cultures and class configurations within individual states, cannot be treated in a proportionate matter. Much of the history of the international system would thereby be excluded.

Ironically, this delimiting relied upon a misreading of the supposedly 'structuralist' *Imperialism* by Lenin: far from being a book about North–South relations, this was a study of why the great imperialist powers had gone to war in 1914, and how socialists should react to it.[17] To examine the relevance of Marxism there is, therefore, a need, not to abandon the emphasis and the theoretical approach of 'structuralism', but rather to broaden the theoretical scope of the paradigm: it could thereby encompass what, in the conventional interpretation, is the high ground of the discipline, and what must remain, for all the 'structuralist' adjustment of the agenda, some of the central themes of the discipline. If the potential of historical materialism is to be applied to the field of International Relations it needs to do so by a double process – redefining the agenda on the one side, and expanding its theoretical scope to embrace the subject-matter of the discipline as a whole on the other.

The Potential of Historical Materialism

It is not possible to claim that the intellectual instruments for such an encounter are simply at hand, waiting to be utilised. Marxism, as a theoretical approach, remains in evolution: while there is much that it has encompassed in the one hundred and fifty years of its existence, there is also much that remains unanalysed, as there is that is contradictory, outdated, confused within its corpus. In this it is no different from other approaches, be these liberalism or conventional economics. The work of analysing international relations is to a considerable extent in the future, its components not present in the works of historical materialists who have written to date. Yet that such an endeavour is possible and can yield a new, comprehensive, paradigm can be asserted, for two general reasons.

First, as is evident from its impact in other social sciences, historical materialism is a comprehensive general theory of political, social and economic action, one that claims to be able to encompass all major fields of social action within its scope. It is indeed the most sustained attempt to provide a comprehensive theory of society elaborated in the past century. Its impact has already been evident in some areas of social science: in economics, history, sociology, to name the three most evident. The fact that it has not yet been accorded a comparable place in International Relations, and has not yet responded proportionately to the challenges of the discipline, is a result of the specific obstacles, theoretical and historical, already outlined.

Many conceptual aspects of historical materialism contain potential for International Relations, and can be applied to the international as other theories have been. As we have seen in Chapter 1, International Relations has derived an immense amount, indeed the majority, of its theoretical tools from other disciplines in the few decades of its existence: from the Chicago school theory of power, through behaviouralism, rational action theory, the first influences of law and philosophy, and conflict theories, functionalism and now 'critical' theory, the influence upon it of other branches of the social science are evident. The scope for such a theoretical enrichment from historical materialism, even where as with history or sociology this enrichment is based on work not directly related to International Relations, is considerable.

Secondly, within its corpus even as presently constituted, historical materialism has produced a body of literature pertaining to the conventional agenda of International Relations, and way beyond the specific interpretation of 'structuralism' that was recognised in the late 1970s: on war, violence, the state, international conflict, transnational economic issues, the development of the international system itself. The attempt by Marxists in the period 1900–20 to theorise the international system around the concept of 'imperialism', by which they meant inter-state strategic rivalry, is one of the most ambitious and creative ever made.

Since the 1970s another considerable body of literature on international issues has been produced under the influence of Marxism: apart from copious studies of imperialism, there have been the world system theories of Wallerstein, the debates on Cold War, and analyses of inter-capitalist relations. Wallerstein's work posits a very different history of the international system to that of orthodox IR: while covering roughly the same historical period, from 1500 to the present. The Wallersteinian approach emphasises the role of economic relations in constituting the system, as distinct from the political and diplomatic analysis of realism; it stresses the creation of hierarchy where the other focuses on the formation of an international 'society', equal at least in juridical claims, and it seeks to link the process of international conflict to internal social and political change, in contrast to realism's denial of the relevance of the internal.[18] At the same time, Wallerstein's work has, from within historial materialism, generated substantial criticism: as a theory that lays too much stress on circulation rather than on production, as a somewhat naive espousal of 'anti-systemic' forces even when these are themselves oppressive, as resting on too one-sided and 'dependency'-theory-oriented explanation of imperialism.[19]

The debate on the Cold War encompassed a wide range of approaches, but was in marked contrast to the reluctance of realism, and of other approaches in IR, to analyse this phenomenon in theoretical terms: for realism, it was but the continuation of inter-state competition, for independence and structural theories it was an embarrassing side-line, a distraction from their main agenda, of inter-developed and North–South relations. The implications of this for IR theory are discussed at greater length in Chapters 8 and 9: suffice it to record here that virtually the only theoretical debate on the nature of this, the dominant international conflict of the second half of the twentieth century, took place within the historical materialist paradigm.[20]

This was by no means the case for the literature on intercapitalist relations, which had been the stock in trade of interdependence literature from the early 1970s onwards, reflected in the work of, among others, Keohane, Gilpin and Strange, writers who also participated in the debate on US 'decline' in the 1980s. But this was, as these authors themselves recognised, an area on which prior to the First World War Marxists had produced a major body of literature, and to which in the new intellectual context they returned: the work of van der Pijl, Kolko, Gill and others represented this contribution.[21]

This work within IR was paralleled by the emergence of another body of work, cognate to, but not formally within, the field of International Relations, namely work in international history. Here conventional disciplinary division combined with the long-standing rivalry between the two academic approaches to prevent IR from taking adequate account of the emergence of a substantial body of literature within the historical field.

Marxism had already made a substantial contribution to other, more specific, fields of history – national, political, social, economic. But from the 1960s onwards there emerged a body of international history influenced by historical materialism and markedly different in approach to the international history of the conventional diplomatic historians. Here, among others, one could note the work of Eric Wolf, Perry Anderson, Eric Hobsbawm. Wolf's study is a comprehensive, and cogent, analysis of the subjugation of the non-European world to the European socio-economic system.[22] Anderson's work traces the evolution of the state up to the epoch of democracy, in relation to both internal social and political development and external competition.[23] Hobsbawm's work, perhaps the most wide-ranging and with the most direct implications for the study of international relations, is to be found in a set of three comparative studies on the evolution of the modern international system: *The Age of Revolutions 1789–1848, The Age of Capital 1848–1875, The Age of Empire 1875–1914*.[24]

Hobsbawm's opus presented work of direct pertinence to international relations and to the issues it addresses: the emergence of states, nations, markets, the role of economic, political and strategic factors in international affairs, the sources of conflict, within and between societies. No comparable body of work emerged either within conventional international history, or within the IR work on 'international society'. While empirically based, and judicious in its judgements and connections, Hobsbawm's work nonetheless located itself within a historical materialist approach and the broad categories of enquiry and explanation that this approach provided. In, for example, his *The Age of Imperialism*, the four decades to the outbreak of the First World War are surveyed, in the context of the development of industrial society and its expansion: whether in the chapters on the spread of democracy, nationalism, imperialism or the events leading to war in 1914 this overall historical and materialist context is maintained, without falling into any simplistic reductions. What Hobsbawm portrays is not, however, the development of some abstracted international society, or yet another exemplar of the workings out of the balance of power, but the civilisation, and crisis, of a very particular historical period.

These two factors – the theoretical potential of this approach as a comprehensive social theory, the specific contributions, substantive and conceptual, it can make to International Relations – combine to suggest that historical materialism can claim to offer a comprehensive explanation of International Relations, without piety about the adequacy of this approach to resolving the questions it faces, or suppression of the weaknesses within it.

In what follows, I shall draw together the implications of the discussions so far and to sketch out some lines along which such an elaboration can go: this will be done first by outlining the general parameters of the historical materialist paradigm, then by discussing certain specific thematic contributions of historical materialism to International Relations. It will then be possible to identify some of the problems involved in such theoretical work.

The Historical Materialist Paradigm

Marx and Engels wrote extensively on 'international' issues, both with regard to theoretical questions underlying the internationalisation of capitalism, and on international political events of their day.[25] There is much in these writings, of substance, concept and tone, that is pertinent to the constitution of a historical materialist engagement with IR. But this classical Marxist *oeuvre* on IR is, on its own, an insufficient basis on which to base such a theoretical endeavour: first, because the two types of writing – theoretical and conjunctural – are markedly different, in that they fail to integrate the theoretical with the analytic; secondly, because focusing on what was written about the 'international' as such reduces the scope of what Marxist theory *as a whole* can contribute to the study of the international. With Marx, as with other theorists, what is most pertinent to the theory of the international may lie not so much in what is explicitly said about IR but in the implications of his broader theory. In looking for their most creative ideas on international questions we do not turn first to what Machiavelli wrote about colonies, or mercenaries, or at Rousseau's musings on the virtues of the Corsican independence movement, or at Kant's views on race, but at their broader theoretical approach and insights.

Amidst the multifarious writings of Marx and Engels, there are four general themes which can be seen as defining, as constituting, the intellectual position they advanced. The first is that of 'material' determination, or, more precisely, determination by socio-economic factors, the word 'material' being used in this particular sense. In simplified terms, Marx saw society as a

totality, a composite within which each element was in a broad
sense governed by the character and tendency of the whole. The
central activity in any society is economic production, and the
main analytic questions are considered in this framework: What is
the 'level' of production, or, in his terms, how developed are the
'forces of production'? Secondly, what are the systems of property
and effective control that define ownership of these forces, i.e.
what are the 'relations' of production?

Combined these forces and relations form a 'mode of production' – feudalism, capitalism, socialism – and through this determination a broader entry, a particular society or 'social formulation' is constituted. Ideas, institutions, events within a social
formation, do not take place in abstract or in isolation from this
context of the underlying mode of production, but must rather be
seen in relation to the totality and to this material determination
within it, defined by the forces and relations of production. This is
not to claim, as 'vulgar' Marxists or many critics of Marxism
allege, that everything has to be reduced to economic activity: this
is not what Marx claimed, and his analyses of political events and
conflicts, be these France in the 1840s and 1870, or the
international events of his time, bear this out. Moreover, his
concept of capitalism embodied not just the specific forces and
ownership of the economy, but the broader set of institutions –
political, legal, cultural – that interrelated with it.[26]

What these broad concepts of the 'mode of production' and the
'social formation' did entail was that analysis of any area of human
acitivity had to be seen in this socio-economic context, and not in
abstraction from it. There is therefore no state, no belief, no
conflict, no power in general, or independent of this context. By
extension, there is no 'international system', or any component
activity, be this war or diplomacy, abstracted from the mode of
production. Indeed, International Relations is the study of the
relations not between states but between social formations. When
this insight is applied to the issues of international relations, a
definite shift of focus becomes visible. Thus the state is no longer
seen as an embodiment of national interest or judicial neutrality,
but rather of the interests of a specific society or social formation,
defined by its socio-economic structure. How far classes control
the state, or are separated from it, has been one of the main issues
of dispute within the field. Sovereignty equally becomes not a

generic legal concept but the sovereignty of specific social forces. Its history is that of forms of social power and attendant legitimisation within a formation. Security is removed from the distinct theoretical sphere in which it has been placed and becomes the security of specific social groups and for specific socio-economic reasons.

The history of the system is also seen in another light: the modern inter-state system emerged in a context of the spread of capitalism across the globe, and the subjugation of pre-capitalist societies. This socio-economic system has underpinned both the character of individual states and of their relations with each other: no analysis of international relations is possible without reference to capitalism, the social formations it generated and the world system they comprise.[27]

The second central theme, embodied in the very term for the paradigm itself, is that of history, and historical determination. In the first instance, Marx argued that history influenced present behaviour. In the phrase he used on one occasion: 'the tradition of the dead generations weighs like a nightmare upon the minds of the living'. But it meant something more than this: Marx argued that the events or character of any society could only be seen in their historical context – one had to ask how the object of study came about, what the influences, of past events were, and what the impact of the past in shaping the current situation might be.[28] Just as he argued that society had to be seen in its socio-economic context, so he believed that the conditions of generation and a recognition of their contingent location, were central to any analysis. To understand contemporary capitalist society, one had to see how it originated and what the problems and tendencies conditioned by the past were, how it limited what people thought of as being their options, and led them to be influenced, or wholly determined, by passions, illusions, identifications derived usually unwittingly from the past.

Anyone familiar with the workings of the international system will, in one sense, be aware of this – the ideological suppression of the origins of the system, a propensity to deny the violence involved in its creation, and the force within international affairs, not least through nationalism, of irrational factors. Thus what Marx said of the role of history in general could be said of any particular country: its domestic and foreign policies, the instincts of its leaders and the responses of its public, the institutions through which policy was conducted, the grievances and fears that drive its population – all reflected the past to a degree larger than was often admitted.

More importantly, as with socio-economic, so with historical determination, Marx also saw these conditioning factors as undermining the appearance which all social events had of being in some way 'natural' or 'eternal': one of the major functions of political socialisation in any society is to make what exists in that society appear as inevitable, and unchangeable. The same is true of the international domain itself, and the attendant forms – nation, state, sovereignty, etc. – associated with it. Location of these features of a society in the historical context of their origin serves to contradict this appearance of being natural and eternal, as well as to suggest that alternatives are also the more possible.

The place of history in the study of international relations is, as already recognised, an uneasy one. This is both for theoretical reasons, in that International Relations seeks to identify a distinct conceptual terrain for study, and for practical and professional reasons, in that it wishes to distinguish and justify itself by contrast with what is regarded as the ideologised approach of diplomatic history, too often a fetishism of archives and dates. The question of historical origin receives less attention. Where history is present, it is usually either as illustration, or, rather too often, as a means of intimidating the reader with a barrage of examples, evident as much in James Der Derian (*On Diplomacy*) as in Martin Wight.

The result, however, is that many of the questions considered within International Relations are to a perilous degree abstracted from their historical context. This applies, first, to the lack of historical culture of most of those writing about and studying the subject, so that the proportion and range of reference to history is often absent. Behaviouralism, of course, made a rejection of history one of its central tenets. It applies equally to the abstracting of specific concepts from the historical situation under which they arose. The claim, frequently made and repeated in the literature, that the contemporary British and American states are examples of a peaceful, non-revolutionary, path of development is one striking example of this. The 'expansion' of Western society or of international society was achieved through the subjugation, plunder, and in some cases massacre, of colonial societies. A more recent case is the prevailing discussion of the concept of 'interdependence' and the related issue of 'ungovernability': this almost elides the importance of the particular event that, at the political level, brought this question to the fore, namely the Vietnam War, and its impact on the US political and social systems.[29]

The third central theme of the historical materialist approach is the centrality of classes as actors in political life, both domestic and international.[30] Classes are defined, very broadly, by reference to their ownership and control of the means of production, a power that is seen as defining the other forms of social power that they exercise. If within a particular state classes act to subject and control those less powerful than themselves, they act internationally to ally with groups similar to themselves when this is beneficial, and to compete with them by peaceful or military means, when rivalry is preferred. Conflict between them, or what is known as 'class struggle', therefore takes place at two levels: between groups at different positions on the socio-economic ladder, and between groups with similar positions. Such struggle also takes place both within specific states and internationally: as the spread of capitalism has increased the size of the capitalist world, rivalry with other ruling classes at an international level has continued side-by-side with conflict within specific states. Each ruling class has been able to use the international character of capitalism both to find support for the preservation of its own position within society, by allying with others, and to see in the international arena a domain for the extension of its own interests and power.

This prominence of classes as analytic tools has two immediate consequences for International Relations. First, it invests the major conflicts of international politics with a distinct socio-economic character. Though it may be untrue to say, paraphrasing Marx, that all the history of International Relations has been one of class struggle, it has certainly been a major and at times decisive component. The competitive spread of the European empires, the outbreaks of the two world wars, the gold standard crisis of 1931, the OPEC price rises of 1971–73, the disputes over trade and interest rates within the Atlantic Alliance in the early 1980s, US–Japanese trade conflict in the 1990s – all now appear as, in broad terms, part of conflict between capitalist ruling classes, between old established capitalist powers and their new rivals, the latter produced by the development of capitalist social relations within their own countries. Many of the disputes that have marked twentieth century history became inter-imperialist and inter-capitalist disputes, beyond their specific national, geographic and historical characteristics: as already noted, this issue of conflict between great powers, not the dynamics of 'North–South' relations was the main question addressed by Lenin and others, in the debate on imperialism before the First World War.

Secondly, in this light, the debates that have flourished within International Relations for so long appear to be founded on some questionable premises. Since the state is not an independent entity, but is rather located in a particular socio-economic and class context, the debate on whether the state is losing power to non-state actors changes character. For the question now becomes not whether the state has recently, i.e. since 1945 or 1970, lost pre-eminence to non-state actors but how far the 'non-state' actors who have *always* affected the power and character of the state act through the state or through other channels. These non-state actors, i.e. classes, have always been there, but have exercised their power in a variety of ways. The question of how far the boundary between domestic and international politics has broken down also acquires a different significance; in capitalism classes have always operated internationally, from the bankers and trading companies of the sixteenth century onwards, and have in turn been affected domestically by changes in the international economic and political situation.[31]

The primacy of classes therefore serves in a dual sense to place in question the concept of the 'nation-state': it shows, first, that the state itself is, to a considerable extent, a function of wider social forces, and secondly that the impermeability of domestic politics is an appearance which conceals a permanent, underlying, internationalisation of political and economic factors. In Marx's own writings, there is an interesting tension on this issue: his political instincts led him to emphasise the international character of the proletariat, the working class, and their aspiration and ability to organise on an international basis against their class enemies; yet his theory contained within it another suggestion, namely that it was not the working class, but the bourgeoisie, who were the most international, since their education and culture on the one hand, and their very economic interests on the other, were such as to lead them to act more and more internationally. The subsequent history of capitalism has, as much as anything, been one in which the internationalisation of the ruling class has proceeded as fast as, or even faster than, that of the working class – hence, as Jeff Frieden, Stephen Gill, Kees van der Pijl and others have shown, the EC (European Community), the Trilateral Commission, the Group of 7 and many others are examples of transnational élite coordination, for the better management of the economy, both national and international.

The fourth central concept of historical materialism is that of conflict and its apogee, revolution. Much of the literature on and within Marxism has been concerned with the issue of conflict at the philosophical and methodological level, as reflected in the question of 'dialectics'. This is a debatable venture, a relic of the Hegelian influence on Marx and of the widespread nineteenth-century view that a single 'method' for natural and social sciences could be ascertained. Conflict is taken here to be a historical and social concept, pertaining to relations between different classes and other social groups, and generated by differences in socio-economic positions. Historical materialism not only argues that such conflict is inevitable, given inequalities in wealth and economic position in contemporary society, but also that it is a major dynamic factor in the politics of the international system as well as being so in that of individual societies.

The culmination of such conflicts can take place in one of two ways, or in a combination of the two: wars and revolution. In Marxism, wars represent conflicts between social classes of similar character, rivals for a monopoly of control over markets, resources and territory. Marx distinguishes between 'political' revolutions, which only change the form of government; and 'social' revolutions that alter the system of class rule: he is concerned with the latter. Revolutions represent conflicts between social classes of different character, within particular states. Revolutions are the events which, arising out of the deep conflicts within a socio-economic structure, lead to changes in the social character of states, and to substantial shifts in the character of international politics. Far from representing aberrations, breakdowns, or interruptions of normal politics, they are widespread and central transition points within the history of nations and of the international community generally. They are, in Marx's words, the 'locomotives of history'.[32]

If this tenet of historical materialism is extended to the international, then it suggests that the central concern of International Relations becomes not security, and the actions of the nation-state directed to defending and enhancing it, but rather conflict, and the ways in which this is generated, conducted, and resolved. Underlying the myriad events of international affairs lies social conflict, within and across frontiers, the pursuit of wealth and economic power as the source of these manifold events.[33] Taking the historical determination of specific states into account, it becomes necessary to enquire whence these came, or, more precisely, out of what historical conflicts they emerged. The most apparently pacific of states may have issued from extremely bloody pasts – the superficially tranquil Netherlands has a history replete with revolution, invasion and sanguinary internal strife. The currently smooth workings of democracy in Germany or Japan betray the fact that this political system was imposed but two generations ago through foreign military intervention. The sudden arrival of close to one hundred new states on the world scene in the period since 1945 is often adduced merely as a numerical addition, a complicating or diluting expansion, of an otherwise continuous states system: the fact that this process was a result of intense conflicts, between colonies and colonial power and, as a major precondion, derived from the weakening of the colonial empires in the Second World War, receives less than its appropriate share of attention.

Marx was aware of this in his writings on the mid-nineteenth century: writing on the challenge to the five-nation balance of power, the pentarchy, he warned of the presence of a sixth great power, revolution. Thus, the dominant problem of twentieth-century international politics is seen by conventional international relations theory as being that of security: but for much of that period it can equally be seen as having been that of containing inter-capitalist conflict on the one hand, and social revolution on the other. In other words, the management of social conflict is the issue that has most concerned politicians and academic analysts of foreign policy alike.[34] As Arno Mayer has shown, an apparently neutral international event like the Versailles Peace Conference of

1919 was preoccupied with the issue of counter revolution and containing disorder. Marx was mistaken to invest revolution with the mystical and deterministic overtones that came to be associated with it, and equally wrong to believe that some radically different and emancipated society would emerge from such upheavals: but he was right to see social conflict, over ownership, power, resources, as a central feature of politics, and to ask how such conflict underlay the apparently autonomous world of political strife and international conflict.

This he was able to do, in part, by introducing the materialist and historical contexts. When it is said that the pursuit of international politics is one of 'order' one has to ask 'order' for whom, and in whose interests? Similarly, when it is said, as by Hedley Bull, that international society is 'anarchical', this both recognises and avoids the question: it recognises it in so far as it acknowledges that there is conflict and that it is endemic to the international system, but it avoids it, in so far as it denies that there is an underlying source of this conflict, beyond the states system, and locates the coherence of the system only at the level of the mechanisms, or so-called 'institutions', evolved to manage this conflict. But the assertion of anarchy conceals the fact that this superficially incoherent conflict is itself the product of factors that are definable and intelligible, even if they cannot be controlled as the principal actors would like. Moreover, for Marxism, it is above all not the anarchy of the states system but that of the market and of capitalism itself that is determinant.[35]

The theme of conflict opens the way to an evaluation of the place within Marxist thought of an issue already touched on, the question of will, and of conscious human activity. Marx emphasised the importance of socio-economic and historical determination: these forces bore heavily upon human actors and set both limits to what they could achieve and directions in which their actions tended.

A central theme of historical materialism is a recognition of the realm of necessity, and of the power of unrecognised factors to influence our behaviour. In this sense, Marx asserted the importance of unacknowledged social and historic factors, in some ways as powerful as Freud's individual unconscious. But, as with Freud, he believed that human will, and the work of making the unconscious explicit and conscious, had a purpose and was, within certain limits, attainable. Moreover, such a recognition was the path not to the celebration of the inevitable, to surrender in the face of the determined, but rather was a precondition for the exercise of that degree of freedom which circumstances permitted. Social groups could the more easily change their position if they saw the extent of the factors that determined their situation.

Similarly, the possibility of action to alter the existing system of international relations, to wage a conflict with some degree of success, depended upon a comparable recognition of necessity. Conflicts are, to a considerable extent, waged by actors who are blind, or who cannot attain the goals they rationally set themselves. In international relations this, in Hegel's terms, 'cunning of reason' encourages the semblance of an international system that is random and anarchical, or one that is unchangeable: historical materialism provided both an alternative explanation and a prescription. It indicated an alternative international system, albeit one that is attainable only through sustained effort and an unrelenting attempt to recognise the degree to which all human actors remain prisoners of the forces, social and historical, that bear upon them. More than other theories it was historical materialism that asserted that human agency had created one world, a capitalist one.

The Inhibitions of Theory

These four general themes provide an outline, brief and inadequate as it may be, of a possible historical materialist approach and a suggestion of the implications of it for International Relations. That this paradigm has not, as yet, yielded either the theoretical or the empirical work on International Relations that is its potential indicates that the paradigm also contains major difficulties, ones that inhibit its development and deflect its practitioners.

The most powerful inhibiting factor in Marxism is the tone of its overall approach, something that inhibited its theoretical development and blunted its understanding by others. This denotes the dogmatism and intolerance of part of the analysis that appears under its name, and, as a dominating part of this dogmatism, the immanence of a historical teleology, i.e. the belief that history was/is moving in a particular, ultimately emancipatory, direction. This dogmatism was a product of the political considerations of many who used it, and in particular of the rulers of communist states, and their supporters elsewhere. Ironically, it was to provide contradictory vindication of perhaps the only international concept produced by orthodox communism that did have general validity, that of the 'correlation of forces', a broad dynamic conception of inter-bloc relations that combined military with cultural, political and economic factors: more elaborated than the alternative, 'balance of power', it was, however, in error on the direction in which the correlation was moving.[36]

But the dogmatism of much Marxism reflects something more than the fact that it is associated with state power in a range of dictatorial countries. It is also a product of factors engrained in classical Marxism itself, and which spring from the belief in the inevitability of the capitalist crisis and the advent of socialism. Consciousness of determinism produces a sense of rectitude, and hence of intolerance. Such an attitude, present as it was in Marx, is in one sense thoroughly un-Marxist, in that it ascribes a permanence to ideas that their very historical and socio-economic contingency precludes. This dogmatism, and unrelenting assertion of specific arguments within a paradigm, is by no means specific to Marxism, as students of International Relations and all other social sciences are well aware. Yet it is a powerful, warping, force within historical materialism itself, one that stunted its growth, made it the easier for its foes to dismiss or distort it, and is still far from being extinct. Nowhere was this more evidence than in the later thinking on 'imperialism', where a set of absolute assertions about the impact of the industrialised countries on the third world blocked analysis of what was actually happening in these societies and the possibilities for change within them.

The first of the limitations within Marxism concerns the very concept of 'determination', the degree to which political events or actors or even the state itself can be seen as mere expressions of the underlying socio-economic structure of a society. This problem is as relevant for International Relations as it is for any other branch of human activity – art, psychology, social behaviour, philosophy. While the writings of independent, 'western' Marxists were able to evade this, the tendency towards reductionism maimed much Marxist analysis for the past century and more.

What appears much more fruitful, and empirically plausible, is to see determination as western Marxists did not in an absolute sense, that evacuates all non-material phenomena of any meaning and individual capacity for action and change, but rather to see it as providing a context, a set of limits and significances within which these other factors can be assessed. To see such factors – be they individuals, parties, governments or ideologies – outside their socio-economic context is to abstract them from the forces that bring them into being and invest them with much of their potency.

This general problem with the level of determination of the socio-economic does much to account for another area of inhibition: the relative autonomy of politics. Although Marx, Engels, Lenin and their successors wrote copiously on politics, as they were avid political practitioners, there remained within their writings a deep and unresolved problem about how to analyse politics itself. This problem is as pertinent for international politics as it is for domestic. Beyond demonstrating the ways in which socio-economic factors influence politics, historical materialists have often been unsuccessful in adequately defining the workings of politics itself, i.e. of that dimension of politics that is not simply an expression of the socio-economic.

Marx's own writings on the politics of his time betray this problem, amidst the tactical astuteness of his observation. Nowhere is this more so than in his writings on the Great Power conflicts of his day, where a deep hostility to Czarist Russia led him into a world of moralising and conspiracy theory that bore no substantive relation to his general theoretical approach. Lenin's naivety about the revolutionary state in early 1917, and his ignoring of the dangers of a new dictatorship after 1918, illustrate the same weakness. The illusion that the state would wither away in its internal dimension, i.e. *vis-à-vis* society, is reproduced in the illusion that the division between states will be overcome by capitalist interdependence or socialist revolution.

Perhaps the greatest and most eloquent example of this underestimation of the state is the abiding difficulty which orthodox Marxists have had in explaining two of the most enduring features of twentieth-century politics: nationalism and capitalist democracy. For all the talk of false consciousness, mystification and leadership betrayal, these major phenomena presented a theoretical problem to Marxism. The former has persistently proved itself superior to class loyalties as a means of mobilising mass support, amongst oppressed and oppressor alike. The latter has secured the loyalty or at least acquiescence of the mass of the population in the more developed capitalist countries for half a century or more, with resort to only limited coercion and intimidation on the part of the ruling classes.

These difficulties have important implications for the study of International Relations. Within International Relations, there are a variety of specific sub-disciplines that go to make up the overall subject-matter of the discipline. These include, international law, institutions, security, decision-making, economic relations, and philosophy. A recognition of their theoretical and practical dependence upon the determinations of the socio-economic and the historical, such that they do not become abstracted and detotalised from their context, can be balanced by a recognition that they are, as in domestic politics governed by rules and tendencies of their own, ones that cannot be reduced to those of the socio-economic. For example, to see the NATO (North Atlantic Treaty Organisation) alliance merely as an alliance of capitalist states, without any geographical, cultural and historical specificity, would be almost as misleading as to see it in International Relations terms as an alliance *in general* without reference to the socio-economic interests, offensive and defensive, of the governments that created and sustain it. Similarly, it is possible to analyse the OPEC states both as insecure oil-producers, the majority of them Arab states of the Middle East, and as products of the combined and uneven development of capitalism in the post-war epoch with corresponding behaviour for commodity suppliers in a *monopoly* position.

Marxism beyond Cold War

Historical materialism, therefore, is a body of concepts that claims to analyse the full range of social behaviour, international relations included. Writers working with its theoretical approach have already produced some specific analysis of issues and events within international relations, and have generated general concepts that have the potential of being applied systematically to this discipline. Historical materialism can present a theoretical and empirical alternative to work within the International Relations discipline as hitherto conventionally constituted. But it can only do so by recognising the challenge which international relations itself pose to it, as well as its own need to develop its analytic potential in open response to the events and some of the alternative theories of the contemporary world.

To argue for the recognition of the relevance of historical materialism in the aftermath of the Cold War and the collapse of the communist system may, at first sight, appear perverse, if not forlorn. Yet such an endeavour is possible not only in spite of, but in certain respects because of, that turn of events. At the most straightforward level, the pertinence of historical materialism as an explanatory system has never been dependent upon the success of dictatorial movements that claimed to speak in its name, any more than has capitalism relied on the success of the authoritarian, racist and belligerent regimes that it produced. The evolution, separate from and in conflict with official communism, of independent Marxism over most of the twentieth century is evidence enough of that. But beyond this consideration lies the possibility that historical materialism may prove to be just as relevant as it ever was as an explanatory system, and one that, in origin and development, takes as its starting point and focus of analysis precisely that phenomenon that now more than ever dominates the world, namely capitalism.

Marxism was wrong to assert the imminence of a revolutionary alternative to capitalist society, and it consistently underrated the potential for change, and improvement within capitalism. As we shall see in Chapter 10, the claim that capitalism inevitably leads to war may turn out to be itself historical, a reflection on states that were not yet fully democratic. But its twin claims, that the mode of production provides the context for the analysis of political phenomena, national and international, and that the capitalist system is riven with conflicts, dangers and failures, grounded in these socio-economic factors, would seem to be as valid today as they ever were.

The concluding chapters of this book provide one set of answers to this, exploring how a broad historical materialist approach may provide explanations both of the Cold War, and of its uneasy aftermath. With the end of the long confrontation with communism, and the attendant compulsion to conceal socio-economic issues, IR may now admit the extent to which specific political and social interests determined its agenda, and the foreign policy of states: in such a context, historical materialism, itself freed from dogmatism and conformity, may become more, not less, significant within the study of the international.

4

State and Society in International Relations

Impasse on the State

Since the early 1970s much of the theoretical debate within International Relations has focused on the question of the state. Some discussion has been around the analytic primacy of the state as the constitutive actor in international relations, while some has focused on normative questions, of the degree to which the state can be regarded as the primary guarantor of what is good, within and between states. 'State-centric' realism has reasserted traditional positions on the state and has, through the emergence of neo-realism, affirmed new ones, especially in the field of international economic relations. Other paradigms have challenged the primacy of the state, either by asserting the role of non-state actors, as in theories of interdependence and transnationalism, or by asserting the primacy of global systems and structures over specific actors, state or non-state. All three of these approaches have been influenced by broader trends within political science: realism by mainstream political theory; transnationalism by the pluralist and behavioural rejection of the state in favour of studying actions; structuralism by theories of socio-economic determination.

By the late 1980s, however, it would seem that this debate within International Relations had reached an impasse. The three paradigms, with their many variations and reformulations, remained vigorous, and the numbers of their adherents waxed and waned with professional development and intellectual fashion. However, there was no sign that any one of them could or would prevail over the others. The challengers to realism were still

74

seeking to refute it and displace it, while proponents of realism repeated the reasons why the challengers are inadequate.[1] The search for a single paradigm, for a 'normality' defined in Kuhnian terms, produced a situation of, for many, unsatisfactory indeed sterile pluralism.

It can, however, be argued that a pluralism of paradigms is, in fact, more of an indication of a healthy discipline than a mono-paradigmatic normalcy in which other perspectives, the research programmes they suggest, the very concepts and indeed facts they point us to, are precluded. The exclusive and chloroforming world of the 1950s in many social sciences, where one paradigm reigned in an institutionalised self-confidence, is one to which few friends of International Relations or social science more generally would want to return. It can, moreover, be argued that the very pursuit of paradigm refutation, on narrowly intellectual grounds, is a misplaced venture, since the reasons for the attractiveness and tenacity of a specific approach are multiple: these include not only intellectual coherence, but also institutional support, the influence of trends and conventional wisdoms within social science as a whole and the broader climate of the times.[2]

To accept the legitimacy and inevitability of paradigmatic pluralism is not, however, to suggest that the reasons for theoretical diversity are not of interest, nor that all paradigms can be treated as equally valid: in the case of the debate on the state, it is worth posing the question as to why the debate of the last three decades has made so little progress. There has been no resolution, and relatively little conceding of ground. One reason, inscribed in Kuhn's own work and in that of his followers, is that paradigms are incommensurable, i.e. because they deploy different concepts and conceptual systems, and ask different questions and select different facts, their arguments cannot be matched one against the other.[3] Any cogent paradigm can provide a plausible explanation of 'anomalies', or trends in the real world, that others might see as threatening its validity: thus realists can incorporate multinational corporations (MNCs), interdependence theorists the continued role of security issues, and structuralists the rise of the newly industrialised countries (NICs). As Kuhn has written: 'All historically significant theories have agreed with the facts, but only more or less'. The impasse on the state is, therefore, in part a product of a deeper theoretical impasse that itself determines a non-encounter on the state. A second reason, identified in, amongst other places, much literature on international political economy, is that the development of perspectives of the state's place in international relations has itself been a contradictory process confirming neither simple realist nor non-realist analyses. The identifying and accumulating of ways in which the state has lost its previous dominance can be countered by another list of ways in which it has maintained or even enhanced it: the state has both strengthened and weakened its position. No simple empirical resolution of these competitive listings is possible, any more than is one in theory. If the realists do appear to be unduly complacent in the assertion that little or nothing has really changed, the challengers often overstate the degree to which states are no longer central actors: this is so both in their analysis of the recent course of international relations and in the recurrent tendency to extrapolate current trends into an apparently proximate and, in most cases desirable, stateless future. The theoretical comprehension of the contradictory process (state-enhancement/state-displacement) is one that can take us beyond the present polarisation.

There is, however, a third reason for the impasse, one that goes to the heart of International Relations, to the concepts it bases itself upon, to the research programmes it stimulates, and to its relation with other disciplines within the social sciences. This is the question of the definition of 'state' which is used. It sometimes appears as if theorists of International Relations are working with the concepts of antique political theorists. For parallel to, but largely unacknowledged within, the International Relations debate on the state over the past twenty years there has been another debate on the state, within sociology and within Marxism, on how exactly the state operates. Most significantly perhaps, at the very time when the innovators and proponents of new paradigms within International Relations have been seeking to reject or reduce the salience of the (undefined) state, the comparable trend within sociology has been to re-examine the state and to reassert its centrality in historical and contemporary contexts, while Marxist debate has focused not on the supercession of the state but on how to analyse its relation to social classes.[4] A major change in favour of the state has been taking place. The title of a collection of sociological essays on this issue, *Bringing the*

State Back In,[5] which resumes this debate and contains articles by many of its leading practitioners, suggests a contrary but crucially relevant development in a cognate discipline to International Relations which has considerable implications for IR's, often unwarrantedly solipsistic, discussion on this issue. Equally, the Marxist debate cuts through any counterposing of states and non-state actors. What these developments suggest is that one way to reassess the debate on the state within International Relations is to study these parallel discussions and in so doing to question the exclusive definition of the state around which much of the International Relations debate has implicitly revolved. The argument is not about whether we are or are not 'state-centric', but what we mean by the state.

This revival of state theory is particularly relevant to those who have claimed the term should be abandoned. In a succession of books and articles published from the mid-1980s onwards Yale Ferguson and Richard Mansbach have argued that so confused and inappropriate is the concept of the 'state', that it cannot provide a basis for theoretical work on international relations. Yet while they are right to draw attention to the multiplicity of meanings attached to the state, they are not justified in many of their other arguments or their conclusions. On the one hand, there is nothing inherent in the concept of the state, as defined below, to preclude discussion of the varieties of state power and value allocation that they draw attention to. On the other hand, they skirt around, indeed fail seriously to engage with, the literature on the state that has developed within the sociological literature and which indeed produced a range of work just at the time when they were pronouncing the concept unusable. The claim that the term 'state' necessarily has normative connotations is quite unfounded. Their attempt to relate the uselessness of the concept 'state' to the broader crisis in IR theory is equally mistaken, based as it is on an electicism of method and an indeterminacy of concept. The conclusion that their work leads to is not so much that, emancipated from the concept of 'state', a new International Relations is possible, but rather that, if this concept is abandoned, further confusion ensues.[6]

Definitions Contrasted

It is not at first obvious that there is a problem about the definition of the state in International Relations, for the simple reason that the operative distinction is implicit and not conventionally subject to extended theoretical or empirical analysis. It is indeed para- doxical that a concept so central to the whole discipline should escape explication as this one has. One can find many discussions of war, sovereignty, institutions and so forth, but one can search in vain in the textbooks for comparable discussion of the state. International Relations theorists assume we know what it is: e.g. Bull that it is a political community. Waltz that it is in practice coextensive with the nation.[7] The reason is that International Relations as a whole takes as given one specific definition: what one may term the national-territorial totality. Thus the 'state' (e.g. Britain, Russia, America, etc.) comprises in conceptual form what is denoted visually on a political map – viz. the country as a whole and all that is within it: territory, government, people, society. There could be no better summary of this view than that of Northedge in the introductory chapter to his *The International Political System*:

> A state, in the sense used in this book, is a territorial association of people recognized for purposes of law and diplomacy as a legally equal member of the system of states. It is in reality a means of organizing people for the purpose of their participa- tion in the international system.[8]

It is not argued by those who use this concept favourably, especially realists, that such a state exists empirically, but only that an abstraction of this kind, derived from political theory and international law, is heuristically the most appropriate for Inter- national Relations.[9] In other words, theory based on this concept explains more about international relations and should, therefore, be maintained. This is a valid reason for maintaining an abstrac- tion: the question is not whether it provides a basis for explana- tion, but rather how adequate the explanation it provides is. It should be evident, of course, that once this concept is accepted then, by definition, the question of non-state actors is largely prejudged.

The alternative concept of the state, as it is used in much recent sociological writing and in the parallel Marxist debate, is of a more limited kind. It denotes not the social-territorial totality, but a specific set of coercive and administrative institutions, distinct from the broader political, social and national context in which it finds itself. Influenced by the German tradition of Max Weber and Otto Hintze, Skocpol defines the state 'a set of administrative, policing and military organizations headed, and more or less well coordinated, by an executive authority'.[10] Many alternative definitions of the state can be provided within this sociological approach. However, this concept of coercive and administrative institutions serves to distinguish a quite separate concept of the state, and to suggest an alternative way in which the concept can be incorporated within discussion of international relations.

Within the sociological discussion of the state that has emerged over the past decades many problems remain unresolved. One is the question of delimiting the extent of the state: if the state is seen as the mechanism for dominating, regulating and reproducing a society under given social relations then the question arises of where to locate institutions that are formally independent but which are influenced by the state and parallel its regulatory and reproductive functions: schools, universities, churches, and, in some of its roles, the family. The debate on Althusser's conception of educational establishments as Ideological State Apparatuses was an example of this.[11] A second debate, well represented in *Bringing the State Back In*, concerns the 'autonomy' of the state: once the state is seen as institutionally distinct from society, the question arises of the degree to which it can act autonomously, and represent values separate from that society, even if it is ultimately constrained by it. The institutional concept of the state is, in part, a means of resisting those Marxist theories that see the state as, to a greater or lesser extent, an expression of class or economic interest. The degree to which those in power can pursue policies against the apparent wishes of much of society (by imposing reforms or pursuing wars that are unpopular and destructive) poses this issue of autonomy quite clearly. One explanation is that the state has the longer-term strategic interests of society in mind. For some, such as Skocpol, there is a distinct area of autonomy which is greatly enhanced by the state's international role. A Marxist such as Fred Block can also take this position.[12] For others, such as Robert Brenner, a division of labour between societal administration and private appropriation should not be confused with any real autonomy, and the Marxist theory of the state as a class instrument remains valid.[13] A third debate, one located more specifically within the Marxist sociological tradition, has concerned the relation of the contemporary state to capitalism and to classes. Going beyond the initial Marxist-Leninist view of the state as a mere instrument of class rule, this debate has generated a variety of alternative theses from the capital logic approach to that which stresses the management of intra-élite conflicts, to the approach influenced by one reading of Gramsci according to which the function of the state is to maintain class hegemony in all its dimensions – coercive, administrative, regulative and ideological. This alternative theory, generally described as 'structural', allows a much greater degree of autonomy to the state.

The difference between these two conceptions of the state is reflected in everyday language. In discussing land, we distinguish between the territory of the state, in its total sense, and the areas of land owned by the state, in its institutional sense. Similarly we distinguish between the population or working population of a state, and the percentage of that population who are directly employed by the state. In revolutions the institutional state is overthrown, but the total state remains. Yet much of the International Relations debate does seem to involve a confusion of these two meanings. Thus when critics of Marxism say it is a form of realism because it is 'state-centric', this mixes up the two concepts of the state: Marxists use the term 'state' quite differently from realists. The result is a prevailing dominance of the totality concept that, because of the very definition involved, precludes other areas of theoretical investigation. This is what a paradigm should do: realists can and do argue that the issues, and data, identified as relevant by other paradigms, are relatively insignificant.

Whether or not the sociological concept has greater analytic and explicatory potential than the national-territorial totality concept is a matter of debate. Yet, whatever the final judgement on this score, two broad contrasts are immediately evident. The first is that, for a discipline concerned with the interpretation of reality, the sociological concept is far less of an ideological abstraction than is the national-territorial totality one. The concept normally used in International Relations is not merely an analytic convenience, but also one replete with legal and value assumptions (i.e. that states are equal, that they control their territory, that they coincide with nations, that they represent their peoples). There could indeed be few concepts less 'realistic' than that of the sovereign state in its conventional International Relations guise. A second immediately relevant contrast is that the sociological approach enables us to pose much more clearly the question of the effectivity of the international dimension; i.e. why and how participation in the international realm enhances and strengthens states, and, in particular, why it enables them to act more independently of the societies they rule. This most central feature of the modern world, that states can be less responsive to, and representative of, their societies precisely because of their international role, is submerged, *ab initio*, by the assumptions of the 'national-territorial' concept.

The least that can be said, therefore, is that an alternative conceptualisation of the state permits analytic questions and avenues of research markedly different from those permitted within the totality approach. In the first place this alternative definition of the state opens up a set of conceptual distinctions that are often confused and conflated in literature on International Relations, but which need to be separated out if the state–society relationship is to be more clearly identified. The very concept 'international' has, as many critics have pointed out, confused the issue by denoting as between nations what are usually relations between states. Morgenthau's classic, *Politics Among Nations* is, like the United Nations itself, symptomatically mistitled.

One distinction is that between the state, in this delimited sociological sense, and society, i.e. the range of institutions, individuals and practices lying beyond the direct control and financing of this central entity.[14] Society itself is not homogeneous, comprising as it does different social classes and ethnic and interest groups, and the access of these to the state will be different, depending upon the power, wealth and political skill of these groups. The state–society relation is therefore variable: it is here that the Marxist debate has been the sharpest, and where many Marxists have most criticised the institutional approach.[15]

A second distinction is between state and government, i.e.,

between the ensemble of administrative apparatuses and the executive personnel formally in positions of supreme control. Conventional political discourse assumes that these are identical, just as the state–government pair are assumed to represent society as a whole. Thus, in orthodox usage, the indications 'prime minister' or 'president' of a country are readily replaced with the name of the country itself: 'Britain's position on disarmament is . . .', etc. However, the state–government distinction may, in some situations, become of considerable relevance as elements within the state resist or actively oppose the policies of government. This may take relatively innocuous forms (press leaks, dragging of feet, arrangements of an agenda) but it can take much more acute forms, culminating in that most extreme of state–government contradictions, the military *coup d'état.*

A third central distinction is that between state and nation. The term 'nation-state', based as it is on an assumption of ethnic homogeneity and political representativity, is, in empirical terms, inappropriate to the modern world. Coercive states may well not represent the nation (i.e. the society they rule) at all; where there is ethnic diversity, as there is in most states of the world, the state may represent the interests of one national group more than those of another. The question is therefore open as to how far the state represents the nation. While some International Relations theory, notably foreign policy analysis, has challenged the realist conflation of these terms, no alternative conceptualisation of the state has so far been counterposed to it.[16]

The sociological approach suggests, secondly, an alternative and less benign view of the origins of states. Its emphasis is on the state as initially an instrument of coercion and extraction, both against the populations subjected to states and against rivals. As Tilly has shown, on the basis of historical investigation, European states began as instruments of subjugation, as protection rackets.[17] It may be that over the centuries these protection rackets have developed a more representational function, but this is contingent, something that varies in degree from country to country and may not be a completed process. It is worth remembering that the principle of one person one vote is only something introduced into major Western states since the Second World War.[18] The fact that in its origins the main functions of the state are the seizure of land and goods, the subjugation of populations, and the waging of war against rivals is rather understated in conventional accounts of the rise of the modern system, which imply that states have been representative ever since 1648.

A third central theme, touched on in Chapter 1, is that states, and their internal organisation, have developed in a world-historical context, i.e. in interaction with, and imitation of, other states. Far from the internal constitution of states and societies being immune, at least until recently, to international phenomena, the international dimension provided the context and formative influence for these states, not only for the majority of the world states that are post-colonial and so shaped by the colonial experience, but equally for European states. The world economy, the Reformation, the values of legitimacy, and above all, the pressures of economic and military competition ensured this.[19] Important as this is in the critique of Marxism (as in Giddens and Mann) it is equally relevant as an alternative international theory to that of realism, which derives the system from states.

A fourth constitutive theme is that states are formative of societies: of national consciousness; of the national ideologies that turn the arbitrary assemblages of people into nations; of national economies. States have always played a role in forming economies, not just through planning, taxation, and the promotion of sectors tied to the national, specifically military interest, but also through the regulation of economies through legislation specifying what is and is not legitimate and through the financial mechanisms of central banks. However international capital may or may not be in the late twentieth century, it recognises the regulatory powers of states. This is nowhere clearer than in the fluctuations of the international money markets in response to varying prospects for elections in major Western states, and in the face of the changing regulatory powers of states, as well as in the sometimes nervous responses of the stock exchanges to the appointment of new central bank chairmen. If the policies of the British, German, Japanese and US states did not affect the money markets, the latter would more easily ignore pre-election polls and the advent of the new forms of regulation. The fallacy of much current writing on the state's role in the economy, in identifying state control only with formal state ownership of productive and financial services, ignores the much broader powers that states have historically maintained and still maintain *vis-à-vis* their economies.

Finally, there is an important set of questions pertaining to the state's own internal composition and relation to society that are raised by the development of historical sociology. As Michael Mann has shown, the question of state capacities, of how states administer populations and territories, and the manifold mechanisms for imposing and extending control, is one that richly repays comparative and historical investigation.[20] This approach frees the study of the state from the concept of sovereignty, the assumption that the state does have a monopoly of power and legitimacy within a delimited territory, and instead asks how, and how far, and with what changes, such control has developed. The premise of much International Relations writing is that the state is sovereign, in controlling effectively the territory and population over which it rules. This is, however, an empirical simplification, even for the most effective of states. It precludes analysis of just how control is exercised and developed and how other factors, including international ones, may modify and affect a state's capacity to control.

These broad themes, recurrent in much of the recent sociological and historical-sociological literature, suggest areas in which the alternative concept of the state can affect the study of International Relations. What follows are some more specific suggestions as to how, given this alternative paradigm, the study of the relations may be developed.

The State as Domestic and International Actor

The most significant theme for International Relations pervading this literature is that the state is seen as acting in two dimensions, the domestic and the international. In its simplest form, the state seeks both to compete with other states by mobilising resources internally, and to use its international role to consolidate its position domestically. For example, a state may appropriate territory, go to war, or pursue an arms control agreement to gain domestic advantage, while it may promote industrialisation, introduce educational change, raise taxes, or treat an ethnic minority better, in order to achieve international goals. Conducted successfully, this two-front policy may work to the benefit of the state, and it is evident that those holding state power have many advantages in pursuing this approach. This two-dimensionality does, however, involve major risks. A state that places undue pressure on its own society in order to mobilise resources for international competition may provoke such an intense reaction that it is overthrown.[21] Alternatively, the pursuit of a domestically advantageous policy may lead the state into destructive conflicts with other states. Successful or not, however, this two-dimensional perspective on state policy indicates that for all actors within a specific society the international dimension is important for the conducting of policy and the waging of conflicts. Those in state power, and those associated with the state, will deploy international resources to contain domestic threats. These resources may be military, up to and including allied troops; economic, whether from other branches of a multinational corporation or from international economic institutions as aid to embattled holders of state power; or political, in the form of moral support, treaties, or alliances provided by friendly states. Much of international relations can be seen therefore as an internationalisation of domestic conflicts, of relations between state and society. Those opposed to states also seek such international contacts, and have, throughout modern history, made much of this dimension. There is certainly room for an International Relations of anti-systemic forces, a substantial study of how those opposed to established states have, and can, internationalise their support. However, the reality would seem to be that here, as in purely domestic conflicts, the state and its associates have a distinct advantage and can mobilise resources within and beyond state boundaries far in excess of those who challenge them. The latter often lack resources and access to mechanisms for appropriate, and sufficiently powerful, international integration of anti-systemic activity.[22] Chapter 3 suggests that Marx's theory of the internationalisation of classes can apply as much, or more, to the dominant than to the dominated classes.

The sociological perspective on the state indicates the need to study, in a comparative and historical context, just how the international functioning of the state has affected the internal workings of the state apparatus itself. This theme in Hintze's studies of state formation involves examining how the international activities of states (war, territorial appropriation, diplomacy) have affected the social origin of personnel in the state, the predominance of some administrative branches within it, the values of state personnel, and the overall size and financing of the state. The role of military elements (the army as a whole, or individual commanders) within states and societies is the most eloquent example of this international determination of state formation. The longevity of aristocratic influence within European states, persisting long after the displacement of aristocratic landed power in the societies concerned, is an index of how the diplomatic function has affected the state as a whole. The influence on the US state of its post-1945 adoption of a global role has been much commented upon and has led some liberal critics to talk of a 'national security state' in the US. In broad terms this was a one-sided argument, in that the Cold War coincided with the extension, not the reduction, of democracy in the USA:[23] but the enhanced power of the president, the ebb and flow of Congressional controls, the rise of new bureaucracies with international functions (the Central Intelligence Agency, the National Security Council), and the changed character of the State Department are all instances of this impact of the international realm on the state apparatus. Nor is it necessarily the case that the ideologies and personnel of state apparatuses reflect only current changes in the outside world: the enduring influence of a colonial and great power past upon the post-1945 British state and its senior personnel is evident enough. In embattled revolutionary states, where the survival of the state is uncertain from month to month, the practicalities of ensuring security against invasion and subversion take an enormous toll on the allocation of resources, and on the time, nerves and concentration of those in power, as well as affecting the conception of what is licit dissent.

State Interests and Social Forces

Equally, the relation of state to society is constantly affected by the international function. This is clear in all four of the dimensions that Michael Mann has seen as constitutive of state power: the ideological, the military, the administrative and the political. The economic benefits of imperialism to the British state have been much debated, but few can doubt the ideological benefits that did, and still do, accrue to the state because of its assertion of British power in far-flung places. The need to sustain armed forces, in peace as well as in war, has given the state a fundamental interest in intervention in the economy and in establishing close relations with those in society most relevant to this issue. This was as true in early modern Europe as it is today. The supportive role of the military lobbies in the US, and the mechanisms (personal, institutional, financial) of interaction between defense contractors, Congress, and the Pentagon have been well documented, as has the link (e.g. in the Irangate affair) between covert operations abroad and private interests at home in the implementation of state policies.

The state recruits sections of domestic society for its international activities. At the same time both the state and society seek to gain support for their internal conflicts from international sources. Earlier, it was pointed out that the institutional concept of the state makes it possible to distinguish between the terms state, society, government and nation. Much of the relationship between these is constituted within specific societies, but there are many ways in which these relations acquire an international dimension: states seek to regulate their own position by obtaining international support; governments, social groups and ethnic groups try to enhance their position, *vis-à-vis* their own states, by obtaining international backing such as economic or military aid; and external actors seek to advance themselves against competitor states by establishing direct relations with elements within the latter's societies. One obvious case of such an interaction is the sponsoring of military coups in independent states: the promotion of government–state conflicts in rival countries. Another is the promotion of social unrest or ethnic upheaval in rival countries through money, arms, radio broadcasts and diplomatic backing. Overall, the existence of the state–society relation permits alternative means of conducting international relations: it encourages states and social forces to pursue international policies that will enhance their domestic positions in relation to each other.

Societies and State Systems

The reciprocal interaction of international society and specific societies is not, however, effected solely through the mediation of the state or with the purpose of eventually influencing the state. There are other processes within society that are influenced by, and which can themselves influence, the relationship of a particular state to the international system, but which reflect processes quite separate from that of state activity on the international level. There are, on the one hand, long-term changes within a specific society that, at a moment of increasing impact on the state and on the politics of the government or executive, have major impact on the international activities of that state. Short of revolutionary upheavals, these can be changes of balance between different social groups, changes in ideology and attitude, and geographical shifts reflecting economic change. The rise of a merchant bourgeoisie in Western Europe in the early modern period, with its resultant impact on state policy and religious-ideological orientation, was one of the constituent influences upon the emergence of the international system. The shifts in the US polity, with the decline of the north-east hegemonic bloc in favour of the sunbelt, do much to explain the sharp changes in US policy between the 1970s and the 1980s. At the same time, the international may have a major impact on the social composition of a society such that it may also shape and influence the state. The most extreme instances of this are conquest and colonial rule, when new state systems may simply be imposed on subjugated societies. Short of such dramatic impositions of the international upon the individual society, there are many other means through which international economic and social changes can affect a particular society, enhancing the position of some social groups, and reducing the influence of others. Incorporation into the world system affects not only the international balance of (military) power, but also the balance of social power within societies.

This focus on the state–society relation may also help in re-examining, and re-theorising, the manner in which social groups that have an international interest themselves relate to state power. Some of this is encapsulated in empirical work on lobbies: campaigns to keep out foreign goods, to back associated enter-prises abroad, to put pressure on foreign states to make conces-sions. Yet much of the debate on the relative influence of states and non-state actors has assumed a polarity in this regard, as if the multinational corporation (MNC) operating abroad wishes to act independently of states. This touches upon the unresolved question of the autonomy of the state: the state is 'autonomous' in some respects, and more so in some periods, most notably wartime, but the least that can be said is that in many areas the state is acting in harness with, and at the behest of, influential interests within society. Herein lies the strength of the 'structural' theory of the state.

Here again, a traditional black box approach to the state makes it difficult to answer the question of the MNC–state relationship, since it only permits us to examine the relationship internationally. Once it becomes possible, however, to examine the relation within a society, and to identify the degree of collaboration in the relative symbiosis of state and some sectors or classes of society, then the nature of the international collaboration and apparent division of labour becomes clearer. There are cases where MNCs defy states by trading with countries, such as in the 1980s Nicaragua, Angola, South Africa or Russia, upon which the state wishes to impose economic pressure. In many other cases the state acts to promote and defend the MNC. When International Telephone and Telegraph (IT&T) ran into trouble in Chile in 1970, Harold Geneen (president of the firm) called the White House. Congress has imposed conditions on US aid to countries that nationalise US firms without adequate compensation arrangements. If the relationship of state and (some parts of) society is seen as constituted domestically, and the international activities of each are seen in this light, then it may become easier to resolve the vexed question of how far states or non-state actors act independently of each other in world affairs.

As we shall see in greater detail in Chapter 6, the state–society relationship is central to another dimension of international relations, namely that of social upheaval and revolutions, and in particular the question of why revolutions have international effects. International Relations literature, in general, has relegated revolutions to a marginal position, while most of the sociological literature on revolutions tends to neglect the international implications.[24] It is the great merit of Skocpol's work that it seeks to interrelate the two, by showing the degree to which revolutions are to a considerable extent a product of inter-state and international factors, and by suggesting how the post-revolutionary consolidation of states and the extension of state power are influenced by international pressures. There could be no clearer demonstration of the interlinking of internal and international politics than the ways in which revolutions can be stimulated by international factors, whether the mobilisation of dominated groups, or the weakening of previously secure dominators. Equally, however, the international consequences of revolutions suggest further consequences of the state–society relation: the compulsion of revolutionaries to promote, if not 'export', revolution abroad, and the anxiety and counter-revolutionary response which revolutions, even in the weakest of states, may provoke in hegemonic powers. The answer to both questions may lie to a considerable extent in the state–society relationship. Revolutionary states see an internationalisation of their struggle as part of domestic consolidation: militarily, in the gaining of like-minded allies; economically, in the winning of collaborative relationships with such allies; and ideologically, in the promotion at the international level of similar ideals to those which legitimate their own regime. On the side of those opposed to revolution, similar concerns may operate: the loss of a comparable society to a rival system weakens a state internationally, but also domestically; it serves to weaken its domestic legitimacy. As Raymond Aron has indicated, and as will be discussed in Chapter 5, it is the preference for homogeneity in political arrangements for international legitimacy and stability that shows up both the crucial, if often understated, dependence of domestic power arrangements upon international factors, and the degree to which domestic factors, including the state–society relationship itself, influence the foreign policy of states.[25] The historical record of the past two centuries suggests that both projects (the promotion of revolution in other states and the overthrow of revolutionary regimes) usually fail in their declared goals. However, as with economic sanctions, the purposes of such ventures may be multiple, and may reflect broader ideological and domestically orientated goals as much as the specifically declared goal of the operation. The study of the international dimensions of revolutions may, therefore, provide insight both into the considerable area of international relations that is affected by such upheavals and into the broader transnational causes of, and influences upon, domestic change.[26]

This theorisation of the state–society relationship also has implications for the comprehensive question concerning the nature of the international system. As discussed in Chapter 1, within current theory the term 'system' is used in a variety of ways, from the realist conception of a system of states, in which the term is used in the loosest sense, to the applications of systems theory to International Relations (with rather modest results) and assertions of an international capitalist system by writers of Marxist or Marxist-influenced persuasion. The problem with the realist theorists is that they avoid the question of the relationship of socio-economic factors within states and internationally to the functioning of the system, the latter being seen in narrowly political terms. The problem with much Marxist writing is that it understates the role and distinct efficacy of states. This latter paradigm begs the question of why, if there is a world economy in which class interests operate transnationally, there is a need for states at all. What, in other words, is the specificity and effectivity of distinct states within a single economic totality? These conundrums (the determinacy of the socio-economic, the specificity of the political) cannot be answered within either a uniquely domestic or international context; rather, they suggest the need to identify how far each level does determine the system, and how states function not only as independent actors in the system, but also as mediators and regulators of a broader set of interactions that, taken as a totality, constitute international society (however this 'society' is conceived).

Beyond an alternative grounding of the concept of system at the international level, and as it affects analysis of the contemporary world, such an alternative theorisation of the state also suggests another variant of conventional International Relations approaches, namely an alternative history of the international system. Hitherto we have been offered a predominant realist view, through which the international system, constituted by states, develops, grows and 'expands' through the multiplication of states and the acceptance by states of what Bull in *The Anarchical Society* has termed the 'institutions' of interstate relations. That such a view has an implicitly evolutionist and diffusionist foundation does not need underlining, i.e. as if it all grew in a relatively easy way. For all the pessimism of the realist view, it tends to suggest an international history that is rather too benign, and at variance with the sanguinary process of imposition, resistance and reassertion of control that is characteristic of international relations in the colonial or third world over the past four centuries. As discussed in Chapter 3, the alternative, and to date minority, view of the system is that outlined by writers such as Wallerstein and Wolf, whose surveys of the expansion of capitalism since 1450 have offered a quite distinct international history depicting a system based on capitalist market relations.[27] The theoretical presupposition of Wallerstein's approach, that the development of international society is constituted by the spread of a social system at the international level, as distinct from the realist stress upon a growth of relations between separate and analytically primary states, is cognate with that of historical sociology with its stress upon the world-historical context of international developments and the multiple conflicts, intra- and inter-national, that have marked it. However, where this history of world society may be questioned, as already indicated, is in its neglect of the political instance, the state, and in its market-based assumption about the capitalist homogeneity of the Cold War world.

To stress the broader, capitalist, character of the international system is not to argue that social relations are in any simple sense transnational. Marx in the nineteenth century and much apparently contemporary sociological thinking make the same mistake in assuming that the state was simply being swamped by trans-national processes. This view, rather, takes the state seriously, but questions more precisely its role within this broader socio-economic context. In other words, it examines the function of distinct states within such a socio-economic context: whether it is to represent different ruling groups, or to represent distinct and autonomous state interests, or to regulate and maintain a system of international hierarchy. There is the further question concerning the implications of a world such as that between 1945 and 1989 composed of two socio-economic systems: in broad terms, one capitalist and one centrally planned. The functions of states, and, not least, of their military aspects, in administering, prosecuting and controlling this rivalry between competitive and contrasting social systems, are discussed further in Chapter 8. Many is the writer on international relations who has told us, on the basis of exhaustive comparative data, that there is little or no correlation between foreign policy output and socio-economic system: at the risk of profanity, students of post-1945 history may be forgiven for questioning this conclusion.

The implications for International Relations of this alternative conceptualisation of the state will take time to work out, and will involve greater recognition of trends in other social sciences, sociology, and the more sociologically literate branches of history, that have hitherto received little recognition. There is no doubt that any such evolution will involve uncertainties and disappointments: a world in which the state is no longer conveniently taken to represent the totality, and in which 'nation-state', 'sovereignty' and 'national interest' are no longer secure landmarks, will be harder to chart. On the other hand, there are substantial areas of International Relations, notably foreign policy analysis and international political economy, where significant work along these lines has already taken place. Since, ultimately, the validity and relevance of any conceptual approach lies in the relevance of its conclusions and the degree of explanatory power they display, it may be that one way to overcome IR's recurrent immobility on the state will be to redefine the state itself.

5

International Society as Homogeneity

The Meanings of 'International Society'

The concept of 'international society' occupies a significant place, at once constitutive and spectral, in the study of international relations. A number of reasons for this ambivalent position will be discussed below, but perhaps the most important of all is the variance of meanings that attaches to the term. Within realism, 'international society' refers to a relationship between states, based on shared norms and understandings: this is the sense in which it is used by Martin Wight, Hedley Bull, James Mayall and other theorists of the English school. Within transnationalism, it refers to the emergence of non-state links of economy, political association, culture, ideology that transcend state boundaries and constitute, to a greater or lesser extent, a society that goes beyond boundaries. Originally pioneered by writers within International Relations influenced by behaviouralism and a liberal Internationalist approach (John Burton, Robert O. Keohane, Joseph Nye) it has been developed in some more recent international relations literature (Evan Luard) and separately but relatedly in the sociological literature on globalisation (Michael Featherstone, Roland Robertson, Leslie Sklair, John Urry). Both of these uses, the inter-state and the transnational, have, within their theoretical frameworks, important explanatory power.

There is, however, a third possible use of the term 'international society'. This denotes a set of norms shared by different societies and which are promoted by inter-state competition. This is based neither on inter-state nor on transnational models, but on the assumption of inter-societal and inter-state homology. This refers to a similarity of domestic values and organisation, i.e. to what has been termed 'homogeneity', in the way societies are organised.

This third concept of 'international society' has distinct implications for the study of International Relations,[1] since it denotes the relation between the internal structure of societies and the international. Briefly, this approach investigates how, as a result of international pressures, states are compelled more and more to conform to each other in their internal arrangements. Unlike the realist concept, 'homogeneity' pays considerable attention to what happens *within* states and societies, and examines the interaction of international activity with domestic legitimacy and stability. Unlike the transnationalist, it accords considerable importance to the concept of the state, in the second sense in which this is defined in Chapter 4; indeed it sees comparative state formation as an important part of the process, and takes competition between states as a factor at least as formative as the growth of more harmonious inter-societal, transnational, links.

This 'homogeneous' conception of international society covers some of the material included in the first two concepts – the organisation of political systems as conceived of by realists, and transnational linkages. Its starting point, however, is rather different, since it begins with the need of societies and of policies that remain distinct nonetheless to conform to an internationally defined model. It is, therefore, a concept that pertains equally to internal development and international relations.

'Homogeneity' is evident, if implicitly, in much social and political theory. The account of economic development found in economic historians such as Gerschenkron and others, focusing on the need of states to 'catch up', is based on this idea of competitive homogenisation.[2] This chapter will explore how 'homogeneity' is used, in political theory, by three thinkers of as different orientation as the historical periods in which they wrote: Burke, Marx and Fukuyama. This concept is based not on international relations between states as in some sense 'social', but on analysis of how social, and for that matter political and economic, relations within states are themselves constituted by the international. If applied, the result would be that part of the subject-matter of International Relations becomes not the study of states alone, important as they have been and will remain: rather International Relations, in its historiographic and theoretical forms, becomes the

study of how international processes contribute to, i.e. both drive
and to a considerable extent are driven by, the internal workings
of states. It is this concept of international society, one denoting
the transnational formation of society, that is characterised here as
the 'constitutive' tradition.

The argument to be developed below is that this 'homogeneous'
concept merits closer attention, not only because of the
importance of the international in forming societies, but, most
pertinently for the student of International Relations, because it
has considerable theoretical implications, analytic and normative,
for the study of the international itself. This stronger, but
displaced, concept of international society has been present
throughout the history of thinking on the international system, if
occurring in systems of thought normally considered rather
disparate. But, beyond the rewards of classical recuperation, there
are particular reasons why it may be of interest to examine it more
closely in the contemporary context.

On the one hand, developments in cognate areas, notably
historical sociology and the sociology of 'global' relations, have
indicated new ways in which the uniquely inter-state concept of the
international and hence of international society may be limited.[3]
They have, if only in reaction to extra-disciplinary intrusions,
prompted the need for students of International Relations to
define rather more closely what they mean by their subject.

On the other hand, a range of developments in the contemporary
world have presented challenges to International Relations theory
that may be elucidated by using this alternative concept of
international society. Students of 'globalisation' and of the
increasing transnationalisation of societies, not least in the
European Community, will find plenty to offer here. But it can
also be argued that the concept is pertinent to the subject matter of
Chapters 8–10 – recent changes in the international system, namely
the Cold War, the manner in which the Cold War ended, and the
prospects for an end to great power military conflict – whose
theoretical implications may not be so evident.

As I have argued at greater length in Chapters 8 and 9 and
elsewhere,[4] theorisation of the Cold War has lagged behind its
historiography, and has been dominated by short-term, rather
instrumental, reflections on 'strategy': it may only be now, with
the conflict over, that the theoretical problems it raises can be

examined. The argument is that international pressure for homogeneity destroyed the Soviet Union: the Cold War was ultimately about two varying concepts of international society, and that it ended because, through international social rather than inter-state reasons, one side prevailed over the other. It was the T-shirt and the supermarket, not the gunboat or the cheaper manufactures that destroyed the legitimacy and stability of the Soviet system. Bruce Springsteen was the late-twentieth-century equivalent of the Opium Wars.

Conventional realism cannot explain the end of communism. The theoretical question posed by the Cold War and its conclusion is precisely that of looking at the mechanisms of international competition and interaction that orthodox inter-state theory obscures; this includes the concept, as defined here, of 'international society'. In sum, the argument being made is not only that this is a conception of 'international society' meriting recognition in its own right, but that it has major implications for the way we look at individual states/societies and at the international system. Its suffusion of other conceptualisations of international society has helped to obscure the explanatory power it may have, for the past, the present and, without any scientistic pretensions about forecasting, the future of the system. In the post-Cold-War era, the question of homogeneity is posed in another way: the issue is how far, if liberal democratic forms consolidate themselves in the major states, a new era of international relations, based on a homogeneous international society, can be realised.

In so far as the term 'international society' in International Relations is generally recognised to be the central concept for a part of the realist tradition, it would seem appropriate to begin discussion of the concept here. The 'part' is important because, although not confined to writers of the English School, the term is far less frequently found in the school of Germanic-American realism predominant on the western side of the Atlantic: by contrast to its position in Martin Wight, Hedley Bull, James Mayall it rates hardly a mention in the work of Hans Morgenthau, Henry Kissinger and Kenneth Waltz. The last, for example, for all his general sympathy for British philosophic traditions, shows no interest in the supposed originator of the English School, Hugo Grotius.

Within the writings of those who do use it, 'international society' serves its constitutive function in three important respects: as explanation for the operations of the international system beyond Hobbesian conflict, as theoretical resolution for the absence of a single authority in the international domain, and as central category in an account of the diffusion of the north-west European system across the globe.[5] Yet while within British realism this concept serves these functions and is given formal recognition of its importance, it remains curiously vague, as much a guardian angel as a hegemonic concept. If this is so for reasons internal to the concept itself, namely the foreclosing of what is meant by the very word 'society', it is even more so because, in asserting one concept of what an international society may be, namely relations between states, this conventional realist category appears to preclude discussion of other, equally suggestive, theorisations of the international system relating to other forms of relation.

The concept of international society as developed by the English realists has been summarised best by Bull, who wrote:

> A *society of states* (or international society) exists when a group of states, conscious of certain common interests and common values, form a society in the sense that they conceive them-selves to be bound by a common set of rules in their relations with one another, and share in the working of common institutions.[6]

And later: 'the element of a society has always been present, and remains present, in the modern international system, although only as one of the elements in it, whose survival is sometimes precarious'.[7] With some variations, Bull's enumeration of what compromises a society – interests, values, rules, institutions – and his historical interpretation designed to prove that at least 'elements' of it have existed for some time, goes for the school as a whole.

In the posthumously published extension of this argument, Wight, trawling history with his usual taxonomic serendipity, gives us three variants of the international society argument: these correspond to his realism, rationalism, and revolutionism schools.[8] These vary in their analytic focus, from Hobbesian war, through Grotian-Suarezian community to Kantian *civitas maxima*. The first corresponds to what, in English School terminology, could be termed a 'system', without any additional 'social' attributes. The third variant, that of Kant, corresponds in some respects to the transnationalist perspective, with a more overt moral programme and an implicit, pacifist, teleology, since peace follows from the gradual breaking down of barriers between states as well as of the authority of states. All three of Wight's variants are based on conceptions of inter-state or inter-social relations, and avoid the issue of domestic constitution or homogenisation. The second corresponds most closely to the Wight-Bull conception of international society itself, i.e. a system plus some additional elements. It is above all with the realist concept, diffused through theory and history, and serving the three functions mentioned above, that students of the international therefore have to contend.

The concept of 'society' is supposedly taken from sociology, and emerged in its main current usage, that which International Relations claims to use, during the nineteenth century.[9] While variations on theoretical usage as between disciplines are hardly surprising (one need only think of the peregrinations of 'structure' and 'realism', to name but two), it is worth beginning by noting some obvious differences between the ways in which the term 'society' is used in the two disciplines.[10] First, within sociology, as within political theory, the concept 'society' has meaning primarily in contrast to the 'state', the very thing whose absence, seen as supreme authority, at the international level realist theorists have emphasised. The consequence of this for International Relations theory is that the term 'society' lacks its counterpart: given this definition of 'society' there can be no realist equivalent of the concept 'civil society', since this, by definition, is that area of political or social activity not controlled by the state.

A second consequence of the definition is that the usage in International Relations seems to occlude what is one of the most central distinctions in sociology, expounded by Tonnies in 1887, that between the looser, more informal, society (*Gesellschaft*) and the tighter, more morally coherent, community (*Gemeinschaft*). Indeed, in the Bull-Wight usage the two are interchangeable, and if anything, their 'society', with its stress on shared values, is closer to *Gemeinschaft*.

Thirdly, the main concern of theorisation of society within sociology is to look at forms of constraint, in other words to get away from the idea of the individual as free and untrammelled. Durkheim's 'social facts', for example, were limits on the individual. Within International Relations this function is performed by the concept 'system', a term which in sociology is not contrasted to society, but serves as the basis for alternative theorisations of social relations, such as those of Parsons. The usage of the term 'society' which corresponds most closely to that within realist International Relations may not be that of sociology at all, but the earlier, and still current, uses of the term: either to denote a club or self-selected group (as in 'building' or 'debating'), or simply to denote a social, often fashionable, élite.[11]

The élitist, exclusionary character of the society of states is, of course, the basis upon which the whole story developed, and the 'expansion' occurred. In origin, the 'society' of European states was a club of (western) Christian monarchs and produced its first forms of organisation against the Muslim, i.e. 'infidel', Turk. This was, indeed, the meaning given to the term by Wight himself, who defined society as, 'a number of individuals joined in a system of relationships for certain common purposes'.[12] As it evolved, its central membership condition, 'sovereignty', was reserved for those states that saw fit, and had the ability, to subject the rest of the world to their hegemonic, largely colonial, rule. Jane Austen's 'polite society' or Cole Porter's 'High Society' may be as close to International Relations' usage as the reflections of Auguste Comte or Ferdinand Tonnies.

Three other broad issues posed by this usage of the term 'international society' need to be discussed. The first arises from within the inter-state perspective, particularly where the influence of Hobbes is strong. This realist usage would deny that the term 'society' can be used at all to define a grouping in which war, and the threat of war, have remained so central. A usage that confined the term to those states, and those alone, which did not threaten force in their relations with each other, would be more defensible, but this has not been a restriction that those using the term, in the tradition of Bull and Wight, have made. Proponents of the concept are usually careful not to define which states are, and which are not, part of the society, i.e. which are, in their terms, in the system but not in the society.

A reading of the literature would, however, suggest that for most of those who use the term, all sovereign states of the twentieth century are part of this society by dint of their participation in diplomatic practice alone. The reply, as in Chapter 8 of *The Anarchical Society*, using the word 'institution' in the functional sense that is particular to the approach, may or may not be convincing: it certainly stretches and dilutes the concept of 'society' much further than a more rigorous usage would suggest.

A further critique of the term stems from an examination not of how far the inter-state system corresponds to a model of society, but from what definition of the concept 'society' itself is being used. Here, as elsewhere in International Relations theory, there tends to be an element of definitional absolutism, achieved not by edict, but by ellipsis: just as with 'state', 'power' and 'nation', so with 'society'. The argument in favour of a particular conceptualisation of the international is reinforced by the simplest mechanism of all, namely reluctance to recognise that there are alternatives, in this case alternative concepts of 'society'. As introduced by Bull, society means norms plus interests plus rules plus values: the only question that remains is how far this model does, or does not, accord with international reality.

Bull's use of his concept of society is certainly consistent, and forms the basis for a cogent picture of the international system. Yet, as with the term 'state', it is precisely here that interesting questions may be foreclosed. The question is not whether international relations, defined as inter-state relations, correspond to one definition of society, but rather to which definition they may most closely correspond. As already noted, within sociological theory, the concept 'society' itself has evolved over the past two centuries to encompass a range of meanings: all those within a community, the élite of that community, or that element of a nation that is distinct from the state (as in the currently revived 'civil society'). There is, consequently, no one single definition of 'society'. Bull's account can be termed 'communitarian' since it implies that 'a society' is a grouping with shared values; it can be contrasted with other understandings of the concept, such as those based on Marxism, which stress stratification and power, if not a formal hierarchical system. One can apply to the international the same arguments that have been applied to specific societies, as to how far the functioning of a society and the transmission of values within it reflects acceptance of a common interest, and how far it reflects coercion. In no society is the answer entirely one or the other: the point is that asking this question raises important concerns about what constitutes a society and the degree of inequality and force within it, concerns that are precluded by Bull's communitarian model.

Inter-state relations may therefore constitute a society, not so much because of the shared values involved, but because it is a grouping established by the coercion of some states by others and maintained, with a variety of ideological and military mechanisms, by the more powerful members. In this vein, the other terms that realists using the 'society' approach invoke will also change meaning: thus 'socialisation' becomes not the inculcation and diffusion of shared values, but the imposition of a set of values by states, schools, families, clergy, media on others, whether or not those who have them imposed actually believe them. The mechanisms identified in Gramsci's concept of hegemony, whereby the subjugated accept their ruler's values, would also apply in the international arena (as would the theoretical ambiguities that Gramsci's thesis raises such as whether those who are subordinate actually accept the values, 'believe' in them, or pretend to, or are in fact subjugated by their espousing a different, subaltern value system).[13]

In so far as Bull recognises this problem with his concept of society, it has produced a tension within his thought between his definition of international society and his actual account – hence the role of the Great Powers, and of war, as two of his five institutions. What he does not do is to develop the implications of this tension to question the definition, explicit and implicit, of society that he gives at the beginning of his exposition. An international society created and maintained by the Great Powers may be the best the human race can come up with, but it is far from being a society based uniquely on shared values.

The third critique of the concept 'international society' arises out of the variation of theories of society, and particularly those, already adumbrased in Chapter 3, which are derivative of historical materialism. Two components of what could be a historical materialist critique have already been suggested – the role of coercion in maintaining a society, and the particularistic, class-specific, nature of the supposedly common or universal values.

But there is a more fundamental critique based on what it is that binds societies together and indeed constitutes them. Opposed to the thesis that it is norms and values, or political institutions, that perform this function, is the argument that it is performed by the economy. What this entails is a definition of the international system as primarily one constituted by economic activity, and the spread of capitalist social and economic relations on a world scale. As indicated in Chapter 3, alternative theory entails alternative histories – Immanuel Wallerstein, Eric Woolf and Eric Hobsbawm – as against the expansion of international society.[14] These alternative histories should not exclude the importance of norms, and the transmission of values through the system. Coercive or not, norms and values are an essential part of the working of any society. But this diffusion of norms, apart from being hierarchical, itself rests on another layer of human activity that sustains and forms the society itself. The spread of Christianity had not a little to do with force. The question therefore becomes not how and how far these norms spread – the historiographic problem of orthodox theories of 'international society' – but how capitalism as a socio-economic system spreads, the role that values and norms, including the concept of sovereignty, play within it, and the changing balance of coercion and consent involved in the reproduction of that society. In this way, alternative theory suggests alternative history: the subjugation of pre-capitalist peoples, the unification of the world through economic processes, the formation of a bloc of economically developed and liberal democratic countries.[15]

Transnationalism and its Limits

The transnational definition of international society and its implications for International Relations theory also need no extensive recapitulation here. As we have seen in Chapter 1, starting from the behaviouralist concern to avoid the paralysis of institutionalism, and an awareness, from an empirical perspective, that many cross-frontier processes were not conducted or controlled by states, transnationalist writers sought from the 1970s onwards to present an alternative picture of the international system in which inter-state relations were increasingly bypassed or influenced by these non-state processes.

Out of this intellectual shift arose the theories of interdependence of Robert Keohane and Joseph Nye, the world society paradigm of John Burton, and much of international political economy.[16] Susan Strange's four structures of power was an outstanding attempt to retain the importance of the military-security dimension while identifying the emergence, growth and in many cases predominance of the non-state processes. In another study, Evan Luard has argued that there is an increasing convergence of domestic and international societies: just as individual societies are becoming less and less homogeneous and centralised, so international relations are acquiring a range of interactions, some organised by states, many not, which produce relationships akin to those within society.[17]

In a parallel development within sociology, a number of writers have come to identify what they take to be a globalisation or internationalisation of social relations and the breaking down of what had previously been discrete social entities: 'society' in the traditional sense. Leslie Sklair identifies three sets of TNPs ('transnational practices'): economic, political and cultural-ideological.[18] The first encompasses the activities of transnational corporations, not least their impact on third world and socialist countries; the second, linkages between political forces, mainly those in power; and the last encompasses the spread of consumerist and other practices and beliefs across the world.

In a cognate field of analysis, strongly influenced by the work of Roland Robertson, and by post-modernist insights into the possibility of multiple ('deconstructed') structures and meanings within the international system, Arjun Appadurai has identified five dimensions of global cultural flow: ethnoscapes, mediascapes, technoscapes, financescapes, ideoscapes.[19] Within each of these dimensions different actors intersect across frontiers, be these tourists, immigrants, refugees, migrant workers, political activists, fashion models or pop stars. In a closing of the theoretical circle, the concept 'international society' has returned to the discipline from which it, putatively at least, originated.[20]

Rich in insight as these various theories of transnationalism are, they leave open a range of questions, four of which can be summarised here. First, the issue of determination and significance is unresolved: it is not clear if we are to regard all transnational processes as equally important, and equally autonomous, or not. Orthodox realists would suggest that the role of the state cannot be dissolved entirely into some mesh of global interactions, and that this is just as much a problem with the globalisation theories as with the world society approach. Marxists and proponents of international political economy might suggest that the role of the economy, and of its hierarchic structures, is central to much of the story of how international society developed. A proliferation of levels, '-scapes' or meanings, may tell us very little. Sudden breathless discoveries of new areas of interaction – the global village or 24-hour financial markets one day, the transnational *flaneur* or satellite communications the next – substitute for measured assessment of what constitutes the global social totality.

Second, and in contrast to a sober assessment of where real change is occurring, there is in much of the transnationalist literature an element of historical foreshortening. Many of the processes – economic, political and religious – that characterise contemporary transnationalism were present, if not to the same degree, decades and even centuries ago. The Reformation, the Industrial Revolution, the spread of universal suffrage, to name but three transnational processes, predate obsession with immediacy and a foreshortened historical framework. Migration was as important a phenomenon in the nineteenth century, and indeed, for some countries, in the eighteenth, as it has been in the twentieth. One can hardly say that states are less involved in this process now than they were in the past. Nowhere is this historical foreshortening more misleading than in much of the literature on 'post-modernity', as something specific to the post-1945 era: this implies ruptures in society or the world that are exaggerations, a product of ahistorical whim. That certain phenomena are specific to the contemporary age cannot be doubted, but the hype of 'post-modernity' as an explanatory concept or historical category often obscures where change has, and has not, occurred.

Third, there is an implicit teleology in much of this writing, whether it be the enthusiasm for European integration found in writings on the European Community, or the belief that a global culture based on youth, satellite TV, sport, or religion is engulfing humanity as a whole. This applies in particular to the speed with which the state itself is dismissed from consideration. The trajectory of Keohane, transcendent of the state in the 1970s, accommodating and rehabilitating in *After Hegemony* of the 1980s, is an indication of the difficulties encountered by those who seek to marginalise its role.[21] There is so much of this underlying optimism and teleology in liberal internationalist writing that as a body of work it is eerily reminiscent of an earlier generation of literature on the transition to socialism: 'setbacks' and 'lags' there may be, but in the end it is all bound to happen.

Finally, theorisation of a globalisation or transnationalisation of culture too often ignores the comparable process of fragmentation and division, at both the global and domestic social levels, which are a direct result of internationalisation. This is, of course, the underlying paradox of nationalism, a global phenomenon, and a response to international pressures, which spawns particularism and fragmentation. Nowhere was this clearer than in the cruelly divided Europe of 1992 with the customs union, Maastricht and the Barcelona Olympics in the west, and genocide, ferocious ethnic strife and murderous hatred in the Balkans. Trans-nationalists often point to phenomena that, in their view, vindicate the claim of a growing common society across frontiers. However, within many of the flows that they identify, new forms of division, chauvinism or particularist hegemony may be arising – religion, sport and satellite TV being cases in point. Any theory of the impact of international processes on the world has to encompass both elements of this process, the integrative and the fragmentary, just as it has to identify the historical continuities as well as discontinuities in the process, and the enduring, often changing, role of the state in international and indeed transnational processes.[22]

The greatest difficulty with the transnational concept of inter-national society revolves around its treatment of the state: precipitate behaviouralist overriding in some cases, eclecticˑmulti-plication of structures and 'levels' in others, or an accommoda-tionist retreat to modified state-centrism.[23] As I have argued in Chapter 4, part of this confusion is the result of two very different meanings of the 'state', which lead to the false counterposing of 'state' to transnational and social processes, and the preoccupation with what is in many ways a non-question, that of the degree to which the state is, or is not, being overtaken by transnational processes. In this chapter, the argument is focused on another consequence of the state/non-state polarity, namely the way in which this false contrast makes it difficult to see how transnational or international processes, far from weakening the state, develop and alter it: how, in other words, the very processes of political and social change within countries are the result of external processes, and how, in turn, the divergence or convergence of states with regard to the norms of homogeneity affect the course of international relations.

The 'Constitutive' Tradition and its Protagonists: Burke, Marx, Fukuyama

So far, the discussion has been about two variants of 'international society' the realist, inter-state, rendering, and the transnationalist account. It is now possible to turn to the other reinterpretation of the concept 'international society', one that does not seek variant interpretations of the inter-state, or the dimensions of trans-national interaction: this conception seeks, while not denying the force of these dimensions, to locate the discussion in another context, to which the term 'international society' may be more appropriately applied. In this context, inter-state relations, and their conflicts, including war, are not dissolved, but are located within a broader framework.

At first sight, this may appear to be but another variant of the sociological usage of the term 'international society' in the sense of transnational society. The latter concept is, however, one that posits a single international society, a transnational entity, linked by a variety of processes and institutions and which is seen to supplant gradually the interaction of states. In so far as this is its focus, it is little interested in the orthodox questions of inter-national relations understood as relations between states. The 'homogeneous' concept offered here is rather different, ascribing a permanent and continuously adapting role to states, but seeking to explain state behaviour by identifying a broader context of transnational relations, and the means by which these two levels of international activity intersect with the domestic. The elements of this theory will become clearer by examining three theoretically and historically disparate writers, in whose work it is possible to discern this third conception of international society.

The idea of separate societies being linked by common

characteristics, and of their foreign policy as being positively affected by such a similarity, was widely held in the thinking of the eighteenth century. The years from the Treaty of Utrecht in 1713 to the French Revolution of 1789 appeared at the time, and in retrospect, to be ones of relative harmony between the great European powers. One, much repeated, explanation is that this peace rested upon the balance of power, but at the time and later, explanations also invoked the shared principles of domestic political and social legitimacy which the states of Europe enjoyed. Thus Voltaire spoke of Christian Europe ('give or take Russia') as 'a sort of great commonwealth' in which the same basic religious beliefs and 'the same principles of public and political law unknown in the other parts of the world' prevailed. Heeren, the Hanoverian analyst of the states system whose work greatly influenced Wight, Bull and their associates in 'the English School', defined a states system in both inter-state and domestic terms as 'the union of several contiguous states resembling each other in their manners, religion and degree of social improvement, and cemented together by a reciprocity of interests'.[24] Commonplace in the relatively untroubled decades before 1789, this idea was, as is often the case, to receive sharper articulation once the assumptions upon which it rested were thrown into question: it was in this context that the idea of an 'international society' based on shared political and social ideas was to receive its exposition in Burke.

The outlines of Burke's theory of politics are well known and need little rehearsal here. Similarly, the general tenor of his views on international issues have been well presented.[25] Burke held the view that society, and political systems, were maintained by intangible factors – sentiments, values, inherited practices, manners – and that, if these were abruptly or too rationally interfered with, chaos would ensue. If he was a conservative, he was not against change, and his record on America, India and Ireland bore this out.[26] His methodology was broadly speaking pre-sociological, innocent of concern with industrialisation or 'modern' society, yet employing, without using the term, a concept of ideology as the precipitate of social development and the main guarantor of peace and stability. His opposition to the French Revolution followed from this: it was not just the actual deeds of the Jacobins – his *Reflections* were written in 1790, well before the worst of the terror or the Napoleonic expansions – that he abhorred, but the very application of reason, the rejection of tradition, and the pursuit of progress and perfection. Instead of the three pillars of stability – monarch, aristocracy and the church – there was a new dangerous trio – regicide, atheism and Jacobinism.

The implications of this, hinted at in one or two passages of the *Reflections* of 1790,[27] are spelt out at greater length in his *Letters on a Regidice Peace*, written in 1795–6. Fragmented and bilious as these texts are, they contain within them a very distinctive theory of international society as homogeneity, and the analytic and normative conclusions which follow from it. In essence, Burke's theory of international society can be summarised as follows.

First, an international society exists by virtue of the common political and social norms prevailing within societies. Burke argues that stable relations between states rest upon their having broadly similar forms of political and social order: they are, in central respects, homogeneous. Applying to the international the conception of social cohesion he had developed internally, Burke argues as follows:

> Men are not tied to one another by papers and seals. They are led to associate by resemblances, by conformities, by sympathies. It is with nations as with individuals. Nothing is so strong a tie of amity between nation and nation as correspondence in laws, customs, manners, and habits of life. They have more than the forces of treaties in themselves. They are obligations written in the heart.

He goes on to talk of the 'confirmity', 'analogy' and 'similitude' between the nations of Europe and their customs and manners and continues:

> At bottom, these are all the same. The writers on public law have often called this *aggregate* of nations a commonwealth. They had reasons. It is virtually one great state having the same basis of general law, with some diversity of provincial customs and local establishments. From this resemblance in the modes of intercourse, and in the whole form and fashion of life, no citizen of Europe could be altogether an exile in any part of it.

There was nothing more than a pleasing variety to recreate and instruct the mind, to enrich the imagination, and to meliorate the heart.

It follows that the threat presented by the French Revolution lies not in any particular policy that the revolution may pursue, but in the very fact of the revolution itself, the very challenge which, by its example, it poses to the whole order upon which British society rests. In Burke's words, the French Revolution constitutes a 'faction' which, merely by continuing to exist, will undermine other states in Europe where other, comparable, factions either exist or may come into existence: as such, revolutionary France is a danger of a very different kind from that which existed before. Burke writes:

> A sure destruction impends over those infatuated princes, who, in the conflict with this new and unheard-of power, proceed as if they were engaged in a war that bore a resemblance to their former contest. I was always steadily of the opinion, that this disorder was not in its nature intermittent. I conceived that the contest, once begun, could not be laid down again, to be resumed at our discretion: that but our first struggle with this evil would also be our last. I never thought we could make peace with the system; because it was not for the sake of an object we pursued in rivalry with each other, but with the system itself that we were at war. As I understood the matter, we were at war not with its conduct, but with its existence; convinced that its existence and its hostility were the same.[29]

In this final phrase, the essence of the theory of homogeneity is summed up: revolutionary France was a mortal danger, merely by dint of its being. The stability of other societies in Europe required that France too be like them. Without homogeneity, there could be neither internal nor international peace.

For Burke, the French Revolution represented such a great threat not just because of the challenge it posed to the 'resemblance' and 'similitude', Burke's phrases for homogeneity of the countries of the *ancien regime*, but also from what he termed 'vicinity'.

There is a *law of neighbourhood* which does not leave a man perfectly master on his own ground. When a neighbour sees a *new erection*, in the nature of a nuisance, set up at his door, he has a right to represent it to the judge; who, on his part, has a right to order the work to be stayed; or, if established, to be removed. . . . *No innovation* is permitted that may redound, even secondarily, to the prejudice of a neighbour.

Burke then applies this to the international arena:

This principle, which, like the rest, is as true of nations, as of individual men, has bestowed on the grand vicinage of Europe a duty to know, and a right to prevent, any capital innovation which may amount to the erection of a dangerous nuisance . . . [T]he vicinage of Europe had not only a right, but an indispensable duty, and an exigent interest, to denunciate this new work before it had produced the danger we have now sorely felt, and which we shall long feel. . . . It violates the rights upon which not only the community of France, but those on which all communities are founded. The principles on which they proceed are *general* principles, and are as true in England as in any other country.[30]

From these principles follows a theory of political and social security, and the programme of international counter-revolutionary intervention, for which Burke is best known. Once the principles of homogeneity and of vicinity are accepted, then it follows that no country or state can defend its interests or its way of life on its own. Reflecting on Britain in the late eighteenth century, Burke argues that while internally it appears to be strong, the French Revolution by dint of its example alone constitutes a threat to it:

If we look to nothing but our domestic condition, the state of the nation is full even to plethora: but if we imagine that this country can long maintain its blood and its food, as disjoined from the community of mankind, such an opinion does not deserve refutation as absurd, but pity as insane.[31]

Burke argues, in effect, for a pre-emptive war against revolutionary France, to strike it down before it engulfs the rest of

Europe. 'Example is the school of mankind, and they will learn at no other. This war is a war against that example'.[32] In Letter II he argues that while some may mistakenly see the conflict with France as a foreign war, and the Jacobins themselves may encourage this, it is in fact a civil war:

> It is a war between the partisans of the ancient, civil, moral, and political order of Europe, against a sect of fanatical and ambitious atheists which means to change them all. It is not France extending a foreign empire over other nations: it is a sect aiming at universal empire, and beginning with the conquest of France.[33]

Burke's analysis of the international consequences of the French Revolution, and of the appropriate response to it, have normally been read in the light of his theory of intervention, or, more broadly, his views on appropriate and inappropriate forms of change within society. Yet present within his *Letters* are the elements of another theory, pertinent to the whole discussion of international relations. For what he is arguing is that relations between states rest above all not on the conduct of foreign policy in the narrow sense, but on convergence and similitude in domestic arrangements, in other words on the prevalence of a homogeneous international society. The conclusion he draws is that for any international order to maintain peace it needs not only to evolve norms of inter-state behaviour, but to produce a community of states with broadly similar internal constitutions.

Few theorists could have a more different starting point, and apparently different conclusions, from Burke than Karl Marx, who, two generations later, produced an alternative theory of the implications of the French Revolution and of what constituted social and political cohesion. If Burke opposed the French Revolution, Marx regarded it as but the beginning of a process of global human emancipation; if Burke invoked tradition and custom, Marx denounced this as ideology and invoked reason; if Burke saw ideas as constitutive of society, Marx saw the productive process, in both its material and social form, as its basis.

Yet beyond or within these enormous differences, there are

three points of convergence of particular relevance to this argument. First, both gave importance in their analysis of society to what we would today term 'ideology', i.e. a set of values about what is desirable in social and political relations, how far it is possible to change them, and who the appropriate agents of change and stability might be. Burke did not derive his concept of ideology from socio-economic relations as Marx did, but he did see that they were tied closely to the interests of those with power in society – monarch, aristocracy and church – and that acceptance by the mass of the population of these values constituted an important form of political and social power: Burke's theory was proto-Marxist, or more precisely proto-Gramscian, providing a concept of hegemony without the concept of domination.

Second, their belief in the importance of ideology within any one society produced a shared international perspective. Burke and Marx saw the stability and development of individual societies and states as being determined by broader, international, processes. This led them to their third common position, that revolutions were international events, in both their causes and consequences, and the ethical requirements this imposed. The normative conclusions of their two theories display a compelling counterpoint: for Burke, the obligation was to intervene to crush revolution before it consolidated and spread; for Marx the obligation was to act to support it, in order to ensure that the international processes it unleashed were sustained. The duty to intervene was common to both, reached from contrasting starting points.

Most analysis of Marx's writings treats his ideas on specific political issues as derived from his general theory, and such derivations are no doubt valid: but in many cases, rather than positing some derivation of a vertical kind, it may be equally pertinent to look at the influence of other thinkers and the general intellectual climate of the time, what one can term horizontal influences. In the case of Marx's views on nationalism this may have much to recommend it: Marx's idea may be as much explained by what others, such as John Stuart Mill, were saying as by his theories of surplus value or capitalist development.[34] A similar, horizontal, linkage can be made with regard to his views on international society, as becomes evident from looking at one of his precursors in the socialist tradition, Saint-Simon.

Saint-Simon believed that European society was becoming more and more homogeneous, and indeed that no major changes were possible in one country alone: 'France does not by any means have a moral life all its own. It is merely one member of European society and a forced community exists between its political principles and those of its neighbours'. Inverting Burke, Saint-Simon argues that the rest of Europe should conform to the changes France was undergoing: 'The French nation cannot be treated and cured in isolation; the remedies which can cure it must be applied to all Europe'. This solidarity arises in part from the moral requirement that they renounce war, but it has a deeper root in the continuing process of industrialisation, which both subjects these societies to a common fate, and produces a new, shared, set of interests in peace. In the end, argues Saint-Simon, industrial society, beyond creating homogeneity, also creates an international peace interest. Homogeneity is therefore both an objective process, and an ethical and political goal.[35]

The clearest statement of Marx's view of international society comes in the *Communist Manifesto*, where he lays out the manner in which the capitalist mode of production, with the bourgeoisie as agent, transforms all societies across the whole world. As much as any liberal thinker of his age, Marx believed in the inevitable triumph of one model of society over the others, and in an increasing convergence and homogenisation of society. Whereas Burke, reflecting on the 'commonwealth' of eighteenth-century Europe, regarded the homogeneity of international society as an established reality, albeit one under threat from the French Revolution, Marx saw international society as an emerging global order being created by the spread of capitalism, in which individual societies were becoming more and more like each other.

> The need of a constantly expanding market for its products chases the bourgeoisie over the whole surface of the globe. It must nestle everywhere, settle everywhere, establish connections everywhere. The bourgeoisie, by the rapid improvement of all instruments of production, by the immensely facilitated means of communication, draws all, even the most barbarian, nations into civilization. The cheap prices of its commodities are the heavy artillery with which it batters down all Chinese walls, with which it forces the barbarians' intensely obstinate

hatred of foreigners to capitulate. It compels all nations, on pain of extinction, to adopt the bourgeois mode of production; it compels them to introduce what it calls civilization into their midst, i.e. to become bourgeois themselves. In one word, it creates a world after its own image.[36]

At first sight, Marx's conception of international society may appear to have more in common with the transnational conception than with the constitutive one. Certainly, he shares the view of liberal internationalists, such as Adam Smith and Richard Cobden whose rightful heirs are the transnationalists of the 1970s and 1980s, that growing contact between societies produces greater integration and unity in world affairs. But the focus of Marx's analysis is not only the growing links *between* societies, the subject matter of transnationalism, but also the degree to which, across the globe, societies increasingly come to conform to each other. Marx recognised the process of international homogenisation and the centrality of this internal conformity to international relations. For Marx, the core issue in international relations is how this growing homogenisation, a result of the spread of capitalism, affects not only the domestic and international politics of different countries, but also their social structure. This is the principle that underlies his most important work of all, *Capital*, which takes one society, Britain, as the exemplar of capitalist development as a whole, and seeks, by examining its structure and development, to posit a universal model. The implicit premise of *Capital* is that an international society is being created by the global spread of capitalism. For Marx, the workings of the economy, and the ownership patterns associated with it, perform those functions which manners and customs do for Burke.

There are, as discussed in Chapter 3, manifest weaknesses in Marx's theory, with implications for this conception of international society, and international relations as a whole. First, the fundamental historical perspective, the teleology, upon which his theory rested was false: capitalism, while riven with irrationality, inequality and cyclical upheaval, was not inevitably creating a set of contradictions that would then destroy it. Furthermore, as he himself began to recognise in some of his later work, capitalism was not creating a homogeneous world, in the sense of one in which an economy comparable to that of the most developed would be reproduced across the globe.[37] Capitalism was unifying the world, and creating its own world system, but this was to be on the basis of manifold inequalities and hierarchies, not the homogenisation assumed, with liberal insouciance, in the *Manifesto*.

Marx was also mistaken about the political and international implications of this homogenisation. For, far from leading to the creation of one single bourgeoisie the world over, or to cooperation between bourgeoisies for mutual economic benefit, this increasing unification of the world, and homogenisation of societies, went hand in hand with growing antagonisms between the bourgeoisies of different countries. It was left to the theoretical generation that succeeded him – Karl Kautsky, Rudolf Hilferding, Rosa Luxemburg, V. I. Lenin and Nikolai Bukharin – to produce, from within a Marxist framework, a theory of how capitalism, in unifying the world, also created uneven development which led the ruling classes of the more advanced countries to go to war with each other. Such, indeed, was the context in which the Marxist debate on imperialism occurred in the first two decades of this century. Later, this was to be formalised as the theory of combined and uneven development.[38]

Yet, if Marx was mistaken in his understanding of both the underlying conception of historical development, and the degree to which homogenisation or harmonisation did in fact occur, he was right in identifying the spread of capitalism and its impact on the economies, political systems and cultures of all countries. Re-examination of where he was right, and where mistaken, was to become rather easier a century or so after his death, with the ending not only of the great interlude in capitalist homogenisation represented by colonialism, but also of the ultimately fruitless attempt by his followers to pursue an alternative, heterogeneous, path of development. Capitalism battered down the Chinese walls not only of the pre-capitalist empires and societies, but also of those who tried to erect a 'post-capitalist' bloc. If nothing else this was, as we shall see in Chapters 8–10, a rather striking example of the workings of international society.

It might appear inappropriate to include in this discussion a consideration of the work of Francis Fukuyama, the American political scientist whose essay on 'The End of History' and later book, *The End of History and the Last Man*, made him one of the more controversial intellectual figures of the early 1990s.[39] Fukuyama has been dismissed by many academic commentators, and there is indeed much in his work that is questionable or unresolved. However, as will be discussed at greater length in Chapter 10, his work, and the moment at which it appeared, do pose a set of important questions for analysing not only the end of the Cold War, but also the course of international relations, not least because, in his idiosyncratic but revealing invocation of a range of classical thinkers, most notably Kant, Hegel and Nietzsche, he seeks to re-establish a connection between contemporary debates and an earlier tradition of political thought.

Fukuyama sets out to examine whether it is possible to write, in the Kantian sense, a 'universal history from a cosmopolitan point of view'. His answer is that it is possible, that history has a direction. This direction is determined by two processes: the dynamic of modern science, and the push towards liberal democracy. He sees the dynamic of modern science as an unceasing process that not only determines how and why economic and social development occurs and evolves, but also explains why this process increasingly produces similar societies.

The first factor Fukuyama identifies here is the impact of military competition which, he argues, encourages the rationalisation of societies and the forming of uniform social structures, a much more accurate account of interaction than one based merely on benign non-state transnationalism. Fukuyama provides many examples of defensive modernisation forcing countries to conform, ending up with Russia in the late 1980s:

> Modern natural science forces itself on man, whether he cares for it or not: most nations do not have the option of rejecting the technological rationalism of modernity if they want to preserve their national autonomy. We see here a demonstration of the truth of Kant's observation that historial change comes about as a result of man's 'asocial sociability': it is conflict rather than cooperation that first induces men to live in societies and then develop the potential of those societies more fully.[40]

The second factor that leads to growing convergence of societies through science is economic development and the requirements this creates for the organisation of labour, the state and education:

> All countries undergoing economic modernization must
> increasingly resemble one another: they must unify nationally
> on the basis of a centralized state, urbanize, replace traditional
> forms of social organisation like tribe, sect, and family with
> economically rational ones based on function and efficiency,
> and provide for the universal education of their citizens. Such
> societies have become increasingly linked with one another
> through global markets and the spread of a universal consumer
> culture.[41]

Fukuyama does not argue that this scientific-developmental
imperative necessarily entails democracy, and his great historical
caveat is that an authoritarian society might succeed in economic
terms equally well, in, for example, East Asia. But he does claim
that in certain respects, as in the freedom of information and of
decision-making, liberal democracy is conducive to such development. He also argues, on quite separate grounds, that liberal
democracy, for all its failings, is better than any other system in
meeting what he sees as the most fundamental of human needs:
recognition and respect. The combination of the two needs,
contingent but reinforcing, provides the basis for his two most
comprehensive claims that a universal history can be written,
replete with teleology, and that, since an answer to the main
problems of human development has been found in theory and to
some extent implemented in practice in the stronger and more
influential states of the world, history, in the sense of a conflict
between global models, is over.

There are two important implications of Fukuyama's theory for
this discussion of 'international society', both of which are, to
some extent, worked through in his book. The first is that as a
result of the processes he identifies, and the conflict and rivalry of
states, countries are forced more and more to conform, to produce
that resemblance, that similitude, that Burke identified. Fukuyama
does not accord to ideology, custom or manners the primacy
allotted by Burke, but he does see culture as an important
constituent of the modernity that all societies are forced to move
towards. Furthermore, culture is one of the mechanisms through
which societies are forced by others to conform: his analysis of the

end of the Cold War, based on the transmission to an educated population within the communist countries of an image of a more successful Western world, makes considerable use of ideological factors.

Second, Fukuyama, taking up the argument of Michael Doyle and others, develops the thesis that liberal democracy will mean the end of inter-state conflict as we know it: since liberal democracies do not, for significant reasons, go to war with each other, the spread of liberal democracy reduces the likelihood of military conflict and military rivalry between developed states and progressively confines war to relations with or between un-democratic states.[42] As liberal democracy spreads, so the domain of war will be reduced. Ultimately the end of history will mean the end of international relations as we have hitherto known it. The creation, for the first time, of an international society in the constitutive sense means that Kant's vision of a universal peace will be realised. Marx will find a perverse vindication, not through the creation of a world-wide communist society, but through the full realisation, a century and half after the publication of the *Manifesto*, of the world created in capitalism's image. The Bolshevik Revolution challenged the capitalist world 'on pain of extinction':[43] in the end, it was extinguished.

The disputes raised by Fukuyama's theory are many, and touch on issues far removed from the analysis of international society. Three, in particular, merit critical attention: agency, democracy, development. I shall return to these in the final chapter, in the context of an overall assessment of his work. Suffice it to say here that the difficulties with his theory, as well as the overall perspective he offers, pertain directly to the issue of international society, and the very meanings of 'society' itself that are deemed to operate at the international level.

Implications for International Relations

Such, in outline, are the elements of what may be identified as the third, 'constitutive', model of international society. As with any theoretical shift, its introduction is designed not so much to deny the coherence and explanatory potential of the other two concepts, although some difficulties with them have been identi-fied, as to point to another interpretation of the concept that may, in its own context, suggest an additional programme of investigation. International society construed as those processes making for 'homogeneity' may help us to look at areas of international relations that have hitherto been under-recognised, or which, by dint of recent developments, be these theoretical or historical, have been cast in a new light.

In the first place, any approach based on the 'homogeneity' concept invites an alternative history of both international relations and the development of individual societies. For the latter, the shift is evident: what may previously have been seen as discrete, isolated, national histories, now appear much more clearly as the result of international processes, of imitation, competition, defensive modernisation and influence. As the work of the historical sociologists on the state discussed in Chapter 4 – Otto Hintze, Michael Mann – has shown, the growth of administrative and coercive institutions has throughout history been influenced by competition with other states. This international historical sociological perspective can be employed to explain not only economic development, but also political and social change within countries. The implications for International Relations are many. If we ask how the 'international' matters, and, by extension, what international processes merit greatest attention, then this process of imitation, homogenisation, and resistance to it, becomes central. Conflict between states, and orthodox diplomatic activity, are not excluded, but form part of a broader pattern of significant international interaction.

One phenomenon that this conceptual approach helps to identify and explain is what one may term, in retrospect, the pathos of semi-peripheral escape. By this is meant the attempt over the past century by a range of countries that were not in the forefront of Western capitalist development to take developmental routes that defied the established model of political and economic organisation.

In one sense these were examples of Gerschenkronian 'catching-up': but what is pertinent here is how, in the end, they had to abandon the exceptional means of trying to do so. What is striking about these attempts is that, while successful for some decades in their own right, they were ultimately broken by international pressures, whether those of war, non-military competition or cultural-ideological influence. The most obvious examples were the communist states, which for a fair period of time, from October 1917 to August 1991 to be precise, sought to map out such an alternative path. Of these, the most significant was the USSR, which although remarkably unbelligerent by the standards of most modern states, nonetheless became involved in protracted military conflict with Great Power capitalist rivals: it prevailed over its first major challenge, that of capitalist authoritarianism in Germany, but succumbed to the second challenge, that of liberal capitalism of the post-1945 period.

The pathos of semi-peripheral escape did not, however, apply only to regimes of the left. On the right, several countries, notably Germany, Italy and Japan, sought their own alternative path in the 1920s and 1930s, only to be brought into line by the firmest instrument of homogenisation of all, namely military defeat and occupation. What the Second World War did for these three countries, the allure of a broader market, and middle-class pressures for cultural and political modernisation, did for the smaller, less belligerent, European states of the right, namely Spain, Portugal and Ireland.[44] Each of these had acquired conservative regimes after civil wars in the inter-war period, but had judiciously prolonged their existence by staying out of the global conflict of the 1940s. Although their strategic exclusion delayed their homogenisation, nevertheless from the late 1950s onwards, they began to experience the attractions of the Common Market and were, by the late 1970s, integrated into the EEC, and appropriately homogenised.[45] The same applied, with some variation, to Greece.

Even the US and the UK, arguably the purest cases of capitalist development, did not escape such abrupt externally fuelled intrusions: the USA tried, up to the 1860s, to maintain the most extreme case of capitalist oligarchy, in the slave-owning South, while the United Kingdom delayed extending suffrage to the working class and women until forced to by the First World War. It is not to deny the importance of endogenous and specific factors, to note how far external factors, and in particular the pressure to conform, contributed to these outcomes.

This understanding of international society as 'homogeneity' has considerable implications for the issue discussed in Chapters 8–10, analysis of the Cold War and its end: first in the explanation it suggests as to why the Soviet system collapsed, a unique case of a hegemonic bloc disappearing in the absence of inter-state war; and secondly in the implications it raises for the pattern of post-Cold-War international relations.

Any International Relations theory worth its salt can, presumably, come up with an explanation of why the Cold War ended. The particular character of the Soviet collapse would, however, suggest that some mechanisms of international pressure, separate from either inter-state conflict or transnational economic interaction, were in play; that, in other words, the mechanisms of homogeneity in the end took their toll. A further illustration of this argument came in 1992 from the rhetoric of the American electoral campaign. Whereas in the Cold War era, the main dimension and leitmotif of international competition as reflected in electoral speeches was the military rivalry with the USSR, by 1992 it had switched to the arena of economic competition, with Japan and the European Community. The solutions offered, by Bush and even more so Clinton, rested explicitly on international comparisons on education, social expenditure, investment policy and wage levels. Both main candidates argued that only by becoming more like their competitors could the United States retain or regain its international position.[46]

As for the future, if the claim that liberal democracies do not go to war holds, and if this political system prevails in a significant part of the world – most specifically if it establishes itself and holds out in Russia – then the establishment of an international society in the stronger, 'homogeneous', sense of the word will mean that a new era of international relations has begun. The 'end of history' would translate into the end of international relations as hitherto understood.

These analytic and historic considerations leave unresolved the theoretical question of how homogenisation works. What needs to be specified is a third dimension of international relationships, interlinked with but separate from, the two identified by the other conceptions of international society, namely the inter-state, and the transnational. This would be legitimately termed 'socialisation', but it would denote not the socialisation of which realism talks, namely getting other sovereign states to accept certain norms in their international behaviour, but the reproduction within societies of norms established elsewhere in the system.[47] This third dimension, that of social, political and ideological influence and homogenisation, may at any particular time be subordinate to the other two, but may at others prevail over them. The least one can say is that, whether the framework, be it the evolution of the system over the past five centuries and the role within that evolution of capitalism or the fate of semi-peripheral countries in the twentieth century, the salience of this homogenisation process seems to be considerable. The end of history may mean the end of international relations as power politics. It may also presage the beginning of International Relations as a comprehensive and adequately theorised interpretation of the multiple dimensions of international society.

6

'The Sixth Great Power': Revolutions and the International System

A Case of Mutual Neglect

The discipline of International Relations has long had an uneasy relationship with revolution. Hannah Arendt's remark that the twentieth century has been shaped by wars and revolutions is often quoted, but it is striking how, within the institutionalised research and teaching on International Relations, these two historically formative processes receive differential treatment. Courses, journals, departments and institutes on war are plentiful. Study of war, in its historical, strategic and ethical dimensions, as well as in policy terms, is central to the academic study of IR. Revolutions, by contrast, have enjoyed a marginal existence. Standard textbooks and theoretical explorations devote little space to them. There is no journal specialising in this question. We have yet to meet the Oliver Cromwell Professor of Revolutionary Studies: there are no invitations to speak at the Thomas Paine International Institute for the Comparative Study of Revolutionary Change.

There is no single reason for this marginalisation. A variety of factors within the intellectual tradition and institutional context of IR have converged to produce this situation. IR itself began as a study of war and the causes of war, and remains focused, as do such war-preventing documents as the UN Charter, on the belief that war between states is to be seen in terms of rationally decided aggression rather than in the internationalisation of social conflict.

The subsequent theoretical development of IR has, in several

ways, confirmed this. In the incorporation of US and British
political science into IR there was a complementary disdain and
neglect of revolutions, which were seen as breakdowns of
otherwise regular processes in national and international society.
With the rise of behaviouralism, the concept of 'revolution', along
with that of the state, was dissolved into a spectrum of violence
and 'internal war' that denied it analytic and historical specificity.[1]
Neo-realism in its Waltzian version, casting all references to
internal and transnational processes as 'reductionist', has in its
turn blocked off consideration of the interaction of international
and internal change.[2]

Other factors can be traced to the broader climate of the social
sciences. The study of revolution is not at home in any of the social
sciences, although it has received more attention within sociology
and history. In these disciplines, however, it has tended to do so
with little reference to the international dimensions of the
phenomenon. Most sociological works until Skocpol's *States and
Social Revolutions* treated revolutions as if they happened within
discrete national-political entities.[3] The other major recent
contribution to the comparative and theoretical study of revolutions, the work of Jack Goldstone and his associates, has drawn
attention to certain international factors in the weakening of
states, notably economic-fiscal pressures, and destabilising alliance
politics; however, these are given a secondary place within what
remains predominantly the analysis of discrete national and
political entities. The most important comparative dimension of
Goldstone's work, that of demographic pressure, is of uncertain
international origin, and, as he himself indicates, international
factors are ambivalent in their impact on states, with the potential
both to strengthen and to weaken them.[4]

Within the theoretical approaches to IR, realism does discuss
revolutions but they are usually invoked not as objects of study in
themselves, but in order to prove the pressures of conformity, the
socialisation, that the constraints of the system impose on even the
most deviant or revisionist of states. No realist textbook is
complete without the assertion, of dubious validity, that the
Bolsheviks had settled into the system by 1922. The lesson drawn
is that even revolutions cannot duck the system.[5]

The most extended discussion of revolutions from a realist
perspective is David Armstrong's *Revolution And World Order:*

The Revolutionary State in International Society. Armstrong departs somewhat from the conventional Wight-Bull conception of 'international society', first by including in the 'norms' of that society issues relating to internal constitution of states, such as slavery, or democratic conduct, and secondly by accepting that, even as they are socialised, revolutionary states may force status quo powers to revise the norms by which states relate to each other, as in the Soviet Union's success in provoking the establishment of the International Labour Organisation in the 1920s and the end of colonialism after the Second World War.[6] However, even if it breaches the realist canon on accepting the pertinence of internal political and social structures, this is at best, a partial adjustment: on the one hand, it avoids the question of what it is in the internal constitution of states that is seen as constituting the norm, not least the issue of property relations; on the other, it neglects the operations of international society in the broader sense identified in Chapter 5, going well beyond the actions of governments.

Other IR trends of the 1970s and 1980s allow equally little space to revolutionary upheavals: international political economy and interdependence are concerned with relations within the capitalist world, and mainly its developed capitalist parts, without much need to look at poorer or revolutionary states. The role of the Vietnam War in provoking awareness of 'interdependence' is forgotten. Strategic studies of the Cold War period, long adrift of its Clausewitzian and historical moorings, examined East–West arms racing in almost complete abstraction of the conflicting socio-economic compositions of the Soviet and US systems. Too little attention was paid to the social and political conflicts of the Third World that, far from constituting another, secondary, dimension of the Cold War, were central to it and a major catalyst of the nuclear arms race itself.[7] In terms of shaping the post-war world, guerrilla warfare, in its revolutionary and counter-revolutionary forms, was at least as influential as nuclear weapons: yet it hardly figured in the orthodox curriculum of strategic studies.

Beyond factors of academic and intellectual climate, other influences, what Kuhn politely terms 'institutional' ones, have certainly also played their part: with the brief exception of the late 1950s and early 1960s, there has been a shying away from a difficult and contentious topic, and, as the price of greater academic integration with the 'real' world, a growing concentration on those aspects of 'reality' deemed suitable for study by donors, at corporate and state levels.[8]

There are, none the less, three respects in which this mutual neglect has not been absolute and where elements of an interaction of IR and revolution can be identified. There is, first of all, the body of literature within IR that has explicitly focused on analytic and comparative issues presented by revolutions: the works of Kissinger, Rosecrance, Wight, Rosenau, Kim, Calvert, and, already mentioned, that of Armstrong.[9] The compensation here is that, despite its exiguous quantity, the quality, the sharpness with which central issues are posed, is usually high. Even those works produced prior to the more recent sociological work on revolutions are of a high standard: the questions they pose have stood the test of time.

Secondly, revolutions have been present within IR in a disguised form, within topics presented from an alternative analytic starting point, but where the existing literature can be re-read and reconstituted so as to be of relevance to revolutions: this is true of some of Rosenau's works on transnational linkages, of the literature on intervention (causes, practicalities, ethics) and, albeit in a most distracted way, in some of the literature on terrorism.[10]

Thirdly, there is some literature in cognate social sciences that is accessible and relevant for the construction of an IR discussion of revolutions: if this is true of certain historical works that stress international aspects of revolution (Palmer, Rudé, Hobsbawm on the late eighteenth century, Carr, Liebman, Deutscher, Harding on the Bolshevik Revolution),[11] it is even more so with the 'third wave' of sociological writings on revolution, and most notably that of Skocpol and Goldstone: via their interest in the weakening and breakdown of states, they stress the role of inter-state competition in the causing of revolutions and in the formation of post-revolutionary states. As with the IR writings on the subject, these sociological texts may be meagre in number, and they may, as already noted, tend to focus on national systems: but their analytic and theoretical implications are considerable.[12]

Examination of the place of revolutions in IR would seem to comprise three broad areas of enquiry. The first is historical: that of locating the place and influence of revolutions in the history of the international system, and in the formation of the international milieu of the twentieth century. The least that can be said here is that the role of revolutions, à la Hannah Arendt, has been systematically understated.

The second area of enquiry is descriptive, the examination of the international dimensions of revolutions themselves, to ascertain how far any regularities of political behaviour can be identified. The existing, mainly realist, account of the international system assumes that it has already ascertained what these regularities are, and finds them confirmatory of realism's assumptions: there may, however, be more to the story than that.

The third, most fundamental, area of enquiry concerns theory, that is, what theoretical issues the study of revolutions poses for IR. This leads to an examination of how far each of the established paradigms can, and cannot, cope with a proportionate acknowledgement of the importance of revolutions, and how far apparently central assumptions of the discipline may need re-examination in the light of such an investigation. This theoretical probing, however, takes us beyond the domain of IR: it involves a two-way process, one that should examine not only how revolutions affect IR, but how far proper consideration of the international context can pose questions for established sociological or political explanations of revolution.

Revolutions and their Effects

The use to which concepts are put within IR depends, to a degree unacknowledged within the discipline, on definitions imported from other areas. If this is true of concepts such as state, power, and system, revolution is no exception. As with all other concepts in social science, the concept 'revolution' has evolved over time, and contains variant meanings. The discussion that follows here uses it to refer to revolutions in the restricted, discriminatory, sense of the term, defined by Skocpol and others: that is, social and political revolutions of a major kind. It rests, in particular, on three major contributions to the study of revolutions which serve to delimit them as separate and comparatively rare historical events, but ones that, far from being marginal or atypical for the history of states and the international system, are points of transition and formation without which the modern world would not be as it is.

The first of these contributions, published in 1979, is Theda Skocpol's *States and Social Revolutions*. This identified revolutions on the basis of degree of transformation of the society, and destruction of the old state, as a distinct category of historical event:

Social revolutions are rapid, basic transformations of a society's state and class structures; and they are accompanied and in part carried through by class-based revolts from below. Social revolutions are set apart from other sorts of conflicts and transformative process above all by the combination of two coincidences: the coincidence of societal structural change with class upheaval; and the coincidence of political with social transformation.[13]

Beyond these specifications, Skocpol, while allowing for mass mobilisation and democratic aspiration, focused on the relation of revolutions to states – they sought both to overthrow existing ones and to consolidate new ones. In doing so, she highlighted how inter-state competition, through economic, military and political domains served to weaken states and so prepared the way for revolution – something evident in the three cases she considers, France, Russia and China.

The second foundation of this study of revolutions is J. B. Barrington-Moore's *The Social Origins of Dictatorship and Democracy*, published in 1967. This examined the contrasting paths to industrialisation and liberal democracy of a range of major states and showed how their contrasted trajectories owed much to the patterns of agrarian power present in the pre-industrial period. But Barrington-Moore's work also developed two arguments that ran in the face of much conventional thinking on revolution. In contrast to the prevailing idea of a 'peaceful', non-revolutionary, path pursued by England and the USA, he pointed to the extremely violent chapters through which those countries made the transition to modernity, the latter including the first industrialised war of modern history, that of 1861–5, which he considered to be a revolution. At the same time, in discussing countries which apparently avoided violent transitions by not having revolutions, Germany and Japan, he brought out the violence that did. accompany their transitions, both through repression within and through aggression without. In sum he argued that there was not a choice between a violent and non-violent path, but that both the revolutionary and the non-revolutionary paths were riven with human cost. Revolutions were, therefore, not aberrations from a non-violent alternative, but one form of an inevitably violent transition to a modern society and often a form that, on the international scale, was less violent than that of the German-Japanese alternative.

The third constituent of the conception of social revolution used here is the as-yet-untranslated classic by the German writer Karl Griewank, *Der Neuzeitliche Revolutionsbegriff, Entstehung und Entwicklung*.[14] Griewank traced the development of the concept 'revolution' from its early astronomical and constitutional sources through to the 'modern' concept that issued from the French Revolution.[15] This enabled him not only to identify different meanings of the term, but also to discern more clearly the constituents of that modern usage: that revolutions involved not only political or constitutional change, but also mass involvement in that process; that the central object in revolutions was control of the state, and, hence, that no concept of revolution was possible before the modern state emerged (the same being true, incidentally, of any concept of the inter-state or international system); that revolutions were now seen as moments of transition to a new, better or even perfect, world, the beginnings of an age when all would be different. It is this 'modern' conception of revolution, analysed by Griewank and inherited from the French Revolution, that has permeated so much subsequent discussion.

The questions of definition and historical role of revolutions are, of course, central to any discussion of these upheavals in the international context. Much of the discussion of revolutions in the IR literature uses revolutions in a much looser sense to include coups and outbreaks of violence, where it does not simply dissolve them into a behaivouralist spectrum. Most IR literature also assumes that revolutions are moments of breakdown, rather than transition, and that these moments are distinguished by violence, in contrast to stable but repressive regimes, which are not. In fact, while each of the major contemporary IR paradigms consider revolutions to some degree, the conceptual bases of these considerations vary to such an extent that their findings approach the incommensurable. This is not only because of general conceptual differences, but because each uses a different concept of revolution. A condensed, necessarily summary, overview of how each of these three main paradigms treats revolutions can make this clearer.

For realists, revolutions tend to be seen in terms of the changing foreign policy styles and priorities of states, such that these now constitute a 'revisionist', 'dissatisfied' or unbalancing factor in the international system and must be suitably tamed: revolutions are a breakdown in an otherwise orderly world. In themselves, they require neither explanation nor historical contextualisation. Even a perceptive realist analysis, such as that of Rosecrance, operates with this model; Kissinger's *A World Restored* exemplifies it. Armstrong, as already discussed, goes some way to locating revolutions more centrally within the course of international history, but at some violence to the realist paradigm itself.

For behaviouralists, such as Rosenau, revolutions are part of the spectrum of violence, and like viruses can spread transnationally: but this violence is seen in psychological terms, abstracted from social cause or international context, and is again implicitly contrasted with a supposedly non-violent, because stable, alternative.

Historical materialism, present in IR in its tamed 'structuralist' variant, pays much more attention to revolutions and sees them as forming precisely the formative, transitional, role identified by Skocpol and Barrington-Moore, and as involving substantial social and political change. In contrast to the realists and behaviouralists, historical materialists regard revolutions in a positive light, and also start by looking at the international factors, defined by capitalism and imperialism, as the context in which any one individual revolution is to be located. In an apt aside, Marx criticised the assumptions of a theory based on the Great Powers by stating that the pentarchic nineteenth-century order, that of the Five Powers, would be swept aside by 'the sixth great power', revolution.

However, such is the focus of historical materialism on the international dimension of revolutions that it has difficulty in explaining why revolutions appear to be confined to specific states and exhibit such distinctly national and nationalist characteristics. Moreover, the historical materialist conception of revolution, in both its practical and theoretical forms, rested upon a view of history as moving, through stages, towards a determinate historical goal: it was, in this sense, 'teleological', and presumed that revolutions were somehow transitions, or staging posts, in a unilinear evolution of human society. While there may be room for some concept of progress in human society, this determinist one was an illusion and constituted a major flaw in the whole Marxist approach. In so far as it is present, in disguised form, in the writings of others influenced by Marxism, including Barrington-Moore and Skocpol, it is also a source of weakness in their work.

A summary examination of three areas of analysis already identified – historical, descriptive, theoretical – may bring these respective anomalies more clearly into focus.

The Formation of the International System

In a striking passage in chapter 6 of his *Power Politics*, itself entitled 'International Revolutions', Martin Wight observes: 'It might well be asked why unrevolutionary international politics should be regarded as more normal than revolution, since the history of international society has been fairly equally divided between the two'.[16] In an attached footnote he develops this point: 'If, taking conventional dates, we regard 1492–1517, 1643–1792 and 1871–1914 as unrevolutionary, and 1517–1648, 1792–1871 and 1916–60 as revolutionary, there are 256 years of international revolution to 212 unrevolutionary'. There can be dispute about a date or phase here or there, but the underlying point Wight is making is cogent: that for much of the history of the international system, relations between states have been determined not by 'normal' factors – Wight names law, custom and power politics – but by abnormal, revolutionary, ones. These are ones in which ideological divisions play an important part, and in which it is the aim of states to alter, in a substantial way, the political and social orders of others. Wight argues that in the end, doctrine gives way to power politics, but his recognition of the importance of revolution in the international system, dominant for over half the history of the system, is striking. The 'anarchy' has been as much one of ideology as of a sovereignless system of states.

The earlier examples of this ideological diversity need only the briefest of mentions: in the sixteenth century, the ideological and political upheavals of the Reformation, itself a case of trans-national 'linkage' and ideological interaction; in the seventeenth century, the wars and revolutions of the 1640s, when no less than six European states saw upheaval in the same year, 1648;[17] in the late eighteenth and early nineteenth centuries, the 'Atlantic Revolution' of 1760–1800.[18]

The importance of revolution in the twentieth century has been immense. The Bolshevik Revolution of 1917 established the fundamental fissure of this century's international relations, one that, on the basis of two competing and distinct socio-political systems, respectively contributed to and then dominated the frictions of the inter-war period and of the post-war world. How far it was the antagonism to the Bolshevik Revolution, and the fear of its impact on central Europe, which provided the spur for the rise of Nazism, is an open question: Hitler himself had other concerns, but the willingness of the German middle classes and army to rally behind him may have been considerably affected by the communist challenge. No such doubt attaches to the course of world history in the four decades after 1945: the already constituted divide between capitalist and communist states was compounded by, and interacted with, the spate of third world revolutions whose very enumeration is that of the major post-war crises – China, Korea, Cuba, Vietnam and, in the late 1970s and 1980s, Cambodia, Angola, Ethiopia, Iran, Nicaragua, Afghanistan.

As discussed in more detail in Chapter 8, the Cold War was an inter-systemic conflict, one between two social and political systems and its extension to, and shaping of, third world conflicts provided the most dangerous and violent episodes of the second half of the twentieth century. From 1945 to 1989 it was these issues of third world conflict above all that fuelled international tensions: one index of this is that it was policy towards third world revolutions that led to US presidents giving their names to 'doctrines'.[19] Equally, it was Third World challenges that did more than anything to challenge the positions of US presidents – as Truman, Johnson and Carter especially had cause to reflect. The partial decline of US hegemony in the 1960s was to a considerable extent a result of Vietnam. The history of the world from the end of the Second World War to the end of the 1980s was largely, but not exclusively, that of the response of the international system to

revolution. In the four decades up to the late 1980s, revolution
provided the historical foundation for the bipolar system, fuelled
the nuclear arms race, provided case after case of great power
competition, and threatened the domestic political stability of
major powers.[20]

The inter-systemic conflict of the Cold War was followed by the
upheavals in Eastern Europe of 1989, which dealt a mortal blow to
the bipolar world that had subsisted since 1945. In one sense, these
revolutions appeared to go against the pattern of the upheavals of
the past two hundred years, the conception of revolution identified
by Griewank: they took place with relatively little violence, and
were carried out not in the name of some heterogeneous
alternative, but in order, or so it was hoped, to bring these
countries into line with prevailing western norms, of society, polity
and economy. In foreign policy as in domestic policy, they did not
seek to defy the prevailing international norms: they accepted not
only the general practices of diplomacy and law, but wanted to be
incorporated into the major institutions of the west, including
NATO and the European Community (EC).

As discussed later, in Chapters 9 and 10, these revolutions were
therefore original in several respects: but, whatever else, their
importance for international politics could not be doubted. The
Cold War ended not because of understanding, or *détente*,
between the great powers, but by the prevailing of one side over
the other: in other words, it was revolution, not mutual understanding, which broke the mould of the post-1945 world and
ushered in a new historical period. It was also these revolutions
which set in train a series of conflicts within and between states of
a kind they had not seen for decades, if at all; these threatened,
and in some cases led to, wars between states over territory. It may
be too early to assess fully the impact of these upheavals; that they
were revolutions, and that they did alter the course of international history, is already apparent.

Historical Patterns

Revolutions are international events in their causes and effects
and, with the partial exception of those of 1989, betray a striking
degree of uniformity. Generalisation on the basis of historical

examples cannot provide a substitute for theoretical investigation, but it can provide raw material for identifying a number of problems that themselves affect theoretical work. In the case of revolutions, there are at least four areas in which such generalisations can be examined: cause – that is, how far international factors produce revolutions; foreign policy – that is, how revolutionary states conduct their foreign relations; responses – that is, the reactions of other states; formation – that is, how, over a longer time-span, international factors, and the system as a whole, constrain the post-revolutionary internal development of states and shape their political, social and economic evolutions.

As already observed, revolutions occur when two broad conditions are met: that the dominated revolt, and the rulers cannot go on ruling. Most intuitive discussion of international causes of revolutions focuses on the first of these two facts, the stimulation of revolt, and critics are quick to identify, or invent, a foreign hand in the subversion and agitation, in some cases arming, of revolutions.

Yet, as the work of Skocpol, Goldstone and others of the 'third wave' have shown, it is mainly via the other dimension, the weakening of states, that international factors promote revolution. International factors play a multiple role in bringing about revolutions, but it is above all because of this weakening of states, that they contribute to change: through defeat or crisis in war, through international economic changes that destroy traditional orders, through provoking conflict between states and societies as a result of the states' mobilisation of resources to pursue international competition, through the removal of guarantees by a hegemonic power. In other words, while states may use the international dimension and the resources it provides to consolidate their position at home, they may also find themselves weakened internally as a result of their international activities and alliances. This was true of many earlier cases, not least France, Russia and China, but it was equally so in 1989. As discussed in Chapters 9 and 10, the collapse of the Eastern European communist regimes in 1989 was in the immediate context a result of the removal of a Soviet guarantee to intervene militarily on their behalf, and, over the longer run, a consequence of the loss of international legitimacy of these regimes, in the economic and political spheres.

The other kind of cause, the encouragement of revolutionaries, is evidently important: arms, political backing, above all ideological encouragement and the force of example. But without the concomitant weakening of states such external stimulation is limited in its effects: witness the example of South Africa, where, despite immense pressure from below, the state retained its power for many years, and only changed in the late 1980s when external economic pressures, specifically the US investment boycott, threatened the regime.

The foreign policy of revolutionary states of the pre-1989 period is a large area in itself, and remarkably under-studied. Some of the literature focuses on the issue of 'new diplomacy', i.e. the role of revolutionary ideology and unconventional action in the foreign policy of revolutionary states.[21] But this ideological challenge to the norms of international behaviour is, at most, a secondary issue: ideology and interference also play a part in the foreign policies of status quo powers, and revolutionary states have distinctive foreign policies above all because of the different goals they pursue, rather than the methods they use.

This last point is significant because in much of the literature, realist and liberal, there is an assumption that the goals of revolutionary states are little different from those of other states. Liberals, for their part, argue that if only revolutionary states were treated better, they would not seek to 'export' revolution, to alter relations within other states. The historical record is rather different: all revolutionary states, almost without exception, have sought to promote revolution in other states. The challenge they pose to the international system is not so much that they propound a new form of diplomacy, or conduct international relations in a distinct manner, but that they make the altering of social and political relations in other states a major part of their foreign policy and regard themselves as having not just a right, but an obligation, to conduct their foreign policies on this basis.

Much of the literature, realist and transnational, understates this, as does much of the policy produced to resolve differences between the USA and third world revolutions in the post-war epoch: with regard to China, Cuba, Iran, or Nicaragua. No such resolution was, however, possible given the internationalist commitment present within the foreign policies of these states: this reflected both ideological components of their revolutions and domestic pressures to pursue such a foreign policy.[22] Over time, such commitments are tempered, but this should not detract from the recurrence of the internationalist commitment in modern revolutions, from the Girondins, through the Comintern, Lin Piao and Che Guevara, to the pan-Islamic appeals of Khomeini, and his espousal of *sudur-i inqilab*, or 'export of revolution': indeed in this, as in many other respects, it is striking how true to form, how conventional, Iranian revolution has been, beyond its particular religious form.[23]

The argument as to which provokes which, international revolution or international counter-revolution, is in historical perspective misplaced: both processes can begin autonomously, for internal and systemic reasons, and, feeding on each other, lead to confrontation. If revolutionary internationalism is an almost universal result of revolutions, so is its opposite, counter-revolutionary internationalism, the attempt by status quo powers to prevent the spread of revolutions and reform and, where possible, overthrow revolutions.

Two more issues that this interaction poses are perhaps more rewarding and take us to the heart of the international system. One is the issue raised by Richard Rosecrance and Raymond Aron, and further developed by Stanley Hoffmann (and discussed in Chapters 5 and 8), of the tendency of the international system to homogeneity, that is, towards a similar organisation not just of relations between states, but of the internal political and social systems of states.[24] Both revolutionary and counter-revolutionary internationalism derive from this tendency to homogeneity, which goes beyond any specific international security considerations about the military threat posed by one state to another (the point is not whether the Sandinista regime in Nicaragua in the 1980s, did, or could ever, pose a military threat to the USA).

The second issue which the record of both forms of internationalism points to, despite the claims of intervention, is the durability of the states system. All revolutionary states have tried to promote revolution abroad to 'export' it; in the straightforward sense of the term, none has ever succeeded. Khomeini's failure to promote revolution in Iraq in the early 1980s, or the Sandinistas to ensure a guerrilla victory in El Salvador in the same period, were true to form: there can be few images of international relations more inaccurate than that of the 'domino theory'. The creation of comparable regimes in neighbouring states has come only through inter-state wars that in the context of broader struggles then permit the implantation of homologous regimes (the *republiques soeurs* in the 1790s, the 'People's Democracies' in the late 1940s). In the same vein, state-led counter-revolution nearly always fails, except in rare cases, either of inter-state war again (France 1815, Hungary 1919) or of severe internal division within the revolutionary regime itself (Finland 1918, Iran 1953, Dominican Republic 1965, Grenada 1983). For all the battering that it takes in periods of revolutionary conflict, the state system tends to hold in the short run.

This 'short run' is, however, significant in that most of the realist discussion of 'socialisation' of states focuses upon the immediately post-revolutionary period and the apparent taming of states. The fact that they introduce truces, abandon internationalist rhetoric and participate in diplomacy does not, however, mean that revolutionary states have been entirely 'socialised'. A brief look at the longer-run record of revolutionary states shows that, as long as post-revolutionary internal orders remain intact, they continue to pose a challenge to the system in other states. The USSR promoted revolution abroad effectively not in the 1920s when it was weak, but in the 1940s, in the aftermath of the Second World War, and in the 1970s when the USA was challenged by a tide of Third World revolutions. The Cuban revolutionary wave failed in Latin America in the 1960s: but in 1975 Cuban forces intervened to consolidate the left-wing MPLA (People's Movement for the Liberation of Angola) in Angola, in 1977 they helped fight off the Somali invasion that threatened, with a degree of external encouragement, the Ethiopian Revolution, and in 1979 the Sandinistas, to a considerable extent armed and encouraged by Cuba, came to power in Nicaragua. In January 1989 most experts were arguing that the Iranian Revolution, humbled by war and economic crisis, would now make its peace with the West. One old man thought differently: the Rushdie crisis ensued.

This longer-run perspective suggests that the 'socialisation' of revolution is less easy than realist orthodoxy would have us believe, and it also suggests that this recurrent, if usually frustrated, challenge of revolutions is a product as much of internal as of external factors. The conclusion this leads to is that until there is a reimposition of homogeneity, that is, until the internal orders of divergent revolutionary states revert to the conventional orders of other powers, revolutionary and non-revolutionary powers will remain in conflict. There could be no more obvious example of this than the decline of the USSR: here, from 1985 onwards, a new, more conciliatory foreign policy evolved *pari passu* with a reform of Soviet politics and economics. The expectation was that, on the basis of greater mutual understanding, *détente* and a settlement of international disputes could be arrived at. Yet, in the final analysis, this reconciliation in the international sphere became possible only when the socio-political system inside the USSR itself had changed. It was the end of the heterogeneity of the two systems, not accommodation in treaties and diplomacy, that ended the Cold War.

The interaction of revolutions and the international system therefore raises questions not only for the study of revolution, but also for IR itself. By way of eliciting these implications, it is possible to outline five areas in which, by placing revolutions more centrally in the picture of IR, some broader theoretical rethinking may follow.

International and Domestic Links

Revolutions force us to question the central, realist, assumption that internal/domestic structures can be excluded from the study of international relations. The major exponents within IR of the international effects of revolutions – such as Rosecrance and Rosenau – have recognised this by arguing *for* the inclusion of domestic factors in the study of foreign policy making and its effects; it is not an accident that Waltz, in his 1979 restatement of realism, should have argued so strongly against this. His division of theories into 'systemic' and 'reductionist', 'elegant' as it may be, is untenable: the briefest examination of how revolutions have contributed to international conflict, to war in its strictest sense, shows how the interactive chain – international system/domestic system/international system – is a central feature of how these wars came about.[25]

The wars of the 1760s contributed to the French Revolution which led to the Napoleonic wars. The pressure on the Ottoman Empire led to the Young Turk Revolution of 1908, which precipitated the Balkan wars and hence stimulated the First World

War. The First World War led to the Bolshevik Revolution which determined Russia's role in the Second World War and beyond. Inter-state conflict, and more broadly inter-societal conflict, led to the collapse of communism in the late 1980s. By focusing only on the 'systemic', Waltz's model paradoxically downplays the force of the international. Following inter-state competition and its impact within society, changes occur that then lead to further inter-state conflict. As discussed in more detail in Chapter 5, this is *the* formative interaction that has shaped so much of international history.

Chapter 4 has already outlined an argument on differing implications of the concept 'state' for international relations: here it is possible only to summarise the implications for the study of revolution. Revolutions are about states, and yet IR operates with a problematic, increasingly contested, concept of the state itself. As much as other developments in IR and elsewhere in the social sciences, revolutions compel introduction of the new, second, concept of the state, a sociological category of the state as an administrative-coercive entity, in addition to the legal-political one normally used in IR.

The concept of the state conventionally used (if rarely defined) in IR precludes examination of precisely those processes that make revolutions international: the effects of inter-state competition on state–society relations, the weakening of state–society links by the impact of revolutions in other states, the determination of revolutionary foreign policy by the state–society conflicts of post-revolutionary periods.

The second, more restricted concept of the state enables us to see states in their Janus-like character, as the two-faced entities that look both inwards, towards the society they seek to dominate, and externally, towards other states and/or societies with which they interact with the goal of strengthening their own internal positions. With this two-faced concept of the state it also becomes possible to re-examine a feature of the international system that conventional theory takes for granted but to which it supplies tautological or axiomatic replies, namely, why states compete; in particular one can ask why, as the realists themselves often note, competition between ideologically antagonistic, i.e. heterogeneous, states is more enduring and comprehensive than those between states of similar orientation. The conventional answers, in terms of maximisation of power in the international arena, leave out the domestic determinants of such inter-systemic conflicts.

The domestic factor in inter-state activity brings us to the still unpacked question posed by Rosecrance, Aron and Hoffmann, and discussed at greater length in Chapter 5, namely, that of homogeneity and heterogeneity. At one level, it might appear excessive to see a tendency to homogeneity of internal orders within the international system. After all, states with different orders can trade and exchange ambassadors with each other. If they respect non-interference and agree to a diversity of internal system, that is, 'co-exist' peacefully, then heterogeneity should not be a cause of conflict: Kim, for example, on the basis of his study of the French Revolution, sees this as a practicable solution.[26]

Moreover, an element of heterogeneity could be seen as beneficial to states, since it provides an 'other', an alien and menacing object in the external world, on the basis of which states can mobilise social and political support within. These are not imaginary considerations: cases where such toleration or re-inforcement through diversity have operated are plenty. But the balance is, on the historical evidence, in the other direction: that is, heterogeneity does promote conflict. There is, in other words, a presumption of homogeneity within the system. This is most obviously true in a negative sense: if states are organised on different bases, then they are more likely to feel threatened by each other.

The most important international and internationalist impact of revolutions lies not in the deliberate actions of states, but in the force of example: the French Revolution proclaimed the rights of man, seized the land of the aristocrats and beheaded the king and queen. The Bolshevik Revolution overthrew the monarchy, nationalised property and proclaimed a state of the working class. Iran's impact has been exemplary and ideological, way beyond the identifiable reach of the Islamic Republic.

Even where states do not seek to promote their model, as most do – the 'malignant charity' denounced by Burke – the knowledge of what they have done, or are believed to have done, acts as a catalyst: it disturbs established orders. The serial collapse of the communist regimes in Eastern Europe in 1989 was a remarkable instance of such a demonstration effect. Once it became evident, in June of that year, that a non-communist government would be able to come to power in Poland, the fate of the other regimes was sealed.

The problem of homogeneity goes, however, beyond this issue of alternative examples, in that it obscures what is perhaps a more fundamental issue: namely, the role of homogeneity in a positive sense in reinforcing states, that is, in reinforcing the 'normal' interaction of stability of states. States are not isolated units: they exist in an international context, and their practices, constitutions, social and economic orders derive reinforcement from the fact that other states behave like them. Nor is this a recent development, as the literature on 'interdependence' too easily implies. Capitalism and the modern state arose in an international context, not the other way around.

This points to the idea that the international dimension is central to explanation not only of the destabilisation of states when there is heterogeneity, but also to the stability of political and social orders when there is homogeneity. Most of the sociological literature on this underplays the international dimension: whether in the Durkheimian debate on common culture and its role in social cohesion, or in the Marxist debate on the dominant ideology, there is inadequate recognition of how the force of international example through similarity and reinforcement serves to consolidate specific social orders.[27] Yet the most important underpinning of any ideology, the claim that what exists in a given social and political order is eternal, natural and immutable, derives confirmation from such a reinforcement. Once it becomes evident that there can be different orders in other states – that there can be republics, or countries where women have the vote, or where houses can be properly insulated – then the 'naturalness' of any given order collapses.

In other words, the key to understanding the ideological challenge of heterogeneity lies in identifying the pre-existing ideological role of homogeneity and reinforcement. If nothing else, this serves to bring out the importance of the 'international' in analysing any one social or political order: the 'international' does not just become relevant when things break down – when there is a political menace from outside, an invasion, a rival economic power – but is equally important in the constitution and reproduction of stable, apparently self-standing and autonomous, states. The 'international' (like health) matters when things 'go right' as much as when they 'go wrong'. As the historical sociologists have reminded us, the 'international' created the state, not vice versa.[28]

Revolutions and War

As indicated in the discussion of domestic–international 'linkage', the relationship of revolutions to wars hardly needs underlining, both in the ways wars cause revolutions and vice versa. If it has often been noted how wars, by undermining states, lead to revolutions, it is equally important to note how revolutions have led to wars: 1789 led to the Napoleonic wars, and the outbreak of the First World War, conventionally seen as a result of the breakdown of the balance of power, was preceded by a spate of revolutions in the semi-peripheral world, from China to Mexico, and, with most direct consequences for the European inter-state system, in Turkey.

This connection was vividly present in the conflicts of the early 1980s: in Cambodia, Afghanistan, Iran, Angola, Nicaragua. The historical record alone suggests that any study of the causes of war, and of means to predict or prevent war, requires identification of the onset and impact of revolutions. Yet to do this involves broaching a difficult but recurrent feature of the debate on international relations, namely the relation of security between states: 'vertical' security, and security within states, 'horizontal' security. The assumption of most literature, and of the UN Charter, is that it is possible to discuss the one, vertical security, without addressing the second, what goes on within states. The reason for avoiding this is evident, since if too close a relation is established, then the unwelcome policy and moral conclusions may follow that those concerned to prevent wars, conflicts between states, should prevent radical changes within them. Security then requires stability and 'counter-revolution'.

Those who establish a close linkage between the two kinds of security are inclined either to be consistent and thoroughgoing counter-revolutionaries, or to argue for a permanent world-wide revolutionary process, on the grounds that conflict between revolutionary and counter-revolutionary states is inevitable and that therefore there cannot be security for revolutionary states as long as its opponents remain in existence. Of those who have drawn the first connection, Metternich and, in his *A World Restored*, Kissinger, were perhaps the most prominent and lucid, but the Brezhnev Doctrine, insisting on the 'limited sovereignty' of communist countries, expressed a similar outlook. Lenin, Stalin and Mao, with their theory of the inevitability of war between socialism and capitalism, have represented the second conclusion.

Even before nuclear weapons, however, it was evident that despite the close link between the two dimensions of security such a combination of the two was not inevitable. The consensus has been to avoid the problem and deny that revolutions lead to war; the result was that the international community was unprepared for the outbreak of wars that followed the third world revolutions of the 1970s. Beyond more realistic and historically informed awareness of how inter-state conflict may follow social revolution, this recurrent linkage also suggests that greater attention needs to be given to ways of making the international system more flexible, so that challenges to security within states do not lead to inter-state war. The greatest mistake would be to maintain the idea that conflict at the international level can be isolated from that within states.

These four issues within IR theory as a whole lead to a fifth one, underlying the way in which each of the major paradigms within IR treats the question of the international dimensions of revolution: namely, the character of the international system itself. As with the concept of revolution, so with that of international system, each of the paradigms presumes concepts that differ significantly from each other.

For realists the system is constituted by interacting states. For pluralists and behaviourists states remain important, but the system allows of other interactions that do not operate through states, variously categorised as linkages, interdependence, transnational processes.

For historical materialists, the international system is constituted by one global socio-economic system, that of capitalism, superimposed on which there exist political structures playing various important, but ultimately secondary, derivative or superstructural, roles. During the Cold War this broad view encompassed two approaches: for one, orthodox, school of historical materialists, the communist countries had abstracted themselves from this system; for others, such as Wallerstein, no such partial escape had occurred. In either case there existed an international system not by virtue of interaction between separate units, as is the case with the realists and transnationalists, but by virtue of the unity of the determinant level, the socio-economic.[29] For structuralists, formation and development of states, later nation-states, takes place within an already established system. International politics is not politics between states but civil war within one, international, social system.

The implications of revolutions for these three models of the 'system' are considerable and parallel the conclusions of Chapters 3–5. On the one hand, the realist and transnational theorists under-state the degree to which the apparently separate states and societies have been formed and continue to exist within an international context defined by common social, economic and ideological features. In other words, their model of the 'system' makes it difficult to discern why revolutions have international effects.

The conventional Marxist model suffers, however, from the opposite problem, namely the exaggeration, on the basis of socio-economic factors, of the unity of the international system, and the underestimation of how states – artificial, arbitrary, interactive as they may be – and associated nationalist ideologies nevertheless act to fragment and cushion the international system as a whole from revolutions in particular states. The argument therefore leads to an examination of how the international character of the economy and of capitalist society and culture as a whole interact with the division of the world into states and the attendant fragmentation of territories, populations, coercive capacities and particularist ideologies this entails. The choice comes down to a theory that sees international relations as, in the end, dominated by states, and an alternative that looks at the system as one of social conflict on a world scale, mediated and fragmented by states.

It may be argued, following upon the collapse of communism and the end, or at least attenuation, of the revolutionary perspective inherited from the French Revolution, that the issue of revolution will cease to be central to the course of international relations. Even were this the case, it would not detract from the need to look again at the history of the international system over the past five hundred years and examine possible theoretical and historical consequences. But there are reason to suggest that, whatever the immediate future may bring, a longer-term certainty in this regard is imprudent.

In the first instance, if we accept that revolutions are unlikely or impossible in democratic states, we are still only talking of around three dozen of the near two hundred states in the world: as Chapter 10 suggests, there may be a very wide gap between the ideological consequences of 1989, 'the end of history', and the realisation of that potential with the generalisation of democracy across the world. Moreover, if we take seriously the implications of Goldstone's argument, that a crisis of state power combined with demographic upsurge is likely to lead to revolution, and combine it with projections of global population, then we may be defining the predominant pattern of crisis for the century ahead.[30]

The historical sociologists, international political economists and analysts of revolution all confront this question of what constitutes the system, also the central issue in IR. The least we can say is that no adequate answer, framed in historical and theoretical terms, has yet been arrived at. The study of revolutions as international phenomena, beyond its intrinsic validity, can provide one means of approaching that question, and quite a few others. It is, moreover, rather to early to suggest that this is merely a matter of historical or retrospective interest; it will take a century or two at least for this question to be resolved. Were it to transpire that revolution was indeed no longer relevant to the study of international relations, we would have to revise Martin Wight's historical summary: a third, rather than a half, of the history of the international system would then have to be characterised as dominated by the conflict between revolutionary and counter-revolutionary states. This would still invest the issue with not a little importance.

7

Hidden from International Relations: Women and the International Arena

The Silence of International Relations

Over the last two and a half decades questions of gender, and particularly those concerning the place and role of women, have acquired much greater importance within the social sciences as a whole. In response to the rise of a women's movement in some Western societies, and to the production of a growing body of analytic literature pertaining to women's position, there has been a marked development in the agenda and concepts studied in a range of academic disciplines. If this has been especially noticeable in history and sociology, it has also been evident in political science, economics and anthropology, and has acquired great importance in the most ideologically constitutive of the humanities, literature.[1] Until the very end of the 1980s there was, however, one outstanding exception to this growing awareness of gender issues, namely International Relations.

A survey of the articles published in, and books reviewed by, the main British and American journals of international relations during the 1970s and 1980s will reveal little if anything on gender questions, and little that reflects an awareness of the expansion of interest in related areas of the social sciences.[2] If one looked at the contents of standard introductory courses on international relations, at the major textbooks, at the relevant shelves of academic bookshops, a similar absence was evident. In the flood of books published on nuclear strategy, terrorism, third world debt and the other preoccupations of the 1980s, there appeared to be nothing, not a single book, devoted to this question. To borrow from the image popularised in Sheila Rowbotham's study of women and history, women have been hidden from international relations.[3] It is as if the issues raised by feminism were simply not considered relevant to the international sphere and did not need to form part of the academic agenda for the study of international relations.

To overcome the invisibility of women requires analysis of why the concealment takes place and of the several reasons that combined to enforce this occultation. One explanation is institutional inertia within the IR discipline. As long as a virtually complete silence on the issue exists, those concerned with it are either discouraged from working on it or choose to do so in other, more receptive academic disciplines – or in extra-academic contexts. In their time-honoured role as gate-keepers, 'refereed journals', often the twentieth-century academic equivalent of the Inquisition, excluded such material.

A second factor is the selective insulation of international relations from developments in other social sciences. International relations is in some respects an enthusiastic importer, one might even at times suggest *comprador*, of concepts from other disciplines. However, there are large areas of social science theory that appear to be unrecognised within international relations: as discussed in Chapters 4 and 5, sociological concepts, except where borrowed in an instrumental manner, as with 'society', are almost wholly ignored; the field of international political economy, while keen to assess the IR of some factors of production, such as money and technology, has been almost wholly silent on the international relations of another factor, namely labour. The growth of women's studies was, equally, long ignored in the IR field.

There is, moreover, the conventional definition of what constitutes the subject-matter of international relations, namely high politics: issues of state policy, especially those concerning security and macroeconomic management. Gender issues have little apparent place in this hierarchy. Even the broadening of international relations to encompass more transnational questions, those distinct from security and not necessarily mediated through states, has done little to rectify the situation. The literature on transnationalism and world society has been almost as silent on gender issues as has the high politics alternative.

Academic reserve is compounded by the fact that the domain of international practice – in foreign ministries, ministries of defence and related policy bodies – is itself an especially male-dominated reserve, beyond even the norms prevalent in policy-making bodies as a whole (as the meagre number of women foreign ministers or ambassadors the world over indicates). In conventional ideology, women are not 'suited' for such responsibilities and cannot be relied on in matters of security and crisis. Nothing could, it appears, be further from the traditional realm of women's concerns than international security and other global issues.[4]

There is a more fundamental reason for the gender blindness of most of the field of International Relations, namely an assumption of separation between the two spheres of gender and international relations. This is, moreover, an assumption which is shared both by IR and by much feminist literature. On the one hand it is presumed in academic writing that international relations as such are little if at all affected by issues pertaining to women. To put it in simplistic terms, the assumption is that one can study the course of relations between states without reference to questions of gender. Moreover, by neglecting the dimension of gender, International Relations implicitly supports the thesis that international processes themselves are gender neutral; that is, that they have no effect on the position and role of women in society, and on the relative placement of women and men. For its part, feminism, concerned above all with the interpersonal, the subjective and the private, has approached its analysis of forms of domination, ideology, division of labour in terms of the classic framework of orthodox sociology and psychology: the discrete society and the family or individual. The chasm between IR and feminism is, therefore, one that both have contributed to reinforcing.

The fact is that, in common with other social practices, international processes do have gendered effects – from military and economic ones to the formation and diffusion of images of women and fashions of feminism. The history of state policy on what may, at first sight, appear to be the most private and individual issue of all, namely human reproduction, is one replete with cases where states have sought to influence the birth rate (until very recently in the direction of boosting the number of children born) as part of inter-state competition. In the nineteenth century, a range of countries – Britain and France included – saw child-rearing, in both its biological and social forms, as a central part of the new imperial and militaristic order; in the words of one imperial eugenist, Caleb Saleeby: 'The history of nations is determined not on the battlefield but in the nursery, and that battalions which give lasting victory are the battalions of babies. The politics of the future will be domestics'. Or in more graphic terms: 'There is no State womb, there are no State breasts, there is no real substitute for the beauty of individual motherhood'.[5] In France, women who bore ten children were given state awards.

What this established was a link between inter-state competition and the birth rate, an ideology and state policy of natalism that mixed stereotypes about women and their reproductive and socialising roles with conceptions of national grandness and patriotic duty. Echoes of similar state ideas can be found in many twentieth-century nationalist states, from the Nicaragua of the Sandinistas, to the Iraq of Saddam Hussein.[6]

The language of international politics also suggests a strong conventional masculine and often homophobic content, with its emphasis on toughness and competition. If this was explicit in the imperial rhetoric of the late nineteenth and early twentieth centuries, with the social Darwinist cult of 'virile' nations, and their right to conquer weaker, presumably less virile ones, it has remained present in the discourse and imagery of Great Power conflict.[7]

In classic political theory, and language, the masculine virtues are held up as those most desired in international relations: indeed, as analysis of Machiavelli's use of the term has shown, the very term 'virtu', the quality of the *vir* or male, contrasts with the fickleness of its feminine alternative, *fortuna*.[8] Among many such possible quotations the injunctions of Edmund Burke can serve to illustrate the point further.[9] Writing in 1796 on the need to confront the threat of revolutionary France, Burke chided the English for their belief in their own weakness, and for accepting the argument that 'a frivolous effeminacy was become the national character'. Instead, he argued, the English overcame their weakness:

> We emerged from the gulf of that speculative despondency; and were buoyed up to the highest point of practical vigour. Never did the masculine spirit of England display itself with more

energy, nor ever did its genius soar with a prouder preeminence over France, than at the time when frivolity and effeminacy had been at least tacitly acknowledged as their national character, by the good people of this kingdom.

One hardly needs to be a post-modernist to deconstruct the layers of gendered symbolism here.

In contemporary political parlance, gendered political language is frequent: it is insulting to be called a Pollyanna, a wimp or limp-wristed. Those women who have come to occupy top political positions have, in the main, sought to reassure their male counterparts, and their male, and female, public opinions, that they can be as strong as men: Golda Meir, Margaret Thatcher, Jean Kirkpatrick all conform to this. The saying 'All's fair in love and war' should suggest a connection between these two Hobbesian domains. Indeed analysis of the language of military strategy, and particularly its nuclear variant, has revealed a striking incidence of gendered language in the analysis of weaponry and its possible deployment.[10]

The emergence of women's issues within International Relations involves a dual challenge to any assumed separation of the two domains, and a challenge to both IR and feminism: if the former would have to recognise the degree to which awareness of gender could subject the discipline, the latter would have to overcome its denial of the relation between gender relations and international processes, and to formulate its analysis, and suggestions for an alternative, in more than abstract or declamatory terms.

One aspect of the challenge is to reveal how gender issues and values could and do play a role within international relations; the second is to analyse the gender-specific consequences of international processes, be these military, economic, political or ideological. The latter modification has broad implications for the study of international relations as a whole, since it rests upon the argument, developed at greater length in earlier chapters, that international relations should study the consequences of international processes within societies, and the resulting impact of these internal changes on international relations, as well as analysing the sphere of international processes *tout court*.

An Emerging Concern: Four Dimensions

Twenty years after the emergence of feminism within the social sciences, some awareness within international relations of the relevance of this topic has become evident. It may be valuable to identify the factors that have prompted the change. There has been some measure of interaction between International Relations and other social sciences on questions of gender, so that questions and concepts raised in cognate disciplines can be seen as relevant to the international domain.

Gender and Theory

The growth of a feminist current within political and social theory has produced analyses with evident implications for International Relations theory.[11] These include critiques of power and its symbolisation in gender terms, as well as discussions of specifically gendered definitions of security, rights and authority. Human rights, for example, have become a much more important issue in international relations and, in so far as they have acquired a gender dimension, it is directly relevant to analysis of the role of states and other actors in promoting or denying rights to women. This is so in the broader political arena, as well as in contested areas such as marriage and family law, contraception and abortion, policies on female employment, and responses to rape and other forms of violence against women.

Discussions surrounding the problems associated with a concept of national interest have made its often partisan and group-specific character more evident. While much of the critique of national interest focuses on differences involving social groups, bureaucratic interests or ethnic and religious groups, this critique could evidently be extended to question whether definitions of national interest are gender specific and benefit men more than women under particular circumstances. The least that can be said is that different policies, be these military or economic, may have variant effects on men and women, and that any assumption of gender neutrality is debatable. Whether this critique of IR categories in terms of feminist theories also has broader epistemological implications, as some feminists have suggested, entailing altern-

ative forms of rationality, conceptualisation and expression, is
another issue, to which I shall return later in this chapter.

Transnational Processes

The second dimension of interaction between women and the
international sphere is the extent to which international policies
and processes, far from being gender neutral, in practice play an
important role in determining women's place in society and in
structuring economic, social and political relations between the
sexes. This is most clearly and often brutally evident in the activity
that is the quintessential domain of IR, and of inter-state conflict,
namely war.

Leaving aside the question of whether or not there is a specific
'women's position' on war itself, there can be no doubt that war
has multiple implications for women: women come to symbolise
much of what war is about (the country or *patria*, the defence of
women from attack) and are also mobilised and reallocated by the
state into a range of new activities, reproductive, productive and,
to a limited extent, military. One of the most revealing dimensions
of this relocation is that of women into areas of work that in
peacetime are the preserve of men, such as engineering and
munitions factories, from which, as the film *Rosie the Riveter* well
demonstrated, they are removed once peacetime returns.

Women are also prime victims of war, not just as ungendered
'civilians', but as objects of rape. The wars in ex-Yugoslavia that
began in 1991 have drawn especial attention to the role of rape, as
a symbol of subjugation and humiliation, a means of propagating
the superior race, and a theme for mobilising ethnic rage.[12] Rape
has recurred in modern wars, as both side-effect and instrument of
policy: a history of world war as a gendered conflict, ranging from
the Japanese 'rape' (in both senses) of Nanking in 1937 through to
the legitimation of rape by the Red Army as it advanced
westwards, remains to be written.[13]

In non-military contexts the impact of international processes on
women is perhaps most obvious in economics: international
economic processes have strongly affected women in both
developed and less developed countries in recent decades. The
newly industrialised countries have seen mass recruitment of
women into high technology industries.[14] In other third world

countries, changes in agricultural employment, as well as high levels of male out-migration to richer third world states or to more developed countries have had great impact on the roles and responsibilities of women. The structural adjustment policies pursued by a number of third world governments in the 1980s, often at the behest of the IMF and World Bank, have had gender-specific consequences: as wage levels deteriorate, women are often compelled to work in the least remunerated areas while publicly financed services on which women and children are particularly dependent deteriorate. Thus women bear a disproportionate burden in debt repayment strategies.

In the developed countries industrial change has promoted the employment of women in some areas and reduced it in others.[15] The growth in some developed countries of an underclass, composed largely of women and children, is in part a product of new forms of international competition.

In the political sphere, the entry of women into political life as voters and political subjects, an international phenomenon, usually experienced and subsequently presented as a purely national one, has been one of the most marked changes of the twentieth century.

Even the most apparently insulated arena of all, family relations, has been affected in many ways by international changes in this century: by changes in medicine, especially with respect to contraception; by the spread of domestic technologies; by the diffusion of new role models and ideologies of male–female and parent–child relations; by, as already noted, state policies, motivated by the supposed needs of inter-state competition, on birth rates. The constitution of women's position in society and economy, and of women's position in the home (for all that it is private and subject to national variations) owes much to changes and trends that are international and transnational.

There is no dimension of transnational relations more contentious and long running than the religious. It is not difficult to see how the changes in religious policy and fashion have, in recent years as earlier, had direct consequences for women. This is true for women in Islamic countries, where the rise of Islamicist movements in the 1970s and 1980s has affected many aspects of women's lives. It is also true within Catholic communities, where the reassertion of traditional doctrine on reproduction has provoked widespread resistance. At the cost of some exaggeration, it is possible to extend the slogan of the women's movement, that the personal is political, to assert that the personal is international, in the sense that interpersonal, micro-political relations are greatly influenced by transnational processes. If there are many ways in which this does not apply, there are far more ways in which it is true than conventional wisdom would have us believe. International processes often are not gender neutral, and gender relations, for all their autonomy, are not insulated from international factors.

Many of these factors have come together in an international process that began in the 1980s and which has marked all the women that were living in the countries affected, namely the collapse of communism. This was, in several respects, an international and transnational phenomenon: the communist regimes collapsed, above all, because of their inability to sustain inter-state competition; the changes that then took place within them involved the gradual encroachment and in some cases imposition of Western modes of social, economic and political behaviour, and the emergence of indigenous nationalist and religious, forms of ideology. The effects on gender relations were multiple: the end of communist controls led to an increase in prostitution and pornography (the latter associated with western freedom and modernity), the unemployment of millions of women, the collapse of welfare systems, including ones specifically designed to help working mothers. The new masculinism stressed the return of women to the home, the need to respect 'traditional' values on the family, as against the imposed or cosmopolitan values of communism.

Women did not experience the transition to post-communism uniquely as victims and in several respects stood to benefit, most obviously in terms of political freedoms. But whether positive or negative the changes to which they were subjected were ones that originated from an international crisis and which had broadly similar impact in different countries.[16]

Women as International Actors

Third, despite the subordination that women have and do experience, they have in recent years acquired much greater prominence as international actors. This has been true on issues of war and peace, in economic and social development, and in the growth of the women's movement itself which, in its concern to alter the position and thinking on a range of social and personal issues, has spread throughout the developed world and has had considerable resonance in the third world as well.

The spread of women's organisations and campaigns across frontiers since the late 1960s is a striking example of transnationalism. Here is one of the clearest cases of *non-state* actors since, it can reliably be reported, women as a group do not hold state power in any of the 190 independent countries in the world. This development is marked by both the growing transnationalism of organisation and debate on women's issues and by the combination of mobilisation on women's questions with action on other, more conventionally international questions. As with many other aspects of transnationalism and feminism, this combination is less novel than is often supposed. One of the most striking transnational movements of modern times was the movement in support of women's suffrage in the first two decades of this century.

While questions of gender are seen as personal or single issues, they have long formed part of a broader political and ideological outlook, as is evident both in the campaigns to promote women's equality and in those that oppose it. The link between women's issues and political and international change was evident at the time of the French Revolution, in the writings of Mary Wollstonecraft among others. One of the originators of socialist internationalism in the 1840s was the feminist Flora Tristan.[17] Similarly, opposition to women's equality may often correlate with certain attitudes to international issues. In the early 1980s one of the most active opponents of the Equal Rights Amendment to the US Constitution was Phyllis Schlafly, a right-wing leader who had also written three books on nuclear strategy in which she called for the US to have first-strike nuclear capability against the USSR and denounced Nixon and Kissinger as dupes of Moscow.

Women and Foreign Policy

Many areas of foreign policy have a gender-specific component. Starting with the question of war, the conventional core of the subject, there is a wealth of discussion about the specific contribution of women to preventing war. There is often a conceptual ambiguity here since, as Ruth Roach Pierson has shown, there is a distinction between deriving a feminist position on peace from woman's role as mother, and arguing for such an approach because women are people normally separate from access to the means of warfare.[18] None the less, the argument on women and peace has a long militant and analytic tradition. If this connection was evident in the 1980s, in campaigns against nuclear weapons, it was equally a feature of the peace campaigns prior to and during the First World War.[19]

In addition, there is substantial discussion of the role of women in war – as combatants in situations of resistance to occupation and as supporters of militaristic policies.[20] The spread within NATO countries of female recruitment to regular peacetime armies in recent years has prompted a wide-ranging debate on how women can and do integrate themselves into military structures.[21] The dispute over the role of women on active duty in the US invasion of Panama and in the Gulf War (where 30,000 women were among the half million US soldiers deployed) served to underline how much resistance to change there is on this question by the military apparatus and the public, as well as the complexity of the underlying issues, not least from a feminist perspective.[22] It was by chance that in 1993, his first year in office as US Defense Secretary, Les Aspin faced three critical issues each embodying an issue of gender – women in combat, homosexual rights and sexual harrassment.

If there is therefore a significant gender dimension to what is supposedly the core topic of international relations, comparable dimensions can be found in other areas of the subject. International institutions have come to devote much more attention to the position of women within societies as well as in relations among them, and the UN Decade for Women (1976–85) prompted widespread interest in issues of international law, development and national policies on women.[23] Both the UN and the EC have produced a substantial body of policy and analysis on the position of women.[24] A great number of non-governmental organisations are active on women's issues, ranging from the general, such as for example the Gender and Development Unit at Oxfam, to the specific, such as the French-based Women Living under Muslim Laws.

The gender dimensions of international economic policy, be these in regard to employment, sexual divisions of labour, development or migration are also, as already noted, receiving much more attention. Foreign aid, one of the most prominent aspects of developed states' international economic policy, has acquired an overt gender component. A commitment to assisting women through development programmes has, since the mid-1970s, become widespread in OECD (Organization for Economic Development and Co-operation) countries. A number of European countries, most notably Sweden, include benefit to women among the conditions of their aid programmes. The Percy Amendment, passed by the US Congress in 1973, stipulated that USAID programmes should spend at least $10 million annually on projects specifically designed to benefit women.

Gender and women in particular play one further role in foreign policy, namely as symbols or instruments of inter-state competition and of the superiority of one society over another. That this has little or nothing to do with concern about women themselves should be evident, nor does the revelation of these gendered discourses mean that foreign policy or international relations are generally or in some ultimate sense solely concerned with women. It none the less illustrates further the intersection of gender with foreign policy in ways that have hitherto been understated.

While Western states, in contrast to an increasing number of non-governmental organisations, have been cautious about making official statements about women's rights in other countries, third world states, opposed to what they see as 'imperialist' values, have not been so reticent. The Islamic Republic of Iran, for example, has often attacked what it considers to be Western mistreatment of women. Thus a report of a speech by the Iranian President Khamene'i in 1989:

> The plight of women in Western society is appalling,' said President Ali Khamene'i and went on to detail their historic oppression as 'mere objects of pleasure' despite the West's deceptive claim of women's freedom and their role in society. In stark contrast with the honour and respect accorded to women in Islam, Western society has degraded her to the meanest level, said the President, and deplored the 'culture of

permissiveness and nudity which gives man a free rein to exploit and insult her personality'.[25]

A striking example of this state exploitation of the gender issues comes from one of the most famous episodes of the Cold War when Nixon and Khrushchev met in 1959 in the model kitchen of an American exhibition in Moscow. This 'Kitchen Debate', known as an argument about which system was superior to the other, in fact revolved around the most domestic and gendered of issues, women and housework. This did not mean that the Cold War was wholly, or even mainly, about subjugating women or reorganising domestic labour: but it did show how symbols of gender were one of the ideological resources used in this inter-state competition. A historian of the Cold War gives both sides of the story, beginning with Nixon's account:

> They left the studio and, with a huge press contingent fighting to get their tape recorders in between the two men, they stepped into a model American kitchen. The argument continued as Nixon pointed to all the latest gadgets. 'Anything that makes women work less is good.' Khrushchev shook his head, 'We don't think of women in terms of capitalism. We think of them better.' Nixon said that a prefabricated home like this one cost only $14,000 in America, well within reach of the average worker . . .

Khrushchev's version of the famous debate with Nixon is slightly different. Completely disregarding anything said in the television studio, he claimed that when they got to the kitchen he picked up a lemon squeezer and muttered what a silly thing it was.

> All you need for tea is a couple of drops of lemon juice. I think it would take a housewife longer to use this gadget than it would for her to do what our housewives do, which is to slice a piece of lemon, drop it into a glass of tea, then squeeze a few drops out with a spoon. That's the way we always did it when I was a child, and I don't think this appliance of yours is an improvement in any way.[26]

Whatever their other differences, of course, both assumed that it would be women who would make the tea.

To sum up, there are at least four distinct ways in which issues pertaining to women and the international arena have, through a variety of processes, received greater recognition in recent years: through the encounter of feminism with International Relations theory; through growing recognition of the gender-specific consequences of a range of transnational processes; through the emergence of women as distinct actors on the international scene; and through an increased awareness of the gender component of foreign policy issues.

States and Women: Nationalism and Human Rights

Many of the questions raised in these four broad aspects of the gender dimension of international relations can be illustrated by examining areas in which questions of gender intersect with established values and policies. One of the most contentious and relevant of all these topics is that of women and nationalism; another, equally difficult, is the place of women's rights in the formulation of inter-state relations. Both lead to what are, in conventional terms, unacceptable conclusions. This alone may suggest that they pose questions that are important in their own right, and also are relevant to the identification and discussion of the underlying assumptions of international relations as a whole.

The shift in meaning of the word 'motherland', within the English language at least, is itself revealing: in its original, eighteenth-century, meaning it denoted land as 'mother', i.e. source, of something, be it minerals or art, and this was the meaning it retained as late as the 1840s. But with the rise of nationalism in the mid-nineteenth century it acquired a new, ideological, meaning, namely one's country of origin.

This fusion of an image of maternity with national identity served its purposes: if there is an assumption that national independence and national interest take precedence over the claims of any specific group within the nation, there has also been an assumption that, in general, the spread of nationalism is beneficial to women since they are a part of the nation. Nationalism mobilises women into political life, exalts particular national traditions pertaining to women, and by granting them political rights as citizens provides a foundation for overcoming specific gender inequalities.[27]

There is, however, another side to the story. Nationalist movements subordinate women in a particular definition of their role and place in society, enforce conformity to values that are often male-defined and make it possible to delegitimise alternative policies on the grounds that these are alien. As the founder of modern nationalist theory, Mazzini, made clear, nationalism was above all about obedience.[28] The use made of nationalist and anti-imperialist arguments to discredit and silence feminist movements in recent years is indication enough of this. States, not least newly independent states, exist to enforce hierarchies. Throughout the world, men have seen in the state and in the ideologies legitimating it – of which nationalism is the most potent – a means of enforcing their control over women: that this control is often exercised via a rhetoric of exaltation and respect, or through state policies that 'improve' the position of women, does not detract from the instrumental and subordinating character of this practice.

Nationalism is far from being gender neutral. It seeks to mobilise women in support of its goals: independence and the consolidation of a specifically defined post-independence regime. Its effects for women are contradictory. How particular national-isms have affected women in the countries concerned is an important topic for research and analysis; so is the broader theoretical question of how far an awareness of the position of women can lead to a questioning of the predominant values in international relations, namely state sovereignty and the primacy of national independence. Here, of course, the long tradition of association between feminism and internationalism may be pertinent, where the latter is seen not just as a faith in international solidarity, but as a moral and political position from which to criticise nationalist claims, and the authority of govern-ments.

Mention has already been made of the internationalism of Flora Tristan, and perhaps the most famous statement of women's internationalism of all is that of Virginia Woolf. Writing of a woman who is asked to support the war effort she replies:

She will find that she has no good reason to ask her brother to fight on her behalf to protect 'our' country. ' "Our country" ', she will say, 'throughout the greater part of its history has treated me as a slave; it has denied me education or any share in its possessions. "Our" country still ceases to be mine if I marry a foreigner. "Our" country denies me that means of protecting myself, forces me to pay others a very large sum annually to protect me, and is so little able, even so, to protect me that Air Raid precautions are written on my wall. Therefore if you insist upon fighting to protect me, or "our" country, let it be understood, soberly and rationally between us, that you are fighting to gratify a sex instinct which I cannot share; to procure benefits which I have not shared and probably will not share; but not to gratify my instincts, or to protect either myself or my country. For', the outsider will say, 'in fact, as a woman, I have no country. As a woman I want no country. As a woman my country is the whole world.'[29]

Powerful as it is, Woolf's argument raises as many difficulties as it resolves. Her formulation of the reasons why women want no country or have none is based on three different considerations: instinct, exclusion from equality with men, inadequate protection by men. The implication is, therefore, that in the latter two cases at least, the woman's position would change if these difficulties were resolved. Her moral appeal clashes also with the history of women in the twentieth century: beyond the symbolism by women of patriotism, possibly dismissible as the work of men, is the very active way in which women have mobilised to support war efforts, and have mobilised in nationalist movements. The mass actions by women in the Yugoslav conflict of 1991–3, acting *as women* to block food supplies going to other communities, is a graphic illustration of this. Resort can always be made to the classic concept of 'false consciousness', but this certainly suggests no automatic political identification by women with internationalism, or with women in other national groups. Yet, whether the relation is a nationalist and patriotic or an anti-nationalist one, it certainly suggests a number of significant, and recurrent, connections between women and the international sphere.

One possible way of approaching the broader question is by way of what one may term a feminist Luxemburgism. Rosa Luxemburg argued that the independence of nations should be seen as conditional upon how far it advanced the interests of the working class; in the case of pre-1914 Poland, she argued that Poland should, on these grounds, remain part of the broader Russian state.[30] A comparable argument could be raised with respect to women and national independence, namely that the independence of specific states should be judged by a range of criteria, including how far that independence has advanced the position of women. In one sense Luxemburgist arguments are no longer relevant: a world of independent states has been created and the question of support, qualified or not, for their creation no longer applies. None the less, it is conceivable that in cases where national and national-religious ideologies subordinate women even more than was the case under foreign domination, the authority of the independent states and their officially sanctioned cultures should not be taken as self-evident: women have the right to challenge the authority of the state that supposedly embodies the nation, or indeed to reject its claims altogether, and depart. In countries such as Ireland and Malta, where divorce is still banned, the identification of nation with clerical authority has especially pernicious effects.

As in the case of the original Luxemburgist argument, there are many obvious counter-arguments: that women's position as members of a nation takes precedence over their position as members of a subordinate gender; that national independence as such is a superior goal to that of the rights of individual members of a nation; that it is not possible to overcome sectoral inequalities of class, ethnicity or gender within a nation until independence has been achieved. These are all strong arguments and would probably carry the day in any context. However, the feminist critique of nationalism and national sovereignty would, at least, open these issues up for discussion in a way that an assumption of the automatic primacy of national independence and sovereignty does not permit. In virtually all cases where nationalism has had deleterious consequences for women, discussion of the implications of this has been silenced or marginalised by appeal to supposedly higher values. Given the predominance of a nationalist framework for argument, women opposed to forms of oppression legitimated as traditional, authentic, popular and so forth have had to argue that such policies are not really those of the nation or are not historically justified. In this way the nationalists have forced the argument on to their terrain, denying the legitimacy of a discussion of the rights of women as such. It should be possible to reject, on universalist grounds, repugnant ideas and practices, be they traditional or otherwise. Similar nationalist distortion is, of course, evident with regard to other political issues, such as the rights of ethnic minorities, workers and intellectuals.[31]

There has, to date, been little discussion of an area in which gender could come to play a significant role in foreign policy, namely human rights. Yet the scope for such a modification is enormous. We have seen, in the 1980s especially, states make the future of their relations with other countries conditional upon their domestic performance with regard to some forms of human rights and impose, or threaten to impose, sanctions of various kinds if expectations are not met. Such demands have not, to date, encompassed the rights of women. But there is no reason in principle why comparable arguments should not be advanced. Countries with a commitment to gender equality could shape their foreign policies accordingly, and could try to mobilise coalitions in the UN, as they do on other issues, to put pressure upon delinquent states responsible for gendered apartheids.

In the latter part of the 1980s, there began to be a shift in the definition of human rights to encompass feminist concerns, a shift that was most evident, as is so often the case, in the work of the non-governmental organisations.[32] At the 1992 United Nations World Conference on Human Rights held in Vienna, a considerable number of groups supporting women's rights attended, and the final declaration included nine paragraphs on 'the equal status and human rights' of women.

A number of cases could, however, be observed where states, or state activity, had begun to make the rights of women an element of foreign policy. One striking case was that of the Republic of Korea which sought compensation from Japan for the treatment of Korean women as 'comfort women', prostitutes for the army, during the Second World War: between 100,000 and 200,000 women were reportedly involved.[33] Subsequently, prostitutes who had worked around US bases in the Philippines also began to demand compensation for sexual diseases they had caught.

A second example concerned an important shift in the immigration policy of the Canadian Government in 1993: for the first time a woman (from Saudi Arabia) was permitted to claim political asylum on the grounds that as a women she was denied her human rights in her country of origin. A third case concerned the pressure put on the Irish Government to alter its absolute ban on abortion, following the rape of a fourteen-year-old girl who subsequently became pregnant. Beyond straining Ireland's membership of the EC, it also created considerable animosity among the Unionist population of Northern Ireland who saw in the ban a mediaeval policy, confirming the fear that incorporation into the South would lead to the domination of the Catholic Church.[34]

The most common inter-state disputes of all concerning women's rights were those surrounding marital disputes, over the domicile of wives, and, most explosively, over the custody of children when divorce occurred. Britain, France and Australia were all involved in disputes with Muslim countries where fathers from those states had, in alleged defiance of court instructions in the original countries, taken their children back to their countries of origin and denied reasonable access to the mothers. At the popular level, these questions, played up in the press, did more than anything to register the importance of gender and international relations.

The development of an international policy on women's rights is not a question merely of recognising the issue: as the Vienna 1993 UN conference showed there are great differences of approach within any such general commitment, notably that between an approach based on human rights and one emphasising equal status, the latter being concerned with poverty and employment, as well as forms of discrimination.

There are, moreover, many practical problems with this option of making the rights of women an issue in foreign policy, not least the problems of backlash and retribution. These dangers, common to all human rights campaigns, should not conceal what is likely to be the most profound source of resistance to such campaigns, namely the belief that while some forms of human rights violation are proper subjects for foreign policy those pertaining to women are not. It is, in conventional terms, 'preposterous' that questions of gender should play this kind of role in relations between sovereign states. There will, inevitably, be much talk of differing national traditions, and official spokesmen and spokeswomen will be produced from the countries concerned to denounce external interference in the internal affairs of the society in question. National and, where relevant, anti-imperialist sentiments will be mobilised to check any such external challenges to male domination, and to the state powers that reinforce and embody it.

There are difficult issues here of both policy and theory: but the failure of such policies to emerge at all, and the probable response to them, illustrates clearly how important issues of women's subordination are in the overall constitution of national ideologies. It also shows how a commitment to gender equality, beyond any domestic or internal political consequences, does pose a challenge to prevailing conceptions of authority and sovereignty in international relations itself.[35]

Implications and Problems

The scope of what is conventionally seen as the discipline of International Relations has expanded considerably in recent years to encompass new thematic and conceptual areas. In the 1980s alone, the rise of international political economy altered much of the academic content of teaching and research. In the case of women, it has been argued here that, on the basis of four general considerations, the discipline can and should adjust to a set of issues that have, to date, received little attention.

It is not as if consideration of gender will alter the teaching and research of international relations as a whole. It will, however, do more than just add another subject to the list of topics already considered, since in addition to the specific questions it raises and the alternatives to established values it suggests, the question of gender and International Relations will reinforce a shift already present in much of the literature on transnationalism and international political economy. This involves asking not only how states and societies relate to each other, but also how international processes, be these inter-governmental or not, make themselves felt within societies. The force of the historical sociological literature lies in its demonstration of how the processes regarded as internal to states and economies are to a considerable degree products of international factors.[36]

One of many potential contributions of a gender and International Relations approach could be to show how gender relations in the economy, polity and family are shaped and changed by processes external to the society in question. This issue could therefore be part of a broader reorientation of International Relations towards the study not only of inter-state behaviour but also of how states and societies interact. That such a development will pose considerable difficulties in teaching and research is evident. The most general source of resistance will be reluctance to accept a general reorientation of international relations, a curmudgeonly rejection of the implications of feminism for the international.[37] But there are also more specific problems, and it may be worth identifying some of them briefly. The production of a literature on the subject has begun, but will take time to consolidate itself: yet some materials are available from related areas – sociology, development studies, history – and can be used as the bases for initial work. There is also the question, recurrent in women's studies, of the balance between autonomy and integration. Should a distinct teaching and research programme be established, or should this work be integrated into the broader, established academic structure? A pragmatic initial response would seem to be that both approaches are needed, with specialist options and research reinforcing the inclusion of gender as a regular item in any comprehensive International Relations course or textbook.[38]

Other theoretical problems can be seen as relevant to this topic, and are well-established points of debate in other areas of social science. One is the problem of cultural relativism – the claim that values pertaining to women and other social actors vary among societies and that it is therefore difficult or impossible to make general statements about what constitutes discrimination or domination in different societies. This has arisen directly in considerations of the position of women in national and religious contexts. For all the dangers of external misunderstanding, there may well have been rather too much concession to this, at the expense of assessing and criticising ideologies and practices that, in the name of national traditions and authenticity, do oppress women. A similar tendency operates with other forms of power, along lines of race, class or age. While an awareness of relativity and difference is essential to an explanation of how and why systems of domination originate and are maintained, such a recognition need not necessarily lead, out of a misplaced anthropological generosity, to denying that forms of oppression do exist and recur in a wide range of societies and historical contexts.

The other theoretical problem is what might be termed precipitate totalisation: that is the tendency, once connections between different levels of social and political practice have been established, to see all as the expression of a single mechanism or process. In this context, assertion of the relation between gender and international relations does not necessarily lead to the claim that gender issues constitute *the* core of international affairs (as if there needs to be 'one') and the key to understanding the international arena as a whole, nor does it follow that all aspects of women's location and experience can be derived from the international – hot wars or cold war, sovereignty or nationalism, can be shown to have significant gendered components, without this implying that gender determines these or that all aspects of any international event or process are necessarily related to each other. To argue this, in some feminist reworking of the Hegelian concept of the totality, would be to distort the case.

At the same time, enough has been done to show that, whatever distinctions prevail, issues pertaining to women do have a place in the study of international relations. Much of the resistance to this linkage stems not from a view of International Relations in particular, but from a refusal to accept the validity of feminist concerns in general. As with other disputes on International Relations and method, it may be best to shift discussion on to this general terrain rather than trying to resolve it in a necessarily restricted International Relations context.

A third issue, and one that pertains to broader methodological debates within IR, involves the relation between this topic and the debate on epistemology and method raised by IR. Post-modernism and associated approaches have, as indicated in Chapter 2, a contradictory import: while providing tools for an innovative examination of discourses and identities, they also introduce a randomness of ethic and explanation that is inimical to substantive analysis and normative engagement alike. In the context of a widespread interest in post-modernism, feminist theory has been increasingly influenced by the latter and this has had its impact in IR, with predictable results. While the authority of traditional approaches has been weakened, the alternative proposed has itself become a new orthodoxy, of a vague and often self-defeating kind. Methodological issues of broad relevance are fought out within the context of IR; alternative epistemologies are offered, but all that is provided is confusion; the very ethical assumption on which the topic began, and on which feminism was initiated, namely a commitment to some form of emancipation through equality, is rejected in a frenzy of wordiness and meandering.

Here, in addition to bearing in mind the general criticisms of post-modernism, as analytic foundation or political position, it is relevant to bear in mind the particular criticisms made of any attempt to promote post-modernism as a general approach for feminists.[39] Those easily scorned as espousing gendered epistemologies or partial remedies may, in the end, have more to offer than the protagonists of hermeneutic verbosity. To their charge that all that is being done is 'add women and stir', it might be replied that their approach comprises an even more unproductive menu, 'add epistemology and stir'. It would be catastrophic indeed if by integrating itself with IR, feminism, as explanation and prescription, was to find itself voided of impact and content by submission to the banalities of intellectual fashion: the result would be that, having overcome the denial of conventional IR, it would be 'hidden' again under the new vapidity.

If these dangers are recognised, they in no way detract from the possibility, and desirability, of a feminist engagement with IR. Without any overstatement, it would appear that there is a great deal of work to be done on women and International Relations. It can only be hoped that this question will find recognition as an important and distinct topic within the overall research programme of the discipline, and that it will become an established element in its teaching agenda. Such a recognition is long overdue.

8

Inter-Systemic Conflict: The Case of Cold War

A Distinct Form of Conflict

The argument of Chapter 5 was based on the proposition that International Relations encompasses more than relations between states and indeed more than 'transnationalism', the interaction and coming together of societies. The 'constitutive' variant of the concept 'international society' discussed here denotes the manner in which societies are affected by the very internal structure of other states and are drawn into particular forms of conflict when these systems diverge, when, in other words, the international society is characterised by 'heterogeneity'. The purpose of this chapter is look in more detail at the workings of such conflict, 'inter-systemic' in the sense that it is between two societies, or groups of society, based on radically different, and incompatible, forms of social and political organisation. The main focus will be on the Cold War of the post-1945 period: but the implications are broader, and go to the heart of the debate on international society, and international relations, themselves.

Inter-systemic conflict is a specific form of inter-state and inter-societal conflict, in which the conventional forms of rivalry – military, economy, political – are compounded by, and often legitimised in terms of, an overall divergence of political and social norms. The conventional forms of competition, including war, may play a role here, but the competition of values is at least equally so, and may time and again be the main dimension in which one party to the conflict prevails over the other. That such conflict is not specific to the Soviet–Western rivalry of the post-1945 epoch is evident from such earlier cases as the rivalry of the Ottoman and Manchu empires with the West, further examples of protracted rivalries in which the military and the strategic were overlain by the challenge which was posed to a system of social and political organisation. In even earlier periods, the conflicts between strategic powers, or blocs, defined in religious terms, had some of the same characteristics.

The picture of a conflict between the 'West' and 'Islam' in the late twentieth century is a myth since, despite diverse claims to the contrary religion no longer plays this role; but much of the period between the seventh and sixteenth centuries took the form of a triangular inter-systemic conflict framed in religious terms, not just between Christianity and Islam, but between two rival branches of the Christian world – the Roman and the Orthodox – and a succession of Islamic empires based in the eastern Mediterranean. The Ottoman and Manchu instances, to be examined at the end of this chapter, provide a comparative example, but also significant contrasts, with the collapse of the Soviet bloc.

Theories of Cold War

At first sight the issue of 'inter-systemic' conflict is almost wholly absent from discussion of Cold War. In the academic and policy-related literature on Cold War and East–West rivalry since 1945 there have been two main debates: one, a historical argument, concerning the causes and 'responsibility' for Cold War, the other, framed partly in the language of the peace movement and partly within IR itself, on the underlying dynamic of the conflict. The former debate fell into three main phases – the initial anti-communist consensus, the 'revisionist' challenge, and a new 'post-revisionist' consensus.[1] Although developed around the first Cold War of 1947–53, the same debate, about causes and responsibility, elaborated simultaneously rather than sequentially, can be identified with regard to the second Cold War, of 1979–1985.[2] Yet although rich in historical detail, this debate on Cold War suffered from two obvious limitations: on the one hand, it arose out of a specific political conjuncture and was dominated by the concerns of that situation – as much for the 'revisionists' as for the anti-communists; secondly, it was conducted in almost complete innocence of theoretical issues as such, reflecting the empiricism both of Anglo-Saxon historiography and of the, off-stage, political debate itself.

The second debate, on the dynamic of East–West conflict, contained some greater awareness of theoretical issues but in neither of its two contexts, the peace movement or the IR literature, was the theoretical underpinning substantially developed: some specific aspects of the conflict – the role of ideology, the arms race, crisis management – did receive theoretical treatment within IR, but not the Cold War as a whole. The analysis of what Cold War was remained very much at the pre-theoretical level, in the sense of having implicit rather than explicit theoretical positions and of failing to ask what the implications of the Cold War for IR theory as such might be. Abstracting from this literature, however, this second debate can be said to have encompassed four main approaches. For sake of convenience, and at the risk of some foreshortening, these can be categorised as: realist, subjectivist, internalist, inter-systemic.[3]

For realism, and those historical sociologists who have recently adopted it, the Cold War was a continuation of Great Power politics, albeit with certain additions such as nuclear weapons, arms racing and capitalist–communist ideological rivalry. The assertion of this continuity within international conflict was facilitated by focusing on the foreign policy of the USSR itself, which was seen as continuing the foreign goals of the pre-1917 regime, and/or of the USA, which was seen as just another imperial power,[4] not only *vis-à-vis* the third world or the Europeans and Japanese, but also *vis-à-vis* the USSR.

By 'subjectivist' is meant those theories that analysed the Cold War in terms of perception and misperception. The IR literature on perception developed in the 1960s and 1970s in the writings of such people as Janis and Jervis. It suggested that foreign policy in general, and foreign policy mistakes in particular, could to a considerable extent be attributed to the perceptions held, individually and collectively, by those making foreign policy and by the populations that influenced or constrained them. This argument was not specifically directed to discussion of Cold War, but had implications for it. Whether the argument was explicitly extended in this way or not, it paralleled and reinforced an argument common amongst liberal writers on the Cold War, and on revolutions generally, to the effect that the conflict could be avoided if only each side had been better informed about the other (a 'different' policy towards Russia after 1917, China after 1949, Cuba after 1959, or, for that matter, France after 1789).[5] Such arguments tended to downplay the necessity of ideological commitments on either side (to world revolution, solidarity/ rollback, intervention and so forth) and to stress the need for better information and contact between states supposedly, but not really, committed to each other's transformation.

The term 'internalist' denotes those approaches that locate the dynamic of Cold War within rather than between the contending blocs. This approach has several variants: it can locate the source of conflict either within the domestic politics and socio-economic structure of the two major states themselves, and, by extension, within the other constituent states; or it can do so within the internationally constituted bloc itself, seen as an ensemble where Cold War is functional to the maintenance of bloc cohesion and the hegemony of the dominant states within it.

The most straightforward version of this is Chomsky's 'two dungeons' thesis, according to which the USA and the USSR pursued the Cold War in order to discipline their own societies and their respective junior partners: 'The Cold War is a highly functional system by which the superpowers control their own domains. That is why it continues and will continue'.[6] Mary Kaldor's work has a similar thrust to it. Arguments such as those of Alan Wolfe, which attribute Cold War to the workings of US domestic politics, are an alternative version.[7] Michael Cox has, in several articles, developed an analysis that is rich in diplomatic detail but which, equally, denies that the Cold War is 'about' anything, other than the conventional rivalry of two broadly similar, blocs.[8]

Many expositions of the 'internalist' thesis focus on the pressure for confrontation from economic sectors, characteristically the 'military-industrial' complex. E.P. Thompson's theory of 'exterminism' is one of the more elaborate variants of this thesis, since it sees the arms race not just as the product of what arms manufacturers themselves want, but of a dynamic that has come to characterise the societies in question as a whole. 'Internalist' arguments tend to deny the efficacy of East–West conflict as such and to imply a degree of homology between the foreign policies and internal structures of the two blocs.[9]

Although mainly formulated in the 1980s, this work had

significant antecedents within the critical approach to society and to international relations: a classic instance of this was the work of the American sociologist C. Wright Mills, whose *The Causes of World War III*, published in 1958, argued that a nuclear war was increasingly inevitable, not because of relations between the blocs or developments in the third world, but because of the power structures within each country. Developing insights first enunciated by Max Weber, on the development of the bureaucratic and militaristic state as a result of international conflict, Mills, whose main contribution to sociology was the theory of the 'power élite' and of the 'military-industrial complex', argued that both camps were ruled by such élites, which would inevitably bring the world to war. What was symptomatic in Mills's work was that, as in Weber, the international was seen as the source of the degeneration of states and the loss of democratic control, and secondly how, in taking an abstract sociological definition of power élites, any substantive differences between the two systems were dissolved. Hence Mills, like Thompson, while striking a timely warning as to the dangers of war and uncontrolled military influence, failed to provide any substantive analysis either of why or how the two blocs were competing on the international sphere, and also of what the underlying political and social differences between them were.

The 'inter-systemic' argument can be quickly distinguished from all three of the other approaches:[10] in contradistinction to realism it denies that East–West rivalry is merely a continuation of traditional Great Power politics, not only by questioning the validity of this supposedly universal and classical model, but by allotting a central place in the conflict to the diverse, heterogeneous, character of the competing states, at both internal and international levels; in opposition to theories of misperception, it asserts that the competing political programmes and ideological perspectives of the two blocs were to be taken seriously, while not at face value, and that the states comprising the blocs were, in broad terms, committed to their realisation; as against the internalists, the 'inter-systemic' approach asserts that international conflict did have a reality, in other words that the two blocs were concerned not just with internal issues, profits, hierarchy or 'order', but also with improving their relative positions *vis-à-vis* each other and with prevailing over the other.

Inter-systemic theory can be summarised in terms of three core propositions: (*a*) East–West rivalry was a product of conflict between two distinct social systems; (*b*) this competition involves a competitive and universalising dynamic; and (*c*) it could only be concluded with the prevailing of one bloc over the other. The term 'system' is not used here to denote the 'international system' in general, as designated in conventional IR theory, nor 'the Cold War as system', in the sense of mutual reinforcement characteristic of the internalists, but to denote the internal organisation of the societies and polities of each bloc.

There was, consequently, something specific and necessary, an underlying contradictory and universalising dynamic in East–West relations. Cold War was, above all, a product of heterogeneity in the international system – to repeat, in both internal organisation and international practice – and could only be ended by the attainment of a new homogeneity. The implication of this was that, *as long as two distinct systems existed*, Cold War conflict was bound to continue: Cold War could not end with compromise, or convergence, but only with the prevailing of one of these systems over the other. Only when either capitalism had prevailed over communism, or the other way around, would inter-systemic conflict cease.

Although suppressed in most of the historical discussion of the Cold War, and denied by the biases of realism, this conception of Cold War was recognised by some of those who participated in it: on the Soviet side it took a range of forms, from the original Leninist view of an ongoing process of world revolution, through Stalin's 'two camps' theory, to the more varied and in its way quite perceptive Brezhnevite theory of the 'correlation of forces'.

On the Western side, politicians had no difficulty in articulating a theory of the contest between the 'communist' and 'free' worlds, but this tended to lead to a set of more immediate, usually military, implications, and to a repeated exaggeration of Soviet capabilities and the threat they posed. One exception to this is the analysis of George Kennan, first formulated in his long telegram of February 1946 and then published in revised form in 1947 in the journal *Foreign Affairs*:[11] this analysis is best known for the policy of military 'containment' construed as the checking of Soviet strategic advances, in Europe or the third world. But perhaps its most important, and in retrospect telling, argument is the prescription as to how, once containment has been achieved, to work towards the long-run erosion of Soviet confidence and hence of the Soviet bloc. In Kennan's analysis the goal is very clear: strategic containment is the precondition for the ultimate failure of the communist system, this latter goal to be achieved by the force of example and by the confounding of revolutionary idealism. He stresses that the conflict will take a long time:

> The Kremlin is under no ideological compulsion to accomplish its purposes in a hurry. Like the Church, it is dealing in ideological concepts which are of long-term validity, and it can afford to be patient. It has no right to risk the existing achievements of the revolution for the sake of vain baubles of the future.

In reply he proposes a strategy equally long-term, and patient, but definitive in its outcome:

> But in actuality the possibilities for American policy are by no means limited to holding the line and hoping for the best. It is entirely possible for the United States to influence, by its actions, the internal developments, both within Russia and throughout the international Communist movement, by which Russian policy is largely determined. This is not only a question of the modest measure of informational activity which this government can conduct in the Soviet Union and elsewhere, although that, too, is important. It is rather a question of the degree to which the United States can create among the peoples of the world generally the impression of a country which knows what it wants, which is coping successfully with the problems of its internal life and with the responsibilities of a World Power, and which has a spiritual vitality capable of holding its own among the major ideological currents of the time. To the extent that such an impression can be created and maintained, the aims of Russian Communism must appear sterile and quixotic, the hopes and enthusiasm of Moscow's supporters must wane, and added strain must be imposed on the Kremlin's foreign policies. For the palsied decrepitude of the capitalist world is the keystone of Communist philosophy. Even the failure of the United States to experience the early economic depression

which the ravens of the Red Square have been predicting with such complacent confidence since hostilities ceased would have deep and important repercussions throughout the Communist world . . . no mystical, Messianic, movement – and particularly not that of the Kremlin – can face frustration indefinitely without eventually adjusting itself in one way or another to the logic of that state of affairs.

Thus the decision will really fall in large measure in this country itself. The issue of Soviet-American relations is in essence a test of the overall worth of the United States as a nation among nations. *To avoid destruction the United States need only measure up to its own best traditions and prove itself worthy of preservation as a great nation* (italics added).[12]

Shorn of its specific references to the USA, and of its vainglorious tone, this presented a clear programme for the conduct of a long-term inter-systemic conflict, based above all on the competition between two systems and the goal, not of peace or compromise, but of ultimately prevailing over the other. What is striking is how this realisation, spelt out in one of the classic strategy statements of the Cold War, found so little reflection in the theory of IR or in subsequent reflections on the underlying character of the conflict.

Sources of Theoretical Resistance

While present in an implicit way in some discussion of the Cold War, inter-systemic conflict theory was little represented in either IR literature or peace movement writing. If it draws its most obvious inspiration from Marxism, it can also be seen as a continuation of a strain of argument within IR that has little or nothing to do with Marxism and which stresses the importance of ideological difference in international conflict.[13] The reasons operating against its acceptance were several. Itemising them may help not only to clarify the claims of the 'inter-systemic' approach, but also to identify what some of the underlying issues within IR theory raised by this issue may be.

For conventional realist theory, as in Bull and Waltz, the issue of systemic determination of foreign policy is irrelevant, indeed technically inconceivable: since all that matters are relations between states, no such admission of the relevance of internal processes, causes or consequences, is allowed within such theory. Relations between 'states' can be analysed irrespective of internal correlates. Moreover, by positing an abstracted 'international system' which determines the behaviour of states and imposes certain rules on component members, realism denies the possibility of fundamentally variant forms of international conflict.

To argue for inter-systemic theory in its fullest form requires having an adequate concept of the difference between the systems, not just in terms of some international slogans and goals, but in terms of the constitution of the societies themselves and the basis of their disagreement. Here the very strong resistance of IR theory both to identifying internal characteristics and to the concept of 'capitalism' becomes relevant: a naive visitor to the field of the international might think that if anything characterised the development of the international system over the past five hundred years it would be this phenomenon. It is at least as important as war, nationalism, statehood and the other familiar terms: yet it is almost never mentioned, except in muffled formulations about the 'development of the international economy' and 'industrial society', latterly, 'interdependence'. To develop a concept of inter-systemic theory involves, however, having some concept of what constitutes the West at both the internal and international levels, namely 'capitalism', and of its comparatively short-lived twentieth-century challenger, whatever the latter may be called. This is something which can be provided either within Weberian sociological or Marxist theory, yet, precisely because of IR's silence, it is almost impossible to do within mainstream international theory.

Even where the internal is considered relevant, as in foreign policy analysis, there is little support for the inter-systemic approach: on the one hand, what are seen as transnational 'linkages' are limited, specific, forms of interaction quite different from the comprehensive view of inter-systemic interaction envisaged here, and based on an often flimsy, behavioural, concept of society; on the other hand, 'empirical' correlations carried out within foreign policy analysis are supposed to not confirm any distinct correlations between type of political system (e.g. monarchical/republican, totalitarian/democratic) and foreign policy output. Since totalitarian societies can be aggressive or defensive the issue of systemic determination does not arise. The alternative explanation would, of course, be that the wrong questions are being asked.

A theory based on inter-systemic conflict is all the more unattractive because of what it appears to resemble: it can easily be assimilated to either, or both, of the paradigms of old Cold War thinking itself, i.e. dogmatic Soviet conceptions of the 'two camps' and of a capitalism–socialism conflict, or Western presentations of the Cold War as a conflict between two rival but morally opposite political and economic systems, a 'free' world versus one of a communist dictatorship. The compulsion to distance themselves from both of these stereotypes does much to explain the espousal by liberal and peace-movement writers of approaches involving a degree of causal, and ethical, symmetry i.e. the subjectivist and internalist. A similar concern can be seen in the liberal writings that accompanied the end of the Cold War in the late 1980s when it was suggested, in the face of all evidence, that somehow *both* sides had been exhausted by the Cold War and were therefore the losers: of course the USA had paid the cost, but it was not Soviet bankers that were coming in to supervise the US transition to socialism. Those using Marxist categories to explain the Cold War were almost inevitably assimilated to orthodox pre-1985 Soviet analyses:[14] this was not only because of bias in those making this assimilation but also because the theoretical underpinnings of the Marxist analysis were not made sufficiently clear.

A further inhibiting factor is that one of the central themes of inter-systemic theory, that Cold War is a product of heterogeneity, does not necessarily command assent. As against the supposedly intuitive view that heterogeneity makes for instability and homogeneity for stability, there is the counter-view, equally intuitive, that it is heterogeneity that makes for stability.

In realist theory this informs the view, espoused by Waltz and others, of the stability of bipolarity. In regard to systemic heterogeneity it is the assumption implicit in the 'two dungeons' theory: it is not explicit in most IR theory, since this is only concerned with relations between states, but in the now fashionably resurrected German theorist Carl Schmitt, who argued the need for an 'adversary' in political life, domestic and by extension international, and earlier, in the general thesis popularised by

Arnold Toynbee of 'challenge and response'.[15] Schmitt, like the inter-systemic theory, has suffered by association, in this case with Nazism: but, as the presence of this thesis within the benign liberal and peace-movement writing indicates, his argument has broader relevance or at least unacknowledged following. It reinforces the view, initiated by denying that capitalism or communism have any serious universalising dynamic, that East–West conflict was a mirage, and was really functional for ruling groups on both sides.

Differing theoretical approaches aside, there are cogent historical, indeed commonsense, reasons for denying the validity of the inter-systemic approach. On the one hand, there appears to be little reason to attribute conflict to the inter-systemic when modern history is so full of conflicts between homogeneous states: from the inter-capitalist explosions of 1914 and 1939 to the disputes and wars of the socialist bloc. On the other hand, the pattern of post-war alliances, and informal strategic alignments, suggests that heterogeneity is no obstacle to such collaboration: thus a capitalist India collaborated with a socialist USSR, while a socialist China aligned with the USA.

The Salience of Heterogeneity

The difficulties with the inter-systemic approach are, therefore, considerable: there are at least three major alternative approaches to analysing Cold War; there are strong reasons, theoretical and empirical, for rejecting it; it has unsavoury political associations. Above all, however, it is underdeveloped in its own terms: those who have espoused it have thrown out occasional arguments as to its validity and components, or have implied that there is a 'read off the shelf' theory within Marxism for explaining such a phenomenon. Once an attempt is made to lay out what the claims of the inter-systemic theory are then it becomes evident that even greater theoretical complexities underlie it and inhibit its adoption. It is, however, only through such a construction and identification of the broader theoretical implications that the argument can be taken further. In the light of this discussion, the inter-system argument would seem to rest on five core propositions:

(i) The socio-economic heterogeneity of 'East' and 'West', i.e. of communist and capitalist societies. This pertains, at least, to the economic and political levels within each state and bloc. The starting point for the inter-systemic argument is this difference, in fundamental, constitutive, terms, between the two kinds of society and polity. This 'difference' may be formulated in Weberian or Marxist terms, but does involve some conception of the political and social system as a whole. Constitutional, bureaucratic or behaviouralist political science approaches, theories based on convergence, or those which saw the USSR as just another form of 'capitalist' society, deny this heterogeneity and will necessarily preclude analysis on inter-systemic lines, as will those that, for diplomatic reasons or out of 'fairness', treat the two symmetrically. If it is not admitted that the Soviet and US blocs were fundamentally different in internal constitution then the argument cannot proceed.

(ii) This socio-economic and political composition must be shown to be determinant, in a broad sense, of foreign policy and international relations more generally. There is no 'foreign policy' as such, but only the foreign policy of specific kinds of state and society. This thesis of determination in some ways overlaps with, but is theoretically quite distinct from, that found in foreign policy analysis with its examination of the domestic determinants of foreign policy output. The difference lies in the conception of what constitute relevant domestic determinants, and in the (unstated) differences in what constitutes the state–society relationship: as in the discussion of heterogeneity, the discussion inevitably leads back to the general conception of society and polity.

(iii) The thesis of inter-systemic conflict implies an internationalising and indeed universalising dynamic within each bloc and system: in other words, it implies that each bloc is impelled to seek not only to protect its own state and economy, to maximise its advantage within the constraints of a 'balance of power', and to appear to challenge the other for reasons of ideological credibility within, but to dominate as much of the world as possible, and to undermine and hopefully abolish the alternative system. Such an argument goes against the orthodox IR conception of international relations tending to preserve whether by design or of necessity, a

'balance of power', and also against the liberal assertion that neither side had any compelling ideological aspirations and that the conflict was all about power maximisation. Yet, apart from a rather large amount of historical evidence with regard to the drives of capitalism, elements of this universal dynamic are recognised in existing theories: the drive of capitalism to maximise markets and access to raw materials, the commitments of the USSR to world revolution, the competition of each for allies in the third world to enhance their military and political security and strength. As already noted, Kennan's long telegram acknowledged that both sides had such an aspiration, and potential.

But these are at best fragments of a broader theory of universalisation, which is as yet obscure.[16] For example, the drive of capitalism is not merely economic: otherwise it would have been quite content to leave the communist states with their political systems intact, provided trade was conducted between them. This drive to universalisation is linked to that of heterogeneity: that each system, beyond any immediate compromises or obstacles, was committed to the transformation of the other. The least that can be said about the outcome of the late 1980s is that, at first sight and more, it lends credence to this. One side did prevail over, and subordinate, the other.

(iv) Inter-systemic conflict operates on multiple dimensions, not just that of inter-state relations as conventionally conceived: the issue of what 'foreign policy' states pursue comprises only a part of how each of the two socio-economic systems operated internationally. Inter-systemic competition took place at three main levels: that of inter-state relations as such, i.e. 'foreign policy' conventionally conceived; that of socio-economic interaction more broadly interpreted to include the actions of entities other than states/governments, most notably financial and industrial enterprises; that of ideological interaction, and in particular the impact on one communist society of the example, the demonstration effect, of capitalist others.

A clear example of this triple interaction, with the mutual reinforcement of each level, was that of FRG–GDR (West German–East German) relations in the late 1980s, up to and through the collapse of the East Germany regime in 1989–90: the project of the FRG as a whole was, in the classic Clausewitzian wrestling sense, to defeat, not annihilate, i.e. to 'throw down' (*niederwerfen*) the GDR. This was inter-systemic conflict in its rawest form and operated at all three levels: Bonn's policies – the undermining of the GDR, the mobilisation of a pro-unification majority within it, the discrediting of any socialist or neutral option – were accomplished by the pressure on the GDR on the three levels. In contrast to what conventional realist theory, with its stress on inter-state conflict, might suggest, the role of the Bonn Government was perhaps the least important and that of West German business secondary: the most influential level was the impact on millions of East Germans of the image they had of the West and then, once the frontier was opened, of visiting the West, the *Reiseschock* ('travel shock'). This demonstration effect was certainly compounded by the pressures of West German banks and businesses on the GDR economy, whether or not this pressure was formally coordinated with Bonn, and the specific actions taken by Bonn itself: conditionality for economic aid, encouragement through automatic citizenship and welfare benefits to GDR population to leave, fostering of rumours about imminent collapse of the GDR economy and so on. It would have been rather difficult to interpret this instance of inter-systemic conflict without some reference to the tendency of capitalism to expand, a tendency realised not just through the actions of states as such but also through the broader social and ideological interactions.[17]

(v) Heterogeneity of internal socio-economic system implies heterogeneity of international relations, conceived in terms of broad goals and mechanisms of internationalisation. The interests of the two blocs were fundamentally opposed, and the kinds of world they aimed to create diverged as indicated. From this it followed that there would be other differences in the foreign policy and international extension of these systems. This did not necessarily mean that they pursued different kinds or styles of foreign policy, i.e. that the instruments, conventions, operating procedures of foreign policy themselves were heterogeneous. This is left open: the states involved in the conflict may, or may not, have been socialised in the realist sense of the term. The argument cannot be settled by looking at 'socialisation' in the formal sense, of whether they had the same kinds of diplomatic conventions or respected sovereignty. The realist argument about 'international society' and

the socialising effects of the system is relevant in limited terms, but does not answer this broader question.

On the other hand, heterogeneity of goals in general, since it arises from a heterogeneity of system, is accompanied by a heterogeneity at least three other levels. First, heterogeneity of cause – the underlying reasons for the universalising dynamic – may well be different in different socio-economic systems, being more or less economic in one, more or less military or political in the other. Secondly, the mechanisms for, and commitment to, creating an international homogeneous bloc around a core, hegemonic, state may well differ, as is at least evident from the very different political and economic policies of the USA and USSR within their respective blocs – the forms of integration and mechanisms of hierarchy were certainly different. Thirdly, the mechanisms for competition with the other bloc may also be asymmetrical – this asymmetry reflecting not just differences in 'power' generally conceived, but the varying salience of different components of a system's *modus operandi*, e.g. economic, ideological, military, as reflected at the international level. The relative balance of economic and military power in the influence of the Soviet Union and USA was very different, just as was the degree of direct political control exercised by each over their respective bloc clients. The competition of blocs may therefore involve not just a conflict of goals, but a conflict of the reasons for which, and the mechanisms by which, international relations were conducted.

Analytic Implications

This outline disinterment of the components of the inter-systemic theory inevitably raises more questions than it answers. Two points are immediately evident. First, whatever its analytic and theoretical strengths, inter-systemic theory is far from having attained adequate development; the appearance of such development in earlier Soviet dogma concealed more than it revealed – not least because of the immanent teleology within its concept of 'correlation of forces', which implied that history was moving inexorably towards the triumph of the Soviet over the Western blocs.[18]

Secondly, any elaboration of a theory of inter-systemic conflict entails a broader theoretical framework, loosely derivative of either Weberian sociology or historical materialism: concepts such as 'state', 'system', the 'international', while apparently common currency between mainstream IR and sociology/historical materialism, are on closer examination not.

More important still, as the above outline makes clear, and not for reasons of canonical deference, the starting point for any theory of inter-systemic conflict is not a generic difference in foreign policy goals or styles, or a divergence derived from geo-strategic asymmetry, but the difference in the constitution of society itself, in both domestic and international variants. The starting point for any related theory of IR is, therefore, the concept of what in Marxist theory is the 'mode of production' and of the relations between this and state: without these the theory of inter-systemic conflict is unthinkable. An ecumenical mixing of differences between an IR mainstream which precludes such concepts and these other socio-economic theories is liable to confuse. There can be no analysis of inter-systemic conflict that cannot admit the category 'capitalism' and its variously named antithesis.

If this argument is valid, then in addition to the development of a theory of international conflict and international relations generally based on social system, there are at least three other areas of theoretical development suggested by inter-systemic conflict theory:

(i) Dimensions and Mechanisms of International Interaction

If, as already indicated, inter-systemic conflict can be seen as operating on three levels – inter-state, inter-socio-economic, inter-ideological – then it becomes necessary to analyse how these interact and how the relative balance shifts from period to period for any specific state, and as between different kinds of state.

What is entailed here is nothing less than a proper sociology of international relations: not in the sense of tacking on some off-the-shelf IR theory to existing sociology, or of making some broad and possibly inapposite generalisations about how international relations have social aspects (law, ideology, convention, etc.), but in the sense of how examining within an international system, constituted by different states, the socio-economic determines both the individual states themselves and, transcending the states, the system as a whole. In the light of the history of the last five hundred years, and of the outcome of the Cold War itself, there is a special need to re-examine and elucidate the universalising drive of capitalism itself, both in terms of why it seeks to mould the world in its image, and the variant mechanisms of so doing: if pop music and T-shirts are the gunboats of the late twentieth century, there is an underlying continuity in the multi-layered and aggressive drive of capitalism to destroy and incorporate all rival socio-economic systems.

(ii) Inter-systemic Conflict and Anti-Systemic Movements

The conflict of social systems, embodied in and mediated through states (USA, USSR, etc.) in Cold War has been accompanied by broader movements within and between states directed against these states and the international orders they embody. In the course of this century, these have taken a variety of forms (revolutions, strikes, guerrilla wars, ideological challenges, etc.) and have been directed against the hegemonic orders in both blocs.

Three standard analyses of these anti-systemic movements are available: the conventional IR approach, which subordinates them to states, and denies their relevance to international relations except where they receive the backing of states – viz. the almost complete silence of IR literature on revolutions, and trades unions;[19] the orthodox Soviet approach which assimilated non-state anti-systemic movements to the state interests of the USSR itself, thus dissolving the issues of autonomy and contradiction involved in the relationship; and the 'world systems' approach (e.g. that of Wallerstein, Arrighi *et al.*)[20] which sees anti-systemic movements as the motor of international history and as capable of overriding the powers and fragmentations of states. In the case of the latter, and analogous writings from the peace movement, these anti-systemic movements are seen as directed against what is still one, homogeneous, system, the divergence of capitalism and communism being denied. Thus the workers' movements in Poland and South Africa are part of one 'anti-systemic' dynamic.

(iii) The Comparative study of Inter-Systemic Conflict

The focus of this analysis has been on inter-systemic conflict of the post-war period, that between the communist and capitalist blocs. This has certain specific features not found in earlier epochs: the technological and economic dimensions of its military competition, the specific ideological forms of hegemony claimed by both sides, the mobilisation of large masses of a population into systemic and anti-systemic activity. This particular inter-systemic conflict would appear to be yielding one other unique feature: namely, the historically contra-cyclical outcome whereby an already established system, capitalism, generated and then suffocated its newer-emerged rival.

Yet in other respects inter-systemic conflict is by no means specific to the Cold War epoch: the conflicts of societies based on feudalism and capitalism from the fourteenth century in Europe to the last redoubts of pre-capitalism in the third world in the late twentieth century would bear comparative analysis, as would more specific localised conflicts between slave-owning and free-labour-exploiting societies. The means by which capitalism has encircled, undermined and then crushed the Soviet bloc have something in common with the earlier capitalist assaults on the Chinese and Ottoman empires, not least in the way alarmed reformers within the besieged bloc have, in trying to alter their own system in order the better to compete, accelerated the decomposition of their social and political systems.

Equally, the economic historians have shown how the inter-action of the more developed world with the less developed world can, short of conquest and direct defeat in war, undermine the weaker states: this was the impact of imperialism even where it did not engage in direct colonial conquest. The fate of the Ottoman and Chinese empires in the latter half of the nineteenth century up to their final disappearances during the First World War are the two classic cases of this. Defeat in war there certainly was, but these were not in themselves explanation for decline (although in the case of the Ottoman Empire the First World War delivered the *coup de grâce*). The process was a more complex one: defeat in war on the edge of the imperial territory led to pressure for administrative and economic reform; an oscillation between reform and traditionalist reassertion marked state policy in the decades prior to final demise; the reform process then provoked greater internal dissension, within the state and in state-society relations; the gradual intrusion of external trade, via concessions and market forces, also weakened state power and promoted social discontent; remoter regions proved harder to govern and gradually broke away; insurrection (Taiping, the Boxers, the Young Turks) challenged established authority.[21]

It is evident that some of these features of Ottoman and Manchu decline are present in the collapse of communism. The Soviet system faced challenge from a rival that was (*a*) organised on fundamentally different socio-economic and political principles and (*b*) clearly superior to and stronger than it in all key respects, except for some dimensions of the military. The conflict was, therefore, both heterogeneous and unequal: the fact that the USSR was, unlike Turkey or China, able to compete with the West in certain selected areas of strategic military activity (space, nuclear weapons) and that it, like the West, had global aspirations, did not detract from its overall weakness. As in the conflict with the Ottomans and the Manchus, the process of erosion was gradual, not cataclysmic, and involved several dimensions: military, economic, diplomatic. Like the earlier empires, the Soviet system tried to sustain the military competition by more intensive but enduringly inefficient mobilisation and concentration of internal resources, while, at the same time, insulating its own economy from the goods and practices of the competitor.

Yet, for all the similarities, the differences are greater. In the first place, the military competition and its impact on the Soviet system itself was of a different kind, strategically and techno-logically. Ottoman and Manchu military policies were designed to prevent the gradual erosion of their imperial territory by hostile colonial powers and in no way presented a threat to the powers themselves. There was no equivalent in the Soviet case to the annexations and conquests that befell the Ottomans from the 1770s and the Chinese from the 1840s.

The greatest loss of the Soviet system, that of China in 1963, while in some degree a result of Western diplomatic policies that split the two, did not lead to the immediate annexation of China to the West and was in any case followed by other advances, military and strategic, of Soviet power in the third world. The two greatest military challenges faced by Soviet allies – in Korea and Vietnam –

were both ones in which Soviet allies survived, and in the latter won outright victory.

In the late 1970s and early 1980s US strategists did begin to talk of 'eroding Soviet power at the margin', i.e. of encouraging revolt in Soviet third world allies, notably, Cambodia, Afghanistan, Nicaragua and Angola. But, draining as these contests were, it was not here that the cracks later appeared, at the end of the 1980s. In military-technological terms, the contest was equally different: here, to a greater extent than in any sphere of competition, the contest was in some respects an equal one, even as the USA was able at almost every point to attain technical superiority over the Soviet Union.

What is most relevant here is that, in economic terms, the contrasts between the Ottoman-Manchu model and that of the USSR were substantial. In addition to losing territory outright to their strategic rivals, the position of the Manchu and Ottoman empires, even in the territory over which they retained control, was eroded by the intrusion of goods from the outside world, which undermined existing social groups and economic systems; in time, both empires accumulated foreign debt which they had to meet by allowing concessions and the supervision of their customs duties by Western officials.

No such processes occurred in the Soviet context. Given the control by the state of economic activity in these countries, the introduction of external goods was mediated by the state and had virtually no impact on employment and status of social groups within the countries. The role of foreign trade in the Soviet system and the manner in which it affected that system were fundamentally different from that seen in the Ottoman and Manchu cases. The provision of Western credit and technology, far from eroding the power of the communist leadership, served to strengthen it and, so the West at least believed, enhance its military capability. Such was the control exerted by communist parties that there was no question of external officials monitoring or affecting its revenue-collecting and other functions. As far as export earnings themselves were concerned, they were boosted in the 1970s by increased prices for oil and gas, the main Soviet exports, whose prices in the world market multiplied in that decade. If economic interaction with, and competition from, the West played a part in undermining the communist system it was not through weakening state control of the economy, by allowing greater space for Western economic actors to operate within these societies, or by altering domestic patterns of production and distribution. It was not the market in any direct sense that did it.

Only spasmodic mention has been made of the outcome of the Cold War, with the rapid demise of Soviet power in the late 1980s. This will be examined in more detail in Chapters 9 and 10. It would, however, appear plausible to argue that in certain important respects this bore out the suggestions of inter-systemic conflict theory: first, in that the collapse of communism came not through the conventional mechanism of inter-state conflict, namely war, nor through the erosion of the Soviet bloc's territory by Western military or commercial pressure, but rather with the undermining of the system via the demonstration effect of Western success in the social, economic and political fields;[22] secondly, that the form in which the Cold War ended was not that of a balance of power, or of a mutual exhaustion, but of the prevailing of one bloc over the other, in other words a systemic victory. Other interpretations of this outcome, and indeed of the underlying character of the Cold War, are certainly possible: the hope must, however, be that at least – even if rather late in the day – the underlying theoretical assumptions and implications of this, the overriding dimension of international conflict in the post-1945 era, are examined.

9

A Singular Collapse: The Soviet Union and Inter-State Competition

New Light on Old Questions

Chapter 8 provided a discussion of the Cold War itself and its underlying dynamic. The collapse of the Soviet system within the USSR and internationally in the late 1980s, in addition to its manifold implications for global politics and policy, raised a range of further issues within social and international theory of a stimulating and as yet unresolved kind which will be examined here. The first question confronting any analysis of this phenomenon is that of explanation, of providing an account that provides reasons, weighted and interrelated, of why a specific political and socio-economic system, one that was in broad terms equal to its rival in military terms, should have collapsed as it did, rapidly and unequivocally, and in the absence of significant international military conflict.[1]

Inexorably, this analytic question raises at least two others. The first, little voiced in these times but of more than arcane interest, is whether this collapse was inevitable, whether communism in the Soviet variety was bound to fail sooner or later, or whether with different fortune, policies or leadership, it could have continued and even expanded or prevailed on a world scale – whether it was always a blind alley or a contingently thwarted attempt to create an alternative, non-capitalist, system.[2] The other, pertinent to both explanation and assessment of communism's overall record, is when and how the terminal crisis set in, whether it can be dated to specific decisions, mainly those of the post-1985 leadership in

191

the USSR, or whether its decline was more prolonged, deriving from, say, the visible onset of economic 'stagnation' in the mid-1970s, or from the failure to democratise and reform the economy in the early 1960s, or whether it was indeed a long-run consequence of the system of command and terror created by Stalin in the 1930s. Even if it is argued that in the long run communism could never have 'worked', that it was necessarily doomed, the timing and manner of its demise were not and require specific analysis.

Challenging as these are, and informed as any answers must be by conceptual and theoretical assumptions, whether explicit or not, these historical questions are necessarily distinct from another set of concerns raised by the communist collapse. The very variety and bewildering speed of the recent changes, and the light they cast on what had previously happened in these societies, constitute a laboratory of uncontrolled social and political processes relevant to the evaluation of conflicting theories. Among many, it is possible to mention four processes which pertain to the interaction of states and the international system; they are at the same time relevant to the evaluation of states, state–society interactions and the forms and limits of state capacities. One, the nature of Cold War and of its underlying inter-systemic character, has already been addressed, in Chapter 8. Here it is possible to examine three other such broad issues: the patterns of transformation from above and the role of international factors in shaping and limiting it; the possibilities and prospects for a hitherto unique transition, that from communism to capitalism; and the variant dimensions of international competition and their role in the Soviet collapse.

Transformation from Above

The fate of communism is a major case for evaluating the thesis that the constitution of revolutionary states involved a strengthening of state control – of an intervention in society – and did so to a considerable degree in response to international pressures.[3] While, to varying degrees, communist regimes issued from insurgent revolutionary movements, and were, in their initial periods at least, based upon mass mobilisations and some popular consent, they all became systems in which policy was decided by a small political élite. The capacities, methods and goals of these élites were in part a result of their own, teleologically conceived, goals, but were also to a great extent conditioned by international factors: the goal of rivalling and supposedly overtaking capitalism, imitation and collaboration with other Communist Party leaderships, in Eastern Europe after the Second World War the support and control by the USSR of the local parties, and the orientation and mobilisation of domestic resources to defend a 'socialist camp' against external challenge, whether real or invented.

The communist leaderships were therefore engaged in a project that was both national and international: it was international as a result of systemic pressure, from other states, but also ideologically, in its own right, as an attempt to constitute a society that was exemplary on an international scale, and to promote similar movements in other countries. Yet if the overall failure of communism must include discussion of how it failed to spread world-wide, the starting point of analysing why the regimes collapsed in the late 1980s needs to be the record of internal, top-down, transformations which the regimes promoted.

These élites, present in the central committees and politburos of the ruling parties, sought to transform their societies in accordance with a theoretical blueprint of where socialist society should be going. We now know that such a project is a failure, not only in the sense that the goal towards which these societies were supposedly proceeding was never reached, but also because much of what had apparently been achieved was impermanent and superficial. If the claims that 'developed socialism' or some other sort of more perfect society had been reached were false, so too were the apparently less apologetic claims that these societies, for all their imperfections, were in some historical, and implicitly teleological, sense 'in transition' to some new socio-economic model and represented some permanent move beyond what capitalism had provided or could provide.

This lack of permanency is as true for attempts to create a viable and self-sustaining planned economy, as it is of those to forge a politically viable one-party system, and for attempts to reform attitudes to major areas of ideological importance, notably work, gender, religion, ethnicity. The simplest explanation of the collapse is to say that such a project was, in an absolute sense, a 'failure': this is the conclusion which many in the communist countries now draw, as those who deny the efficacy of 'social engineering' have always done. There are, however, reasons for resisting such a conclusion. In terms of evaluating the capacities of states to transform society from above, the record is not as absolute.

First, it is far too early to see how much of the legacy of communist rule will in fact endure and whether some of it may not in fact survive. Secondly, it would be mistaken to take as evidence of the failure of communism the emergence of forces that appear to mark a return to pre-communist forms of behaviour, since many of these have a character that has been shaped by the very impact of communist transformation – ethnic conflict being an obvious case. Similarly, as many who analysed the emergence of Gorbachev have shown, the change in Soviet society was in some respects a product of the very achievements of communism – expansion in education and urbanisation being obvious contributory factors.[4] Thirdly, even if much or all of that which is associated with communist rule does disappear, say in the space of a decade or two, the historical fact of the communist achievement over at least some decades will remain: this is evident in socio-economic transformation, the raising of living standards and the implementation of a widespread social welfare system, the sustenance and reproduction of a political system and, not least, a considerable success in the most testing area of all, inter-state competition.

It may be that the success of the latter – Soviet victory in the Second World War, plus four decades of rivalry with the West thereafter – itself inflated the illusion of communism's overall efficacy, at home and abroad. But the record of inter-state competition alone would suggest that the characterisation of the communist record as a 'failure' is simplistic. Such a verdict would have come as rather a surprise to, for example, the 250,000 Germans captured at Stalingrad as it would have to military planners in the Pentagon faced with Soviet space advances in the late 1950s or missile developments during the 1970s and early 1980s.

Assessment of why communism 'failed' involves, therefore, looking at both its internal and external records even as far as state performance and capacity is concerned. This involves a disaggregation of different kinds of inter-state and inter-societal competition: in the more conventional, military, dimension of international competition communism was reasonably successful – not only in the Second World War, but in subsequent Great Power arms races and third world strategic competition; its failure at the internal socio-economic level was, however, also an international one, since it involved not an absolute failure but a comparative, perceived, failure to match the performance of the competition. It will be suggested that a central question in analysing the collapse of the Soviet system is how, and when, this perception of comparative socio-economic failure came about, at both leadership and mass levels. Given the compulsion to compete, a result both of a general systemic compulsion to do so and of the particular ideological commitment to competition inherent in communist ideology, and given the near impossibility of war, the comparative domestic record of communism compared with its main capitalist alternatives became the key dimension of rivalry and ultimate demise.

The Transition from Socialism to Capitalism

The collapse of communism as a socio-economic system involves what is, in effect, the transition from one socio-economic system, in Marxist terms, from one mode of production to another.[5] What that 'non-capitalist' mode was, and how far it had realised its potential, is the subject of much debate: all we can do here is use working definitions; but if the agonies of the current transition make nothing else clear it should at least be that this system was in fundamentals different from capitalism. It is, moreover, evident that, as in the case of other transitions, the form, pace and outcome of 'transition' cannot be decided by uniquely internal factors, and that, in each country and in the post-communist world as a whole, international factors play a major role.

The end of communism has involved a double disillusionment: first, the realisation that the prevailing command economy, based on centralised planning and the predominance of the state sector, could not be expected to continue because of its increasingly evident difficulties – what these 'difficulties' were is something to which we shall return later; but secondly, that this system could not be maintained in a reformed, liberalised, version – the fate of

Yugoslavia and of the new economic mechanism in Hungary was indication of that.[6]

If the Soviet leadership under Brezhnev held to the former illusion, Gorbachev appears to have entertained the second for the first few years of his period in office, before accepting the impossibility of a reformed centralised system, a 'regulated market' in the communist sense of the term, in 1990. Just as he came into office believing in the one-party system and the 'leading role' of the CPSU (Communist Party of the Soviet Union) and in the success of the Leninist policy on the nationalities, so it took some time before he realised that the economic system as a whole needed transformation, and it required even longer for many members of the CPSU to come to this conclusion as well.[7]

The mere acceptance of this inevitability is not, however, sufficient to ensure that such a transition takes place in the way its proponents would like to see. History is not without cases of transitions from one socio-economic system to another, but there has not to date been one of this kind, from a centrally planned to a free market system. Certain factors favour such a process: the educational and social strengths of the societies in question, the relative willingness of the advanced capitalist countries to provide assistance through state and private channels, the probable decrease in inter-state competition, the availability of an alternative, and comparatively viable, model.

The difficulties are, however, evident: lack of capital, legal and administrative context, entrepreneurial and other personnel, as well as the conflicting pressures of political accommodation and economic change. The end of communist rule has introduced a new period of political, social and ethnic diversity in these societies, producing struggles that will affect how, and how far, a post-communist system is created: the social conflicts in Poland and the GDR alone in the first half of 1990 indicate that no simple 'planned' or 'managed' transition can occur. Inter-state competition in the narrow sense may well decline, but inter-social conflict may well not.

If history has any lesson to offer, it is that, in addition to the character and relative strength of social forces within these countries, the international character of this transition is of great importance. In a broad historical scale, it is possible to distinguish between what one can roughly call self-determined transitions, i.e.

ones such as that from feudalism to capitalism in Europe, which happened at a pace and through processes largely generated from within the societies in question, and imposed transitions, resulting from the impact upon weaker, less developed societies, of stronger ones, as in the colonial encounter.

The former were, we hardly need reminding, of an often protracted and sanguinary character, from the wars of late mediaeval Europe to what Arno Mayer has aptly termed the 'thirty years' war of the early twentieth century, that of 1914–45;[8] yet imposed transitions were even more costly and disabling, since they involved genocide, the enslavement of subject peoples, the extermination of indigenous societies, and, not least, the apparently chronic if not eternal locking of subjugated peoples into a position of inferiority within the world system.[9]

The aspiration of many in Eastern Europe and the USSR is that they become like Western Europe in a relatively short time-frame, of five to ten years. Many in the USSR now express their aspiration as being that their country become in some generic sense 'civilised'. The reality may be one of enduring political conflict, on social and ethnic grounds, and a cycle of Latin-American-style instability at both political and economic levels. If the international precludes long-term heterogenicity, it simultaneously inhibits successful imitation. In the aftermath of Marxist regimes, these societies would appear to vindicate the Marxist theory of capitalist development as *both* combined *and* uneven.

It is here that it becomes possible to address a question of both historical and theoretical importance, namely how far and in what ways external competition contributed to the evolution and final collapse of the communist system. That system was not destroyed by war, nor was its collapse solely exogenous. Nor can the outcome be understood solely by looking at states. But, in ways that require some greater examination, external forces, including economic ones, did contribute to the final collapse of 1989. Various factors in inter-state competition will be examined: the conclusion will be that, above all, it was neither of these but competition in the fields of perceived economic and ideological performance that determined the outcome.

Mention has already been made in Chapter 8 of the record of inter-state competition between communist and capitalist states, and of the need to distinguish between different dimensions of this competition in order to ascertain why the communist system failed. In the light of what the historical sociologists have written, there are certain obvious starting points: war itself, the pressure on state–society relations of the need to mobilise domestic resources in preparation for possible war, the formation and deformation of domestic institutions as a result of external competition. It is not necessarily war itself, but also the costs of past wars and the increased pressures placed by the concern with new ones that can, as in France after 1763, lead to the increased tensions within and ultimately to collapse of a political and social system.[11]

International Factors and Cold War

Mention has already been made of the international factors involved in the collapse of communism, and of those associated with the fates of the Ottoman and Manchu empires, i.e. those derived from the record of anterior interactions of heterogeneous and unequal systems. The other set of international factors often cited in connection with the fall of communism are more recent and more singular, those which are commonly held to be responsible for the collapse of the communist regimes, and in particular for the crisis of the USSR, in the late 1980s. These revolve around the argument that in one way or another the pressure that the West placed upon the communist system from the mid-1970s onwards, embodied in the policies of the Second Cold War, was such that the Soviet system could not endure.

Breaking this general argument down, three specific factors are often cited: the burden of the arms race, the economic and NATO technological embargoes and the anti-communist guerrilla movements in third world Soviet allies. On their own, or in some kind of combination, these were, it is frequently argued, the forms of international competition and pressure that brought the USSR to its knees.

The Arms Race

Enough is now known for us to be able to chart the history and significance of the East–West arms race to a reasonably satisfactory extent. In summary form, its record was as follows:

(*i*) From the late 1940s onwards the USSR and the USA were engaged in an arms race, conventional and nuclear, involving growing expenditures, and a technological race, in which, for all major dimensions except space in the late 1950s, the USA was in the lead, in the technological field, and remained, in most dimensions, in the lead in the quantitative domain.[12]

(*ii*) Despite this US lead, the relative burden on the USA was significantly less, representing between 5 per cent and 10 per cent of GNP (Gross National Product), whereas for the USSR arms expenditure represented between 10 per cent and 20 per cent throughout this period – some Russian officials now say it was as high as 25 per cent.

(*iii*) Despite the lack of a direct US–Soviet military confrontation, conventional or nuclear, this arms race represented, in a Clausewitzian sense, a continuation of politics by other means: it reflected a search for an elusive but strategically meaningful measure of 'superiority' over the other, it embodied a pursuit by both sides of prestige and status in the international arena, and it constituted a means of pressure on the budget and hence on the state–society relationship within the other.[13]

Given the burden on the USSR, its inability to compete with the USA, and the evident Clausewitzian rationales of the arms race, it is frequently argued that it was this race which forced the USSR into strategic retreat in the mid-1980s.

At least three variants of this argument can be noted: an economic one, that the level of expenditure on arms and the diversion of resources to the military sector were such that the USSR could not continue to compete, and needed a drastic reduction in military expenditure in order to divert resources for domestic economic reorganisation; a technological argument, that it was the continued US lead, acutely represented in the early 1980s by two developments, SDI (Strategic Defense Initiative) and the cruise missile, which forced the Soviet leadership to realise that it could not continue to compete; and a political argument, that the dangers of nuclear war and the costs involved forced the CPSU to abandon the idea of the world as one divided between two camps, locked in social conflict, in favour of a stress on universal human values and the common interests of human kind.

All three of these are, in varying degrees, found in the writings of Soviet and Western writers and each must certainly have played a role. Gorbachev himself consistently evoked the third, political, argument: while the appeal to 'universal' values has a long history in Soviet – and before that – Russian thought, the power of nuclear weapons and the accident at Chernobyl in 1986 certainly served to reinforce this awareness of the dangers of nuclear energy and, by extension, nuclear weapons.

Important as it is, there are significant reasons for qualifying the import of the arms race explanation as the major factor behind the Soviet collapse. Certainly, the economic argument must have considerable force: indeed the very quantitative figure of 10 per cent or 20 per cent of GNP being spent on defence understates the qualitative and distorting impact, with the allocation of the best administrative and scientific personnel and of key material resources to this sector.

On the other hand, military expenditure as 10 per cent or more of GNP is far from being an adequate explanation for the failings of the Soviet economy. Israel and Taiwan had comparable defence allocations in the same time period, but enjoyed higher standards of living and greater rates of growth.[14] Moreover, the very high rate of military expenditure as a percentage of GNP is but another way of saying that GNP itself was rather low – the figures for overall expenditure as between the US and USSR show that in absolute terms the USA was outspending the USSR.[15]

The focus must, therefore, be as much on the efficiency and allocative mechanisms of the civilian sector as on the claim of the military on GNP: had the Soviet GNP been rather higher and had the remaining 80 per cent of the Soviet economy been more efficiently organised, the 'burden' of military expenditure would have been less and would, given reasonable efficiency and growth rates, have represented a lower percentage of GNP anyway.

Similar problems arise with the technological argument: the assumption of much analysis of the arms race, and of the conventional Soviet approach prior to this, was that, more or less, the USSR was compelled by the necessities of inter-state competition to match the USA in qualitative and quantitative terms. Previously, the USSR had imitated US advances – as in the development of multiple-warhead missiles after 1972 and of a submarine-launched intercontinental capacity: the challenge of SDI and of cruise missiles were that the USSR had no comparable riposte and that there was no evident antidote which it was capable of producing.

Yet the USSR could have, without a mimetic rivalry, produced counter-measures to these US challenges – low-flying strategic missiles plus a system of decoys would have done much to invalidate SDI, even had it proved viable. A policy of what was termed 'minimum deterrence' would have made a substantial difference and enabled the USSR to escape from its self-defeating pursuit of 'rough parity'.

The third argument relevant to the arms race, the political argument about the threat to humanity of nuclear weapons, had great validity in itself and it is to the credit of Gorbachev that he articulated it more clearly than anyone else: but it does not entail the overall process of political and social change within the USSR that accompanied the adoption of these universal values associated with 'new thinking'. It is conceivable that the USSR would have opted out of the nuclear arms race as previously pursued but insisted on preserving its distinctive political and socio-economic system. To explain the latter involves looking beyond the realm of the arms race and its economic, technical and political costs.

Economic Pressures

The second set of factors commonly adduced to explain the Soviet retreat is the economic, and in particular the impact on the USSR of Western embargoes and restrictions in the field of high technology. It is worth repeating here that this line of argument runs counter to what would hitherto have been taken to be the impact of international trade upon a distinctive system: in the latter case it would be assumed that increased trade would undermine the other system and so contribute to its demise, whereas in this East–West contest it was argued that trade would benefit the rival bloc and its demise be hastened by denying it such interaction. Most post-war discussion of the relationship between trade and security in the East–West context operated with the assumption that increased commercial interaction between the two blocs would contribute to the stability of the Soviet bloc: the argument, as it developed in the 1970s, was between those who believed that greater trade, by making the Soviet Union more secure, would reduce areas of conflict between it and the West, and those who thought it would encourage combative behaviour. If the former view, drawing on theories of 'interdependence', was dominant in the early 1970s, it was the latter view that prevailed in the period of the Second Cold War.

On the basis of the partial evidence available, it would appear that economic interaction and pressure of various kinds both contributed to the collapse of the communist system, but that the most important factor was not the vulnerability of the centrally planned system to it, so much as its inability to make use of the advantages which trade with the capitalist world brought.

In the case of certain Eastern European countries – Poland is the most striking example – the opening up to the West in the early 1970s had short-term gains, in terms of availability of consumer goods and investment, but led to a longer-run crisis, with foreign debt and increased pressure on domestic earnings once debt-repayment became necessary. The centrally planned economic system could not make use of such external support adequately to develop its own economy, and ended up being trapped by its international commitments.

In the case of the USSR, all the evidence suggests that straightforward commercial interaction with the capitalist world had the effect of strengthening the existing system in the short run: most obviously, higher oil prices bought time in the 1970s and wheat imports provided a means of off-setting failures in agriculture. The rise in the price of oil in the 1970s gave the USSR a windfall profit for much of the decade: however, as Soviet writers have recently pointed out, the longer-run consequences of these profits were inhibiting, since they enabled the central planners and managers to postpone changes that might otherwise have had to be introduced more rapidly.

The same applied in the field of technology: the record of technological innovation in the USSR is by no means as bleak as is often suggested, but there is no doubt that most of the major technological innovations of recent decades originated in the west. Here the USSR was at a disadvantage, in two respects, the second of which was probably more important than the first. Self-evidently, it did not make many major innovations itself and was therefore compelled, in the civilian and military spheres, to copy or simply steal new technologies from the capitalist world. The degree of Soviet insulation from the international market was never as great as conventional images suggest: the industrialisation of the 1930s relied heavily on capital goods imports from Britain and Germany; the history of Soviet aerospace is of reproduction of Western aircraft and technologies. Yet in this pursuit of technological development, the USSR was always behind.

Even more important, however, it was unable to make proper use of the technologies it did have: there was little interaction between the military and civilian sectors; the system of central planning contained built-in disincentives for innovation and encouraged the use of inefficient and traditional methods of production; political and ideological constraints inhibited the use of information technology throughout the system. The pattern of 'conservative modernisation' identified as endemic to the centrally planned economies operated in this regard.[16] It was for this reason above all that the third industrial revolution, of microtechnology and computerised precision engineering, which began in the early 1970s, outstripped it more than ever.

The role of economic pressure and its political impact is two-sided even when it comes to the embargoes. Here it has been argued that Soviet behaviour in the international arena was affected by Western restrictions, both those of a strictly national security kind, through CoCom (the Co-ordinating Committee on East–West Trade), and broader political embargoes announced in the wake of Afghanistan. The former, it was said, would make it more difficult for the USSR to compete in the arms race, the latter would act as disincentives for unwelcome Soviet foreign policy actions. Given the degree to which the USSR protested about these restrictions, it would seem that their impact was considerable.[17]

Yet these pressures in themselves can hardly explain the change in Soviet orientation from the mid-1980s onwards: the USSR, faced with a dire technological lag in the military sphere, could have made substantial concessions, such as withdrawing the SS-20s or cancelling the SS-18 strategic missile, without placing their overall strategy in question; in the short run at least, they did not respond to Western political sanctions by making major foreign policy concessions and were indeed more intransigent up to 1985 than had hitherto been the case. The very same factors that diminished the import of Western commercial and technological impact served to lessen the impact of their withdrawal: the centralised political and economic system could absorb the shocks as well as it could inhibit the diffusion of new technologies.

Erosion of the Bloc

A third major factor adduced to explain the retreat of Soviet power was the cost of supporting its third world allies, at both the economic and military levels. Numerous reasons for such an explanation suggest themselves: Soviet writers themselves complained openly about the costs, economic and diplomatic, of backing third world allies and reversed the earlier Khrushchevite view that the national liberation and third world revolutionary movements made a positive contribution to the power of the USSR;[18] the concept of 'imperial overstretch' would seem to apply here and provide a comparative perspective on the Soviet retreat; the very character of Soviet relations with third world allies, resting as they did on substantial economic subsidies in return for political and strategic rewards, made this set of relationships especially burdensome; for US strategic planners in the early 1980s the weakest link of the Soviet system lay in the third world and this is why there evolved the 'Reagan Doctrine' of support for anti-communist guerrilla movements.

On closer examination, however, the pressure of third world commitments may have been different and in some regards less than at first sight appeared. The greatest cost to the USSR of its third world commitments was in the diplomatic field – in the way that Soviet support for revolutionary allies and movements worsened US–Soviet relations and, with the invasion of Afghanistan, provided a means through which the West could for the first time break the USSR's relationship with the third world as a whole.

The other factors normally adduced, economic and military, may well have been less significant. First of all, the figures for Soviet 'aid' to the third world comprise a variety of forms of support, including, in the case of the largest commitment – Cuba – major long-term trading agreements that gave Cuba far better terms of trade than it could have got on the world market (higher prices for sugar, lower for oil) but were not net transfers of resources in the ordinary sense. In the case of Cuba there were benefits to the USSR – getting sugar and nickel that could be paid for in rubles, rather than having to pay in hard currency; in other cases, the third world ally was able to provide the USSR with valuable imports – Afghan gas being one example. Secondly, and despite current Soviet overstatement of their aid record, the amount of aid, even on an extended definition, was in comparative terms very low – 0.25 per cent of GNP, roughly equivalent to the US record.[19] Politically convenient within the USSR as it may have become to blame third world allies, who certainly were mismanaging their economies, for the economic woes of the USSR, this was hardly a major factor in the economic crisis of the Soviet system.

As with military expenditure within the USSR itself, the focus of criticism must go back to the overall system of planning and production and the inefficiencies it contained, and which were, incidentally, reproduced by Soviet aid programmes within third world states themselves. The strategic cost of sustaining third world allies in the 1980s was certainly rising, as a result of the 'Reagan Doctrine': but if the purpose of the anti-communist movements was to weaken the USSR at its most vulnerable point this turned out not to be the case. One of the major reasons for Soviet and Western involvement in Afghanistan was the demonstration effect of a ruling communist party being overthrown: the impact on Eastern Europe of Kabul falling would, both sides believed, be potentially enormous. Yet in the end it was not in Nicaragua nor Afghanistan that Soviet allies were first overthrown, but in Eastern Europe itself. It was what happened in Warsaw, Berlin and Prague that did so much to affect developments in Managua, Aden and Kabul, and not the other way around.

A Comparative Failure

The argument so far has identified two categories of external factor, the traditional-imperial, discussed in Chapter 8, and the more recent and specifically East–West Cold War ones, discussed here, which can be considered to have played a role in eroding and undermining Soviet power. While both categories have some explanatory power, reasons have been suggested as to why these may prove inadequate in themselves. If this is so, then it pushes the argument towards a re-examination of the reasons for the collapse of Soviet power, at both historical and theoretical levels: i.e. a re-examination both of what actually happened, and of how our conception of inter-state competition may need modifying in the light of the Soviet case.

The phenomenon that needs explanation is that an international system of states collapsed in the absence of the most evident forms of threat: it was not defeated in war (even in Afghanistan); it did not face political challenges from below that it was unable to contain – Poland being the only, partial, exception; it was not, despite its manifold economic and social problems, unable to meet the economic levels that its citizenry had become accustomed to. It did not, therefore, 'collapse', 'fail', 'break down' in any absolute sense. What occurred, rather, was that the leadership of the most powerful state in the system decided to introduce a radically new set of policies, within the USSR and within the system as a whole: it was not that the ruled could not go on being ruled in the old way so much that the rulers could not go on ruling in the old way. The question is what it was that led these rulers, who cannot be accused of having in the past lacked a desire to retain power or of being initially covert supporters of the West, to introduce the changes they did.

Two kinds of reason, one endogenous and the other exogenous, seem to have led to this conclusion. They can be termed, in summary form, as socio-economic paralysis and lack of international competitiveness. The paralysis was evident in a wide range of spheres: falling growth rates, rising social problems, growing corruption and disillusionment, ecological crisis. Not only could the system not go on reproducing the rates of growth and improvement in welfare provision characteristic of earlier phases – the 1930s, the 1950s – but it seemed to have run out of steam in a comprehensive manner. These phenomena were often referred to in the Soviet literature of the late 1980s as 'stagnation', yet in many ways this was a simplistic term:[20] it understated the degree to which there was continued progress in some spheres, not least the political; it still contained within it the teleological assumption that the system could, under other circumstances, have continued to grow and develop.

Most important, however, 'stagnation' left out what was in

many ways the vital factor in forcing the Soviet leadership, faced with this trend, to introduce change, namely the awareness of the system's *comparative* failure *vis-à-vis* the West. It is here, above all, in the perceived inability of the Soviet system to catch up, let alone overtake, the West that the central aspect of the Soviet collapse may be seen. It was a failure to compete internationally that led to the post-1985 changes in the USSR: once begun, an attempt to reform the system the better to survive and compete quickly capsized into the failure to save the state as such.

The awareness of the system's inability to compete in the 1980s was the final in several stages of such loss of hope. The first, historical, disappointment was that immediately after 1917 when the Bolsheviks realised that their revolution would not be reproduced in Germany. This realisation led to a double redefinition of strategy – temporary abandonment of the idea of world revolution, proclamation of the idea that a socialist regime *could* be built in the USSR. With the victories in the Second World War and the increase in the number of third world pro-Soviet allies it appeared for the 1950s and 1960s as if the initial encirclement of the USSR could be overcome concomitant with the development of socialism within the USSR itself. The successes of post-war reconstruction and space technology in the 1950s seemed to confirm this: hence the new, secularly optimistic, programme of Khrushchev which combined continued rivalry with the West in the third world with a policy of socio-economic development designed to 'catch up with and overtake' the West in two decades. It would seem, difficult as it is to believe now, that this perspective, modified by Brezhnev, dominated Soviet thinking until the early 1980s: there were continued advances in the third world, the USSR attained 'rough parity' with the USA in the arms race, and at home it was official policy to state that the USSR was now at a new state, a stage of 'developed socialism'.

The reality was, however, rather different, as each of the major areas of inter-state and inter-bloc competition showed. In the most public and privileged area of competition, the military, the USSR was, as we have seen, always inferior, in numbers and quality, except for its conventional strength in Eastern Europe. In the early 1980s it faced new challenges which it was both forced to accept and constitutionally unable to respond to, and it lacked anything like the global deployment capabilities of the USA and its allies. If this was the area where the Soviet Union was to compete the most, it was evidently not doing anything like well enough.

In the second place, the international system created by the USSR was markedly weaker quantitatively and qualitatively than that created by the West. Not only was the international capitalist market far stronger in terms of economic output, technological change, and numbers of countries included within it, but its degree of integration was greater: one of the paradoxes of planning within the USSR and the Soviet international system more generally was its inability to integrate sectors beyond giving them separate, if supposedly co-ordinated, production targets. In the military sphere a similar disparity and qualitative inferiority prevailed in the comparison between NATO and the Warsaw Pact. For all the talk of constituting a new world order, the Soviet one was less integrated and much weaker overall.[21] In many respects, not least innovation and pricing, it remained dependent on the capitalist system, and ineffectually imitative of it.

This failure to compete in international terms would, in itself, have been a major problem, given the fact that underlying East–West rivalry and Cold War was an attempt by both sides to provide a new basis for an international order and to demonstrate the superiority of the one over the other. But this external blockage, one going right back to 1917 and only obscured by subsequent international triumphs, was compounded by the internal limits of the system in many spheres: the failure to match levels of output in the West, the growing gap in living standards between developed socialist and developed capitalist states and, obscured by rhetoric about 'socialist' democracy, the contrast between a substantial degree of democratic success in the West and centralised political control in the East. Had the USSR been able to rival the West successfully in other spheres these internal deficiencies, those denoted by 'stagnation', might have been concealed the longer, but it was the failure at the international level that forced the leadership to face up to them.

Here we come to a central feature of the collapse: almost impossible to believe as it may now be, it would seem that up to the early 1980s this contrast in internal achievement was hidden from, or at least not recognised by, most Soviet observers, in the leadership or elsewhere. The underlying self-confidence of the

Soviet system, a product of the revolution's historic claims and of victory in the Second World War, seemed to have lasted up to that time, but at some point in the early 1980s it began to erode, first amongst the leadership and then within the population as a whole. The awareness of how most people lived in the West, and of the enormous gap in living standards, produced a situation in which the self-confidence that had lasted from 1917 evaporated in the space of a few short years. It is not possible to disentangle the economic from the political dimensions; but the evidence suggests that it was the economic which played the major role in getting this process going. Once the living standards gap became evident then the legitimacy of the political system was swept away and that of the alternative system, the Western variant of pluralism, was enhanced.

Here it is worthwhile looking at the mechanism by which this change of attitude seems to have occurred. The insulation of Soviet society was both physical – lack of communication, radio jamming, absence of travel, punishment of those who sought contact with the outside world – and psychological – a belief that whatever went wrong, *'u nas luchshe'* – 'things are better with us'.[22] Those who travelled abroad or had access to comparative data were condemned to silence, even when they realised the truth. Here the change of heart of the leadership was of pivotal importance and opened the flood gates to popular discontent: the breaking of the secular self-confidence of the top leadership must certainly have been encouraged by the failures of international competition in the military and economic spheres, but it would appear that the very perception of the contrast in living standards, highlighting the reality of internal paralysis in the late 1970s, played the crucial part. In Gorbachev's case, for example, it would seem that his visits to Canada provided such an occasion: it would only take five minutes in an average Canadian supermarket for the point to become clear, and for the specific experience of shortages and administrative problems he experienced in running the Stavropol region to be set in its decisive, internationalised, context.

Once this change had occurred, then the process of broader awareness followed. The liberalisation of the political system within the USSR alone allowed of greater information about the capitalist world, almost all of it favourable when not uncritical, and for a more negative assessment of the record of the USSR.

It is noticeable too how, in speeches made after 1985, Gorbachev himself would make telling comparisons with the capitalist world, in the field of social indicators – infant mortality, hospital conditions, alcoholism, availability of basic foods – as well as in broader macroeconomic and political terms.[23] His own process of self-education seems to have followed such a path: already dissatisfied with socialist performance, he came into office in 1985 apparently believing that the socialist system could reform itself by applying technology in a more intense way, the better to 'accelerate' production; but by 1989 he had moved much further on both the economic and political fronts, in the face of the evident inability of the system to reform itself within orthodox socialist political and economic parameters. In other words, the international comparison that had brought him to the point of initiating major reform in 1985 pushed him after 1985 to envisage a much more radical reform of the system. The fact that, though forcing the comparison onto the Soviet public, he had unleashed widespread additional dissatisfaction, only served to confirm this trend.

Whether his project, in whatever form, could have succeeded, given the difficulties of such a transition and the subordinated international position of the USSR was, as indicated above, an open question: what is clear is that under the combination of international pressures, and in particular the perceived gap in living standards, the top leadership decided they could not go on in the old way.

Here it may be possible to distinguish between two broad phases of the collapse: a first, conscious and controlled phase, from 1985 to 1989, and a second, uncontrolled phase, when the situation, in Eastern Europe and the USSR itself, then got out of control, culminating in the failed coup of August 1991 and the subsequent dissolution of the USSR itself.

The first phase gave way to the second not because Gorbachev and his associates foresaw what would happen, but rather because they did not: they believed that some modified, reformed, humanised, 'accelerated', socialist system could work and, more-over, that the regimes in Eastern Europe would endure beyond the removal of the Soviet military guarantee. Had they realised the fragility of the communist system, in the USSR itself as in Eastern Europe, and even more so had the military and political élites realised the impossibility of sustaining such regimes, then it is possible that matters would not have taken the course they did: the communist regimes could, with increasing demoralisation and entropy, have survived for years, or even a decade or two more.

Once the military guarantees were removed, the Eastern European regimes collapsed. Within the USSR, once the restrictions in information and contact with the outside world were removed, and once the role of confrontation and rivalry with the West ended, then the political cohesion of that system collapsed. In both cases, the removal of international constituents of the stability of the system led to the later outcome.

To all of this must be added one further factor – the political calculations, and selective initiatives, of Western leaders: this was particularly the case with Germany where Helmut Kohl, realising his historic opportunity to reunite Germany and abolish the communist system in East Germany, applied a mixture of pressure and enticement to achieve his goal. This conscious, political, intervention was decisive in the course of events after the Berlin Wall came down in November 1989, but it was possible only in the context created by another set of international circumstances.[24]

Three Levels of International Competition

This analysis of East–West competition up to the late 1980s and of the subsequent collapse of the USSR and of the communist system more generally has a number of implications for International Relations theory generally and for theories of inter-state and inter-society competition in particular – ones that return to the conclusions of Chapters 4, 5 and 8. No one analysing East–West conflict can deny the relevance within it of what can in IR phrasing be termed 'realist' concerns, of conventional inter-state forms of competition – at the military, economic and political levels. The rivalry of the Soviet and US systems in the post-war period involved a comprehensive competition in which the innovation was not the role of states but rather the way in which this inter-state competition developed into new domains – the nuclear arms race, on the one hand, the comprehensive mobilisation of ideological resources on the other.

Given its strong position in the economic field, it was natural that the West should seek to use its economic strength to place pressure on the USSR for security reasons: the international political economy of East–West relations was, in essence, one of the use of economic instruments by the stronger bloc, that of Western states, for political and military ends. In the final phase of the conflict, and once the communist states had opened the door to Western influence on policy and its attendant conditions, then the pressure was even clearer, general prescriptions on political liberty being linked to specific conditions on the role of the state in the economy.

This was most evident in the ten-point programme enunciated by Kohl after the fall of the Berlin Wall: while presented in the form of a set of agreements between two states, it was actually a programme for the subjugation of the German Democratic Republic. Points one and two spoke of cooperation between two states, but point three made all this conditional on 'a fundamental change of the political and economic system in the GDR' which was to be irreversible i.e. capitulation. As his adviser made clear, Kohl used the term 'confederative structures', not 'confederation', in order to preclude the two state-relationship from acquiring a lasting character.[25]

This inter-state competition, comprehensive as it was, is not sufficient to explain how, why and when the communist system collapsed, how the West succeeded in prevailing over the East. Earlier cases of inter-systemic conflict – the Ottoman and Manchu cases – provide at best partial points of comparison: despite some similarities, theirs was fundamentally a very different story. The specifically Cold War instruments of inter-state competition – arms race, embargoes, third world harassment – do not, in themselves, explain why the Soviet leadership took the decisions it did after 1985. To analyse this rivalry it is necessary to take a broader look at East–West rivalry as a whole, one that encompasses the competition of systems within which state competition plays an important, but not exclusive, role.

In this perspective, it becomes possible to apply the three dimensions of competition, interrelated but analytically distinct, that were discussed in Chapter 8: the level of activities of states, that of social and economic entities, most notably firms, and that of ideology and culture – inter-state, inter-socio-economic, inter-ideological. In addressing the question of 'how' the West put pressure on the East this tripartite distinction may be helpful.

Operating on the first level, Western state action had effects, but it was not the only story. The ability of Western states directly to put such pressure became greater than ever before as the linking of economic assistance to socio-economic change within the USSR and Eastern Europe showed: *perestroika* created the conditions for, not resulted from, such a socio-economic intervention by the Group of 7. In the case of Eastern Europe, Western firms – industrial enterprises, banks – also played a role, especially in dealings with Poland in the early 1970s and in the handling of the Soviet oil output. In the opening up that took place from late 1989 onwards, West German business enterprises have taken a role and a lead, somewhat co-ordinated with, but separate from, that of the Bonn Government itself. Once the wall had come down it was the pressure of the West German state, plus the impact of West German firms, and particularly banks, that combined to render impossible any reformed regime in the East. It would be analytically misleading either to reduce state policy in East–West relations to the wishes of multinational corporations, or to see the latter as acting simply within parameters laid down by or at the behest of Western states. Their actions were parallel and usually – though not always – convergent: the response of sectors of the business community to political embargoes on communist states was evidence enough of divergence in this regard.

The ideological and cultural dimension was, however, of even greater importance: its role in the collapse of communism and in the East–West rivalry that preceded it was in some ways decisive. What above all forced the leadership of the CPSU to change course, and what destroyed the support or acquiescence of the peoples of Eastern Europe and the USSR to communism, was the perceived contrast in living standards and in living conditions between East and West. This ideological dimension is certainly something that states help to promote and regulate, and which their information and propaganda organs disseminate, and it is something which rests upon economic performance, on the output and sales policies of business corporations. During the Cold War Western radio stations broadcasting to the East were, in a general way, aware that programmes on Western culture and life-style would erode the confidence and legitimacy of regimes in the East, in a drip-by-drip process.[26] But this process is something distinct from governments, encompassing as it does popular culture, the media, fashion, and in broad terms the image of what constitutes a good life. It combines the traditional concept of ideology with that of consumerism. Moreover, the dissemination of images pertaining to this is not simply the result of state or business enterprise decision: it takes place in an uncoordinated but pervasive way, through television and film, through popular music, through impressions gained from travel and personal encounter. It is informal and diffuse, but constitutes the most potent interface between two societies. The abandonment by the majority of the inhabitants of East Germany of any belief in a separate socialist way or entity was above all a product of this encounter: years of exposure to West German images on television, followed by the direct encounter itself, the *Reiseshock*.

In so far as this distinction is valid, and the importance of ideological-cultural factors in international relations is accepted, then it suggests another interpretation of the Cold War and its end, and of international relations more generally, one involving the pressures for homogeneity and the force of example already discussed in Chapter 5. Relations between states retain their importance and the particular mechanisms of conflict and resource mobilisation at any one time are open to analysis on a contingent basis. The denial of state efficacy and the premature reduction of its role is as misleading as the realist insistence that all international relations can be seen, or deemed, to be ones between states.

At the same time, international competition involves two other major dimensions: the unofficial, socio-economic, and the ideological. The latter has always operated – it would be impossible to follow the history of Christianity, its diffusion and division, without it. But the ideological has a special salience in a world where material well-being, fashion and consumerism occupy a special role in the constitution of specific societies, and in an international situation characterised by immediate transmission of sound and images. There is clearly a relationship between power in one domain and power in the ideological – through control of images and their means of diffusion. Never was Gramsci's conception of hegemony, in the sense of ideological and cultural factors as instruments of domination, so relevant as in analysing the international system today. If communism surrendered, almost without firing a shot, it was because the instrument of international competition in the late twentieth century was as much the T-shirt as the gunboat.

10

International Relations and the 'End of History'

The preceding two chapters have examined the Cold War and its outcome in the light of two of the themes that run through this book: the role of 'heterogeneity' of values in international conflict, and the contribution of socio-economic and ideological factors to the collapse of the Soviet model. This chapter takes a broader look at the evolution of the international system, including the collapse of communism, in order to suggest some ways in which these events may cast light on the questions raised in preceding chapters and the degree to which new issues, and priorities, are raised by them.

In the late 1980s and early 1990s the world underwent a strategic and intellectual earthquake, comparable in effects – though not, at least initially, in the human suffering – caused by the First and Second World Wars. A hegemonic system, and its attendant distribution of power, collapsed. The map of states was redrawn, and around twenty new sovereign states were created. A degree of uncertainty unparalleled since the 1930s prevailed in the international arena. The world created by this set of changes corresponded to no easy model, and rightly provoked considerable bewilderment. The following chapter, after some general observations on what it is that occurred in this period, examines different interpretations of these events, and some contemporary responses to them. If it avoids prediction, it does, none the less, hope to offer some analysis of where the international system is going, and of some possibilities for the future.

Aftermaths of the Cold War

The historical outlines and hence originality of what happened in the late 1980s can be summarised in brief.[1] A bloc of states, dominated by the USSR, which had since the 1940s been engaged in great power competition with the West, and which had, in the form of the USSR itself, been challenging the Western world since 1917, collapsed. The originality of this system's collapse needs recognition: as discussed in Chapter 9, it occurred without inter-state war, in a very short space of time, without the presence of evident forms of political vanguards or organisation and without significant bloodshed. Moreover, in contrast to other revolutions since 1789 which had to some degree claimed to defy the international norm or propound something 'new', those pro-pounding change in this context wanted not, as had hitherto almost always been the case, the creation of something 'new', an alternative to the prevailing world order, but rather conformity to that order, a recruitment and incorporation, as rapid and painless as possible, into what was deemed to be the prevailing norm, be it 'civilisation' 'democracy', the 'west', or 'modernity'.[2]

Certain qualifications to this picture of a major kind are necessary: most of those ruled by Communist Parties in 1988 (1.7 billions) still were (1.4 billions); there is no certainty about what kinds of government will emerge in the former Soviet Union, or in many of its former allies; the future pattern of Russian foreign policy is obscure. None the less a cataclysm of great proportions had occurred, and one that brought to an end not only the Cold War and the challenge of the Bolshevik Revolution but also a longer period of international history in which a move-ment of contestation of the hegemonic capitalist form was identifiable.

At the risk of what one could term 'megalo-presentism', it could be suggested that 1989 brought to the end a period of history that began in 1789 with the French Revolution. In this sense the argument of Fukuyama, that what was new about the contemporary situation was that there was only one set of answers now acceptable on a world scale, was to a degree valid. It is in this, above all, that the historic importance of 1989 consists: a year that began with a political and journalistic élite of the West nervously opining that, on the eve of the bicentenary of the French Revolution, such upheavals and changes could not occur, and that the 'masses' no longer made history, if indeed they ever did, produced as much surprise, or what Hegel would have called 'the cunning of reason', as any other dramatic period of modern history.[3]

In this perspective the 'end of the Cold War' was a composite phenomenon involving several broad historical trends, with the prospect that they would take a long time to work themselves out. In the first place, and in many ways in the most important, the end of Cold War marked the end of the inter-state conflict that had dominated the world since 1945 and the end of the Soviet–US nuclear confrontation. Two obvious prospective issues were whether this marked an end of Great Power military rivalry as a whole, at least for a generation or so, and whether a new pattern of inter-state blocs and of hegemony would emerge to replace the old.

The argument for the former would seem to have had considerable historical force – that for a century since the Sino-Japanese war of 1894 Great Powers had been engaged in major military confrontation, or in the threat thereof. The prospect of this now seemed definitely to have receded: while there were those who foresaw new Great Power conflicts in the near future, the pattern of the past century would appear to have been broken.[4]

There was speculation about new conflicts emerging around trade blocs – a dollar bloc, a yen bloc and an ecu bloc. But while trading blocs in a loose sense were clearly forming, and while there was friction over trade, the world was a long way from trade wars or exclusive systems of the kind that had prevailed before the Second World War, and it was hard to see them forming. Moreover, even if there was conflict over trade and a flood of nationalism directed against commercial competitors, there was no inevitability, and initially not much likelihood, of this leading to a military confrontation.

As for hegemony, and the dangers of a new imperialism, we now saw a situation of great fluidity in which no bloc of states seemed likely to emerge to match the USA, but where the USA itself appeared reluctant to play the 'Roman' role which the collapse of the USSR had allotted to it. The argument that war between states is almost precluded when they are liberal democratic states, well explicated in the writings of Michael Doyle, has much to recommend it, although it has been put to apologetic use in obscuring the degree to which democratic states wage war against undemocratic ones:[5] if true in a strict sense, it would focus our attention on the revival of authoritarian regimes in some major states, and hence of whether some of the great powers, Russia or Japan, or depression-ridden US, UK or Germany, may in the longer run diverge from this model.

The second dimension of the end of the Cold War was the end of communism as a political force. As already indicated this was, at first, a phenomenon confined to Europe and the Asian regions of the former USSR: but the trend within China seemed to indicate a move towards capitalism, if not liberalism, and the remaining communist states were unable to provide an international alternative (Cuba, Vietnam, North Korea). Two large questions arose here: first, what the future of an alternative to capitalism now was, and if it had one at all, and secondly, what the historical import of the whole communist experience was.

In regard to the first it seems that no programme of revolutionary political challenge to liberal capitalism from the left now had any serious credit or support: the communist challenge was now exhausted. What remained were variants of social-democratic adaptation within advanced capitalism, but ones that were more and more restricted in part by international conditions, in part by changing social and political configurations within individual countries themselves. It is conventional to state that the collapse of social democracy was in part a result of the failure of communism: the reverse may, however be the case – the dynamic of social democracy and its equivalents was broken in most advanced countries in the 1970s (Britain, USA, Australia, Germany). The very lack of a credible middle, or third, road meant that the choices facing communist reformers in the late 1980s were all the starker.

The question of what was communism, too near to allow of an easy perspective, has occasioned several candidate explanations: a dictatorial tendency whereby revolutionary élites seized control of societies, a flawed movement for the self-emancipation of the working class, an expression of Judaeo-Christian messianism, a product of oriental despotism, a failed developmentalist project.[6] One judicious author suggested that communism may end up being comparable to the Jesuit experiment in Paraguay, a rational attempt at insulating a section of the world from international pressures and sustaining an alternative development path, and one that was much idealised by intellectuals at the time, but one which was in the end to collapse almost without trace.[7]

Some explanation involving different elements of the candidates listed above may be most appropriate: it is easy, in retrospect, to say that it 'never worked', but this attempt to escape the conventional path of capitalist development was for a time remarkably successful, not least in the ideological and military challenge it posed to the West, even if it was in the end forced to capitulate, and to do so almost without resistance. Although now seen as inevitable, this was not how the communist experiment appeared for many decades: both amongst those who supported it, and those who feared it, there was a belief in the efficacy of socialist state intervention that subsequent events have belied. If nothing else, as suggested in Chapter 9, the communist collapse deserves careful study from the perspective of those who believe in élite-led or state-dictated social and economic development.

The third element in the end of the Cold War was the break-up of the USSR, and of its attendant alliance system. Here it was not at all clear if the process was complete by the end of 1991, not only with regard to Eastern Europe but also to Russia itself: the Russian Federation was subject to substantial centrifugal forces and could yet break up into three parts under international and internal pressure. Yet even if the process of fragmentation was complete already, it had unleashed powerful changes in the international arena. It had created a situation in which, with the break-up of the pre-existing order, new regional alliances and new potential hegemons have emerged: in Europe, Germany; in the Caucasus, Black Sea and Central Asia, Turkey. In the Far East the realignments were less major, because Soviet power was weaker, but it encouraged, and coincided with, an increase in both Chinese and Japanese power. The Far East was indeed the area with the greatest political and economic range, and promised to be the fulcrum of the twentieth-first century: whether it could contain these changes without major military conflict was as yet not evident. The impact on Indo-China, with the removal of the Soviet role in Cambodia and Vietnam, and in the North-East Asian region, was none the less substantial and continuous.

Some of these regional changes took the world back to a situation before 1914 – the pattern of alliances in the Balkans and in the Baltic were cases in point. Others were new – the Turkish–

Iranian contest in Central Asia being only a remote descendant of earlier ones. It would seem probable that some of these powers would assume major international responsibilities and roles in the century ahead: Germany and Japan, politically quite different from their Second World War characters, were reluctant to play such a role, especially in the military field, but would in the end be forced to do so. Some saw this reticence as a just recognition of their criminal pasts: but the problems with their pasts did not lie in their contemporary foreign policy. What was most worrying about these countries was not any proximate danger of their becoming aggressive military powers again, but the evasion and euphemism that still prevailed in much of their internal life. A healthier recognition of the past could have enabled a more commensurate international role in the economic and security dimensions.

The fourth broad consequence of the collapse of communism was that it broke a 'regime' that had prevailed since the end of the Second World War, in terms of which the existing map of the world, with its iniquities and arbitrariness, was maintained. For all the talk of secession and unification that marked the post-1945 epoch, it is striking how, until 1989, the map more or less held. States became independent, some lost bits of territory, but the actual division into 170-odd states was more or less frozen. Unification or fusion occurred only by force and at moments of uncertainty arising from decolonisation (Palestine, Western Sahara, Timor and, it can be argued, Tibet), or through the voluntary merging, again at the moment of independence of formerly separate colonial entities (Cameroun, Somalia). Secession only occurred in the case of Bangladesh in 1971, but that was of an entity that was already geographically separated from the rest of Pakistan.[8]

After 1989 both fusion and fission came again onto the order of the day: it was expected that the fusion of the Yemens and the Germanies would be followed, albeit with some delay, by that of the Koreas and probably, in some form or other, of the (three) Chinas. On the other hand, fission was the fate of the multi-ethnic states of the former communist system (USSR, Yugoslavia, Ethiopia, Czechoslovakia), with the result that in the space of two years over twenty new sovereign states came into existence.

No one could yet tell what the longer-term demonstration effects of this process were going to be, but there could be little doubt that the breaking of the post-1945 regime would encourage many others to think that they too could achieve separate statehood. This affected some areas more than others, and it may turn out that only those states where communist regimes had been ousted would actually fragment; but parts of Europe and Africa, as well as India, were likely to be subject to increased strains, now that it had been shown that secession is allowed. It is for this reason above all that it was essential for states and international bodies to develop some more adequate means of assessing and regulating this process. The behaviour of the international community over the issue of secession has been a striking example of the void between ideal and practice: while the system is founded on the claim that peoples are sovereign and are entitled to their own states, the practice has been to oppose secession until the last moment, except where a direct self-interest (often of an expansionist kind) prevails. The break-up of the USSR, and of its three associated multi-ethnic states in the period 1989–93, occurred despite, not because of, international encouragement. The international response was one of reluctant and belated acquiescence, well summed up in the informal observation by the British Foreign Secretary Douglas Hurd in June 1993: 'I hope we do not see the creation of any more nation-states'.

Varieties of Historical Evaluation

In broad terms, there were three kinds of response to these changes. One was a secular pessimism, a gloomy sobriety of the right, which saw the breakdown of the Cold War order as in many respects a return to the world before 1914, or between the two world wars, leading to greater inter-state conflict, nuclear proliferation and hyper-nationalism. The second was a pessimism of the left which asserted that we were in a new imperialist epoch – that the north was incapable of assisting in the development of the South, that ecological destruction was ongoing, that the USA would, on its own, or in association with its old allies, use the new opportunities to dominate the world. The third approach was an optimistic one, that saw the world as having moved decisively forward and as being in a period when certain desirable goals – peace, democracy, greater prosperity – were now available to all.

Though these approaches had the merit of providing broad interpretations, in some obvious respects they were all deficient.

The pessimistic perspective of a return to 1914 appeared to draw sustenance from new forms of inter-state conflict and from the rise of nationalism, but it forced the analogy too far: the major powers were not in the grip of nationalism directed against each other, and were relatively uninterested in preparing for military action against each other; there was a torrent of nationalism, but it took a communal, inter-ethnic as distinct from strategic, form.[9] Much was made of the cruel fate of Sarajevo, with the sombre joke that only world wars which begin in years with even numbers start there. But for all the horror and suffering, and the differences of approach between Security Council members, this was not a conflict that threatened to provoke war between great powers. The states themselves involved on the international scene had changed dramatically since 1914, most notably by the universalisation of democracy (no major states had universal suffrage in 1914) and by the growth of economic prosperity. Germany, for one, was not the state it was in 1914, or 1939: neo-Nazi youth was repugnant, but it was not yet dangerous for other states, as was the Kaiser or Adolf Hitler.

In a mood of historical analogy, some compared this period of history to that of the *belle époque*, the decades preceding 1914 when industrial Europe appeared to be at a new height of economic, political and culture success, only to plunge into the wars of the twentieth century. There are analogies with the *belle époque*, not least the complacent belief that the rich states of the west have solved their problems, and the modishness of various forms of irrationalism.

But there are striking differences, not least all that had happened in the intervening century. Few in the industrialised countries now believed, as many did a hundred years ago with varying degrees of social Darwinist conceit, that war was a viable, let alone desirable, means of resolving conflict between major states. Equally importantly, the world was not in a period when new ideological challenges were emerging from situations of social and political conflict: one of the most striking, and in its way depressing, features of the post-1989 international conflict was that no one was saying anything new, and many were making the same kinds of claim as had been heard a century before. The verities of Balkan nationalism or the conflicting aspiration around Nagorno-Karabagh, were, whatever their other problems, not the communism or fascism of their day. Indeed what was in some ways most dispiriting about all this fractious and strident clamour is how utterly familiar it all was. We knew Mr Karadzic, the Bosnian Serbian leader, group therapist for a second division football team turned demagogue: we had met him many times before. The world was, therefore, in what was in many respects a new international situation, both with regard to the pattern of the post-1945 period, and more generally.

The contrary position, the pessimism of the left, received much support from the Gulf War, and there were many who sought to draw general lessons about the post-communist world from that event.[10] Leaving aside the, often solipsistic, analysis of why the war occurred, the critics of the war were, in most respects, and not least with regard to the longer-run significance of the conflict, proved wrong. First of all, and for all the destruction visited on Iraq, the cost was far less than its critics suggested at the time: total Iraqi dead were around 10,000 – a twentieth of what was claimed – and, despite rhetoric about Iraq being bombed back to the stone age, most of the war damage had within a year or so of the war been repaired.[11] Despite imperial dreaming on the right, and speculation about the character of a new world order on the left, the US was not able to use its victory to put pressure on its economic rivals, or on other third world countries; militarist sentiment showed no permanent increase in the US, as George Bush found out to his disappointment; there was movement on a range of Middle Eastern issues, including the Arab–Israeli issue and freedom of expression, for Kuwaitis at least, in Kuwait. The Gulf War was an important, but essentially diversionary, chapter in world affairs.

Where the critique of the left pessimists had more force was elsewhere: first, in regard to the marginalisation of organised dissent and of radical criticism within the developed and under-developed world, and secondly in regard to the issue of inter-national economic relations and the question of whether the wealth of the richer countries can, given constraints historical and new, be diffused in any reasonable way to the rest of humanity. The latter is an issue which will be discussed later in this chapter, and where the conventional certainties of left and right can no longer be deemed to prevail.

Both the pessimism of the left and of the right share a common view, on the reduced role of the state, and the increasing globalisation of the world at the economic, political and cultural levels. At the theoretical level, the most challenging issue to confront is that of producing a response to changes in the outside world, but a change that has now been reflected in a growing body of academic literature: namely, how to conceive of the growing internationalisation of the world. This internationalisation is apparently clear for all to see: in international trade, in the growth of communications, in the shrinking of distances, in the creation of a global financial system and the decreasingly national locations of specific enterprises.[12] Within Europe we have a process of increasing transfer of powers to the institutions of the Economic Union, and the introduction of a single market in 1992. This picture of growing internationalisation is usually accompanied by two other concerns: namely, the beliefs that the position of the state as previously established is eroding, and that the nature of power in the contemporary world is changing, from being largely confined to military power to being more based on economic and even cultural factors. The world is, we are led to believe, becoming more and more international.

At the same time, there is a strong pessimistic argument to be made about the global trends – demographic, technological, ecological – and their differential national implications: a cogent example of this approach is that of Paul Kennedy in his *Preparing for the Twenty-First Century*.[13] He is a qualified, and unenthusiastic, prophet of doom: in contrast to Fukuyama, he neglects politics and the role of ideas almost completely, focusing on economic and scientific change. On the other hand, his pessimism is of a baneful and resigned kind, free of the Nietzschean or social Darwinist undertow found in writers of an earlier age.

Kennedy begins with the analysis of Thomas Malthus, first published in 1798, according to which the rise in world population would outstrip the rise in food output. He argues that, in his time, Malthus was wrong, for at least three reasons: emigration drained off surplus population from the countries with the fastest growth rates; agricultural productivity rose faster than he expected; industrialisation provided new forms of employment. His claim now is that, two centuries later, a pessimism comparable to that of Malthus is far more valid: world population is increasing at a rate faster than ever before; demographic, economic and social pressures are creating ever greater tensions in the third world; technological change, through robotisation and the biotechnology revolution, are reducing the number of jobs available, and promoting greater inequalities of wealth and productivity.

Hence he is not saying, as Malthus did, that the world will run short of food, but rather that a set of other contradictions will provoke internal and international conflict: population is rising where ecological crisis is most extreme, technological change is separated from demographic explosion, the number of jobs available is being reduced. While he stresses, in a set of country and regional analyses, that performance and potential vary enormously between countries, he warns against any idea that the richer countries of the world can be fenced off from the tensions in the third world: migration, political and military upheaval, economic clashes and, above all, ecological degradation ensure that this is a global conflict.

Kennedy is not fatalistic about these trends, but he does stress that most of them are unavoidable over the next decades and that the state, while remaining the main instrument for addressing them, is increasingly inadequate to the task of confronting what are global problems. He has nothing to say about one often-proposed solution, global governance and international institutions, and he manages to paint a grim picture without discussing the revival of nationalisms and ethnic conflicts. Kennedy does not claim that the world is bound to deteriorate in the manner he indicates, and he suggests, as Malthus did before him, that there is something states can do. But he is far from sure that all, or indeed any, states will respond, or that, if they did all that was in their power, this would be sufficient.

There is, therefore, a considerable amount of truth in this claim of globalisation, but it needs qualification. First, many of the themes to which people refer – migration and transnational religious movements are obvious examples – long predate the contemporary world. Secondly, the indisputable trends towards globalisation in some domains coincide with – indeed to some extent stimulate – greater division on the other: the politics of ethnicity is one such obvious response. Most important of all, both suggest, for better or worse, and usually worse, that the power of states has been eroded by these transnational forces and that there is less and less that elected governments, or indeed unelected ones, can do to manage the affairs of their countries. Here, there has to be considerable caution. First, as discussed in Chapter 4, globalisation is itself to a considerable extent the work of states, who direct, stimulate, assist companies to do what they want to do: no one believes that Japanese or German business operates independently of the state, nor is it true of their French or Anglo-Saxon competitors. Moreover, there is much that states can do to stimulate competition on the internal plane, even if they have lost some of their control of capital flows and interest rates.

We may, indeed, have to distinguish between two questions: the first, whether any form of human agency – state-based, or other – can cope with the problems we face; the second, whether, given that some purposive strategic response to these questions is possible, this should be based on the state or an international body. The concept of 'global governance' has gained currency in recent years and, shorn of unrealistic aspirations, can be seen as having several components: the strengthening of existing global and regional institutions, the evolution of law and norms prevailing to international behaviour, the protection and promotion of international 'public goods', be these the environment, space, minerals, or the high seas. Yet however far we go, and can go, down that road, the components of that governance structure will, in the main be states, and the considerations that move politicians or publics to accept them will have to encompass a state-based ('national') interest as much as a global one.[14]

The same applies to the domain of legitimate international competition, and of the major global trends threatening society which Paul Kennedy has surveyed. If we take the three factors that Paul Kennedy considers to be the keys to a state's long-run international competitiveness – the quality of education, the status of women, the quality of political leadership – then states, and societies, retain a large measure of freedom in all of these and have only themselves to blame if they fail to act, or blame everything on external pressures. The same applies to the great ecological and demographic threats which Kennedy rightly points out as hanging over the next century: these are not going to be addressed, contained or solved, by a global community, or by transnational forces. States, and only states, albeit urged on and assisted by unofficial bodies, have the power to do something about these. If anything, the challenges that Kennedy and others have identified make the need for states greater than ever before: the disciplines, and the cost, of adjustment policies are ones that only they can impose.

The growing importance of the international, both real and apparent, is therefore a more historically complex, and two-sided, process than a simple assertion of how international the world has become would lead us to suspect. The world is moving in at least two contradictory directions simultaneously. That much was evident in the broad process of change already taking place: it is even more clear in the world we have entered most recently, as a result of the changes of the latter half of the 1980s.

This brings us to the last of the perspectives on the contemporary world, the optimistic one that somehow we have found an answer, both internationally and domestically, and that things are going to be better. If I would agree that military competition between major states is, for a time at least, improbable, this does not mean that conflict in international relations will decline or that anything approaching a 'new world order' has been, or can be, created. For a brief period in 1988 and 1989, when the USA and USSR were working together to reduce points of tension, the term 'new world order' had a real, if limited, meaning. The collapse of the USSR has deprived it of that meaning, and the proliferation of conflict, not only in the third world, but in the Balkans as well, shows how unfounded this oneiric outlook was. Even in its liberal internationalist form, according to which the great powers will do their best to help sort out the world, it is misleading, since it overstates the willingness of the governments, or populations, of the developed world to assume their global responsibilities.

The 'End of History'

The collapse of communism and the apparent spread of liberal democratic political forms to a range of countries, post-communist and third world, has led some to suggest that a new era of global democracy is at hand. This is in essence the argument of Francis Fukuyama, although he is careful to state that he distinguishes between the claim that there is no other viable model on offer from the claim that its consolidation in all countries is imminent or even plausible. The discussion of the end of the Cold War may, therefore, serve as an introduction to the last of the underlying themes brought out by this survey – the question of whether we are now confronted with what Fukuyama calls the end of history.[15] By history, Fukuyama means a period in which humanity is in conflict over fundamental values and marshals its forces in the international arena for such a competition of values. It has been fashionable to denigrate Fukuyama, but there are several ways in which his arguments merit more serious attention.

First is his assertion of the importance of progress in contemporary history: Fukuyama is not saying that progress is without costs, nor that it is destined to continue, but he does assert that humanity as a whole has made progress of a significant kind over recent centuries and that it has the capacity, ecological and nuclear disaster aside, to continue. In this way he rejects both the pessimism of the right – that history is circular, unintelligible, or straight decadent – and that of the left, based on various forms of historical romanticism or, in the case of Wallerstein, on a combative assertion of overall human decline since 1400.[16] This cautiously but confidently optimistic note is worth asserting, not only because there is something which most people would recognise as progress (like 'imperialism' and 'patriarchy' it leaves much to be desired as a concept, yet *faute de mieux* we need to go on using it) but also because in order to argue about progress, and whether or not one accepts that it has occurred, one needs some universal analytic and moral criteria. In the contemporary intellectual climate, of nationalist and religious particularism, and postmodernist confusion of all kinds, this firm eighteenth-century assertion of the possibility of universal criteria, whatever their historic, social and geographical origins, is to be welcomed. In that sense those who deny there has been progress, Wallerstein included, are themselves allies against those who say we cannot know.

Secondly, Fukuyama has something important to say about the Cold War. His account of why and how communism collapsed is contestable, but his judgement of the end, that one side won and the other side lost, needs asserting. This may seem rather obvious, and no doubt it is to those who have been on the losing side and who are scrambling to get as much of capitalism as they can. But it has to be said that it is not obvious in much left and liberal discourse in the West. As has been discussed in Chapter 8, prior to 1989 the dominant view here was that the Cold War was not about an ideological or inter-systemic conflict at all – this was the myth of the Pentagon, the KGB and odd people such as myself who tried to say so – but about a *pas de deux* of two hegemonic systems. Each pretended to rival the other, but in fact used the pretence of conflict to hold down their own people, make money out of useless military production and so on. Such analysis went from the perfectly justifiable claims that some people, such as arms manufacturers, benefited from the Cold War and the attendant arms race, that many of the ideological claims about free worlds and socialist democracy were false, and that the Cold War enabled other forms of intra-bloc hegemony to be preserved, to the quite different and unwarranted conclusion that the inter-systemic conflict was an illusion. Even after 1989 there was a solipsistic argument to the effect that, while the former Soviet system collapsed and failed, so in some ways did the West – viz. the social and economic crisis in the USA: as if anyone could fight and win a war without some losses, or that the end of one titanic conflict, be it the Second World War or the Cold War, would not lead to further conflicts in the future.[17] The reality, as Fukuyama underlines, is that the advanced capitalist West did win the Cold War.[18]

The third issue on which Fukuyama is interesting is that of liberal democracy itself. Of course, his invocation of this concept is selective and ahistorical. That most classical liberals did not believe in universal suffrage, or the equality of nations, and did believe in an interventionist state is not recognised by him. He seems to espouse the view that 'markets' can somehow effect social change, neglecting the fact that markets, like houses and sausages, are man-made: there can no more be a market-led account of history than a house-driven or for that matter a sausage-driven theory.

The main thrust of his argument is, moreover, inclined towards the complacent, that a solution has been found, in 'liberal democracy', and that it will, more or less, last for ever. But there is another reading of Fukuyama possible, not least in this age of the dethroned author: namely, that while liberal democracy will prevail as the dominant solution to politics in the contemporary world it is itself inherently unstable, and liable to self-destruction. This, eminently Hegelian and pre-Marxist, argument rests upon the destabilising effects of *thymos*, what he regards as the human drive for recognition and respect, both with regard to relations within states and to those between them. His reasons as to why this model may not mark the end of history are to be questioned, but are less important than this cogent assertion of the inherent limits and contested future of the political form now claimed to be the solution to humanity's problems. And even those Marxists who still hold the inevitability of revolutionary socialist outcome as capitalism digs its own grave, need to be reminded that there is an alternative path which liberal democracy could take: namely, a regression to various forms of barbarism, national and international, via the prevailing of some mixture of capitalist-authoritarian, nuclear, ecological, racist and recidivist trends.

The fourth area where Fukuyama's argument is to be welcomed concerns his analysis of the trend towards universalisation in the contemporary world, the theme of Chapter 5. Here again his thesis might appear to be self-evident, were it not for the fact that substantial theoretical resistance to it can be detected from several quarters. One source of this resistance has already been noted with regard to the argument on the Cold War, on the part of those who denied that both Soviet communism and Western capitalism sought to prevail over the other. Underlying this view is a belief that persists even in a post-Cold-War situation, namely that capitalism in some way 'needs' an enemy.

The theoretical import of this idea has been discussed in Chapter 8. Here it is worth spelling out the practical consequences: with communism gone, it is suggested, some other bogey, such as ethnic minorities, or Islam, has to be evoked. In some cases, this is used to explain the genesis of the Gulf War. In fact, as Marx and Engels pointed out so well in section two of the *Communist Manifesto*, capitalism does not need an enemy at all, but seeks to make the world like itself, 'on pain of extinction' – more or less what happened to the Bolshevik Revolution. Rarely articulated, this 'needed enemy' argument underpins much of the critical literature on Cold War, in its reluctance to see why and how capitalism has developed a universalising dynamic, not just at the level of markets and productive relations, but also in political forms and cultural patterns.

Resistance to this idea is also found in a theoretical school that Fukyama criticises, but not enough, namely the 'realism' of state-centric International Relations theory, epitomised by Waltz and discussed in Chapter 2, according to which all that matters are relations between states, and the internal character of them is to be disregarded as 'reductionist'. Fukuyama criticises realism as being inapposite to a post-Cold-War situation where inter-dependence is growing:[19] but here he fails to see the import of his argument as a whole, which is that realism was never an adequate explanation of international relations. There was always a universalising element in the system, ever since capitalism began to develop transnationally in the sixteenth century.

Prospects for Liberal Democracy and Peace

The problems with the Fukuyama argument are many, but suggest, for their part, what a programme of future theoretical and historical work may be. Absent from the 1989 article, there is here a powerful psychological component to the historical thesis based on the Greek term *thymos*: his interpretation of this may raise as many problems as it solves.[20] Much has been made of how Fukuyama's confident extrapolations are supposedly wrong – wars will continue, Islam is a threat, the 1.4 billion people still lived under communist party rule as opposed to 1.7 billion before 1989, and so forth. These do not really challenge his central theme, since neither post-Maoist modernisation, nor Islamic fundamentalism, are challenges on a global stage: the 'Islamic threat' is little more than a malign combination of clerical bombast and Western paranoia. The real challenge to the 'West' (a hypostatisation we could well do without) is from Japan, not Iran or Algeria: where, one might ask, is the technological or investment challenge from these latter states?

Where Fukuyama is, on empirical grounds, more shaky is in two other respects: first, in his belief that capitalism can bring the whole of the world up to current developed levels; second, in the degree to which he believes liberal democracy is now spreading. In the former, a restatement in RAND corporation terms of the view cogently expressed by Bill Warren, he is right to criticise the myths of dependency theory, but ignores the facts which stare at

one every year from Table 1 of the *World Bank Report*, namely
that while few countries outside Africa are getting poorer, the gap
between rich and poor states is widening. Moreover, as Giovanni
Arrighi has so well pointed out,[21] the membership of the club of
rich states has remained constant for over a century – no one has
left, although the members have changed places in the pecking
order, and only one state has joined, namely Japan.

The belief in liberal democracy understates the degree to which
capitalist democracy is precarious: it needs to last for a generation
at least before it can be assumed it will endure. One only has to
think about the Weimar Republic, or about such states as Sri Lanka,
Liberia, Argentina, Lebanon in the 1960s to see how dictatorship
can be re-established. In this, historically more cautious, perspective, there are only about two dozen established liberal democracies
in the world today, out of what are now over 180 independent
states.

This historically superficial view of democracy is linked to an
idealist and most misleading account of how democracy came
about. The dates he gives for the establishment of liberal
democracy – 1790 for the USA, 1848 for Britain etc. – are those of
constitutional myth. The reality, which Goran Therborn has so
well shown, is that full democracy, including, among other
criteria, one person, one vote, and only one vote per person, came
to these two states in the 1960s, and, as a result not of the
evolution of the system in some idealist manner, but of political
action, of struggle.[22]

Here we come to the central theoretical problem of Fukuyama's
work which is not about whether history has come to an end, but
of what constitutes history and, more specifically, historical
agency. Behind all theories of the end of history there lies a theory
of agency. That most people have some working answer to this
question is evident if we just list some of the candidates for motor
of history that have occurred in recent centuries: God, gods, the
stars, Reason, the balance of power, the working class, the
bourgeoisie, the peasantry – indeed virtually every class except the
one that may have done more than any other to shape the
twentieth century, the petty bourgeoisie – the intelligentsia,
conspiracy theories of all shapes and sizes, the economy, and, as
we have recently seen, the market. No doubt more are to come.

Fukuyama's answer is idealist, it being economic scientific

development combined with the evolution of human freedom that constitutes the motor of history, or, as he calls it, 'the Mechanism'. Here there is a lot to disagree with. His account of the evolution of science is singularly innocent of the Kuhnian and other institutional studies of how power relations determine scientific progress – compare the amount of money being spent on arms as against AIDS research. He seems to ascribe to it a direction independent of human intent and interest. More to the point, he ignores what is the main motor of human history, in this and previous centuries, namely collective political action, action by groups be these classes, nations, states. The span of world history since Hegel and Marx, and not least the collapse of communism, encourages us to rethink how collective action operates and to enlarge the range of such possible actors, while taking away the priority and historical role ascribed in socialist theory with too much ease to the proletariat.

Indeed it is the retheorisation of this question that constitutes the major challenge of Fukuyama's book. Faced with the evident discrediting of the teleology and the agency underlying most Marxist theory, it is not necessary to revert simply to the idealist assertion of a world spirit, now presented as science and *thymos*, shaping the course of events, any more than it is to collapse into post-modernist vacuity and frivolity. The problem with Fukuyama's theory, and his account of history, is fundamentally the same as that of Hegel himself. There is, of course, a classical solution to this problem: to do to Fukuyama what Feuerbach did to Hegel, namely turn him on his head.

In International Relations we have been rather too cavalier about this issue, moving from states to system and back again, and ignoring other candidates. We have been particularly coy about the word 'capitalism', a term of which sociologists are not shy and which one supposes can characterise the international system of the past few centuries as aptly as any other. International Relations has indeed proceeded as if agency was a marginal category, compared to the various determinations of the inter-state or global hierarchical systems that are normally upheld as the proper objects of study. To answer Fukuyama involves, however, an answer to this level of his argument, the positing of an alternative theory of agency in international affairs, and hence of both an alternative past and an alternative present. This would seem, in the face of the rather deplorable record of much of the twentieth century and of the daunting problems that confront the world as it heads towards the end of that century, to be a task with some normative as well as analytic urgency. It is also one that brings International Relations into the orbit of other social sciences. Exculpatory abstractions about history, system, structure and the like have little more validity than the invocation of the divine, or the astrological. We are all participants in the making of the future.

11

Conclusion: The Future of International Relations

This book has been concerned with ideas as to how the international has been, or may be, changed; it has also suggested processes and mechanisms for such change, be it the transnationalism of society and ideology, the 'emancipatory' forces of class and group, or the construction of forms of global governance. Any such agency evokes questions not only of efficacy, but also of ethical foundation. The preceding chapters have been focused elsewhere, on the relationship between domestic and international politics, and on the implications of this for analysing how the international system works. In conclusion, however, it seems appropriate to turn to the moral questions raised by the turn in international events of the the late 1980s and to offer what any theoretical approach should offer, a programme for future work.

The Challenge of the Normative

International affairs are, notoriously, the area where moral considerations apply least, and we have come to accept different moral criteria for states than for individuals. But at the same time the international is a domain replete with moral claims and counter-claims, not least from nationalists, and even to accept a supposed reality is itself to take a moral position. It is worth noting, as well, that in recent years some moral questions, separate from the claims of nations and states, have come, if anything, to play an even greater role in public discussion, and public justification, than before: economic justice, human rights, ecological responsibility. The 'ought' will not go away. What turns out to be less developed is the set of criteria and discriminations which we are able to make in this domain.[1]

Two normative questions raised most directly by recent international crisis, and indirectly by the fall of communism, are those of nationalism and of intervention. Most of the work done on nationalism in recent years has been on its historical and sociological aspects: yet what has attracted much less attention are the normative claims underlying it. These are that we all belong to a nation, that the nation, embodied in its leaders has a claim over us, that it gives us an identity. Closely related, and brutally present in the Balkan wars of the early 1990s, is the further normative claim that nations, defined by their leaders, have claims, given by God, gods or history, to territory.

It is utopian, in the bad sense, to envisage a world in which the claims of nations, on people or on territory, have no salience at all. But it is important to note just how threadbare both of these claims are: there is little beyond a casual utilitarianism to justify why one should owe loyalty to a motley collection of people into whose midst one happens to be born, or why one can assert one particular claim over territory when every bit of the earth's surface bears multiple claims, if not from the living then from the dead. Here there is considerable force in the views of Ernest Gellner, who stressed the contingency of national identity and the existence of nations and of the late Elie Kedourie, who saw in the spread of both these principles – the claim of community over individual, and of these self-defined communities over territory – a bane of the modern world.[2]

These principles do, however, now prevail, but we have to find ways to temper and to reduce them. And yet much of what we aspire to introduce into the international system still rests on the acceptance of both as valid and permanent features of international relations. People have a right to live in communities and in a way that meets their wishes, and that usually means, and will go on meaning, in national communities, with, hopefully, a state and territory to reflect this. But we have gone far too far in accepting either of these principles as supreme, given the ethical weakness, and nefarious consequences, that accompany them.

The issue of intervention abuts not so much onto the question of ethnicity or national rights, but onto that of state sovereignty, and it was sharply posed by the end of the Gulf War and by events elsewhere, in Bosnia and Somalia. This is arguably the greatest change in the international agenda in recent years, and poses a set of questions, moral as well as practical, for us all.[3]

In the case of the Gulf War it was posed not so much by the war over Kuwait as by decisions taken, after the war, and after the Iraqi popular uprising, to establish a 'safe haven' in northern Iraq.[4] For in the post-war situation, the US, UK and France intervened to establish a form of separate state within northern Iraq, and in support of the indigenous Kurdish population.

There is no precedent for this in post-war history: seen in some of the Arab world as a form of colonialism, or of the old imperialist policy of partition, it nonetheless accorded with the wishes of the Kurdish people themselves, whose subsequently elected leaders made clear that they wanted the safe haven policy to continue. This was a practical and innovative implementation of the policy of humanitarian intervention, meaning by this not that the intervening powers had only humanitarian motives, a condition that would be impossible to meet, but that it had in part a humanitarian motivation and that its consequences were of clear and substantial benefit to the populations concerned. This action constituted a direct challenge to the sovereignty of Iraq, and a dramatic innovation in the field of human rights policy. The questions which it raised on the moral level were several and were posed in classical form by John Stuart Mill: first, what degree of tyranny or oppression justifies or obligates such an intervention; secondly, at what cost such an intervention could be carried out; thirdly, whether it could be carried out only in support of an identifiable ethnic group or more generally. But once the principle is admitted reasonable, and general, answers to these questions can be formed.[5]

At one level intervention involves not norms, but prudence. But there is nonetheless a normative question here, pertaining both to the issue of state sovereignty and equally to the obligations of states. Much of the western discussion focused on the issue not of what the consequences of not intervening are, itself a consideration of moral import, but of whether 'we' meaning Britain and other states ought to have done so. From where does this 'ought' come? From where, indeed, does the 'ought' come with regard to third world poverty, or individual cases of human rights? The answer is that, in the first instance, it comes from the UN Charter, paragraph 24 of which obligates the members of the Security Council to 'assume primary responsibility for the maintenance of international peace and security'.

Here we come to a question that is much discussed in the literature of international relations, but which public discussion fights shy of for understandable reasons, namely the role of the great powers. In law, all states are sovereign and equal, but in reality they are not, and they are far more unequal than individuals in a state. For much of the past century, the international system was run by great powers through the mechanisms of imperialism, which held subject peoples down, and which led these imperial powers to contend with, and fight, each other on a variety of pretexts. Imperialism in the sense of formal domination or colonialism, even in the rather peculiar Soviet form, is over, and, so might it be thought, is any pre-eminent role for the Great Powers.

As I have argued, conflict *between* the great powers may no longer be the motor of international politics, and the public opinions of the major states are reluctant to incur the kinds of risks once acceptable. But this only poses, in sharper form, the dilemma for international diplomacy, since, if these powers are not going to take the lead, who is? The record of the Gulf crisis is clear, and in the eyes of many discredits it: without the US lead nothing would have happened. In the case of the Balkans, one of the reasons so little did happen, and why the Serbians believed, rightly, that they could press on with their campaigns, is that the US appeared to regard this as a European matter. One of the arguments used for Congress's refusal to ratify Woodrow Wilson's support for the League of Nations was, precisely, anxiety about becoming involved in Balkan wars.

Yet some leading role for the great powers would seem to be inevitable and indeed desirable, just as the role of the major economic and financial powers is desirable and necessary in the field of international economic managements. The question is not whether they do or do not play a role, but rather whether this is unilateral, competitive and short-sighted, or whether it is a multilateral, more cooperative, and long-term policy. The alternative to Article 24 is not international harmony, but a world in which no one takes primary responsibility for the maintenance of international peace and security. The inhabitants of the Balkans saw quite a lot of this in 1991–4: one can doubt if they would recommend it to the world as a whole.

These two questions, of nationalism and intervention, and the related issues of the great powers, touch upon what is perhaps the most pervasive and difficult of all the normative issues confronting the world at the moment, namely that of universal versus particular values. Since the eighteenth century there has been a current in Western thought that has asserted the validity of certain universal, rationally based, moral principles of relevance to political life – the rights of the individual, secularism, democracy in some form or another. It has been amplified in recent times to include more explicit recognition of the equality of gender and of race. These values are by no means universally supported, nor do they permit of unequivocal interpretation. But they are now enshrined in political documents, national and international, and it is very much part of the optimistic post-Cold-War view of the world that they are now set to prevail. It has already been suggested in Chapter 10, that, in any immediate sense, they are not set to prevail, because the conditions under which, say, democracy can sustain itself are not given in most countries in the world.

But there has increasingly been another challenge, to the effect that these values are in themselves questionable, and that other value systems, of other provenances, have equal or even greater value. The proponents of religious fundamentalism are front-runners in this regard, but there is a broader current, evident in East Asia, of contesting what is said to be a Western and ethnocentric value system. Out of sympathy, or support for a position loosely termed post-modernist, many in the West have also subscribed to this relativistic challenge to any single grand normative code.

There is, historically, much validity in this critique: these codes were produced in particular countries, reflecting their background and values, and it was not accident that these were in large measure the same countries who occupied and dominated much of the rest of the world.[6] Increasing liberty at home coincided with spoliation abroad. There has also been a great degree of hypocrisy in the claims made for normative rectitude on the part of the dominant Western powers: they did more than any others to violate sovereignty over the past century or two; the greatest crimes against humanity have been committed in this century on European soil.

But these reservations do not invalidate the larger claim that on matters of primary normative and political concern there is a measure of international consensus around a set of values that, on grounds quite independent of their origin, can be based on reason and which bear, for reasons that social scientists can happily argue over, some relationship to economic prosperity and peace, both domestic and international. It is a pity, indeed it is very dangerous, that just at the moment when a new international situation emerges, there should be a faltering of political nerve in the countries with the greatest international influence on what does, and does not, constitute a desirable political system. This may please the more critical in these societies, but one may doubt if it will do much to help those in the rest of the world who, when asked, tend to want more rather than less of the universal principles happier countries take for granted. In the international debate, it is often those in power, and who benefit from current variations in international norm, who are the first to tell us that universal criteria do not apply: governments, clergymen, indeed men in general, are those who trumpet normative exceptionalism. Yet independence, secularism, equality, the rule of law, and a range of economic and social privileges, constitute a good life as internationally defined.

Here we come back to the issue of intervention and how far, and in what ways, the international community should seek to enforce these norms, pertaining not just to relations between states, but also to those within them. We cannot construe international relations, or the role of the great powers, primarily in terms of a muscular normative police: but we can see that any realistic, and cooperative, policies designed to further respect for these principles is desirable, and develop policies to make it so. If we do not do so, this will constitute a great abdication, even if it is defended in the name of individuality, anti-hegemonism or plain post-modernist whimsy.

Alternatives in Research

The neglect of the normative in most International Relations literature of the post-1945 epoch, be it in its north American or British variants, is in part to be attributed to the fear of falling into the mistakes of the inter-war 'utopians', in part to the rather too close identification of the discipline with the priorities, and temper, of states. Methodological orientation, in this case a complacency of value, is as much the servant of power as is apologetic explanation. Yet the neglect of the normative is, as much as anything, highlighted by the uncertainty which has come to prevail in public discussion, academic and other, in the aftermath of the Cold War, with anxiety about the overall direction of political life intersecting with the vacuities of post-modernism and ethical relativism. The only suitable response to this double crisis, of international analysis and ethical meandering, is to offer an alternative set of themes on which to base research and analysis.

What this particular survey of International Relations suggests is one such agenda for the study of international relations, based on greater awareness of a range of concepts that have hitherto had a secondary or marginal place in the discipline, and on a methodological orientation that eschews the cult of quantification, prediction and 'scientificity' for a commitment to theoretical and historical explanation. In this light, the preceding chapters can be summarised to suggest the following research programme:

(1) the forms of expansion of the capitalist system, from, the fifteenth century onwards, its contradictory impact on the pre-capitalist world, the evolution of forms of inter-capitalist relationship and capitalism's conflict with the transitory non-capitalist bloc of twentieth century communism;

(2) the examination of how capitalism operates as an international system and of the specific political forms, the sovereign state and the ideology of nationalism, that it has produced and maintained, with, in the present context in particular, a measured assessment of the changing forms of interaction between states and global processes;

(3) the manner in which agency, including but not specifically that of classes, operates transnationally, both in its constitution and in its influence, taking into account the impact of informed and active non-governmental actors, e.g. on matters of ecology or human rights, the international organisation of

hegemonic social groups, and the, fragmented but recurrent, international actions of subordinated groups;

(4) the study of conflict in its social and political context, the analysis of war, beyond the fetishism of arms races and balances of power, and of the role of both ethnic mobilisation and social revolution in fracturing and constituting the international system;

(5) the formulation and potential implementation of moral principles, and, where agreement is not possible, a minimal agreed form of legitimate moral debate, on issues pertinent to the international – loyalty, identity, security, equality, freedom, amongst others.

Given the combination of political turmoil and theoretical confusion that appear to be accompanying the end of the twentieth century, the challenge, and responsibilities, of a discipline concerned with the international would appear to be larger than ever. The greatest dangers would be agnosticism, analytic or moral, or a relapse in the conformities of either side of the Atlantic. Those conformities may now have exhausted themselves, as much as the international context in which they originated. However, it would be equally mistaken to confuse what is undoubtedly a major turning point in world history with an assumed necessity to overthrow all established conceptual systems. The 'presentism' of international affairs need not, though it may, entail a revision of theoretical approaches, analytic or moral. The least one can say is that the two issues, of change in world history and change in philosophical and theoretical orientation, have to be kept separate: the collapse of the Berlin Wall, or the internationalisation of capital and labour, do not imply that there is no longer a distinction between 'ought' and 'is', or that basic forms of rationalism are now invalidated, any more than it means the earth is flat or the moon is really, after all, made of cheese. The research programme outlined here, and developed through the critical chapters of this book, would suggest that there are many conceptual tools available to analyse, and provide moral orientation in, the post-Cold War world.

If there is validity in the claim that we have as citizens, as politicians, as academics, been 'sleep-walking' through history, then the conclusion, evident enough, is that we need to be a little more alert and awake. We shall hear, and indeed are already hearing, much reflection on the end of the century, and the start of a new millennium. All of this may be portentous irrelevancy, not least because for much of the world the millennium corresponds to another chronological system: there are at least six other systems of counting the years to be found in the world to date — the Judaic, the Muslim, the Zoroastrian Persian, the Ethiopian, the Chinese and the Japanese – and their millennia come and go at different times. There is nothing more ethnocentric than the year 2000. But if the idea of millennium, like that of examinations, helps to focus minds, so much the better.

Political leaders, elected and unelected, have had a pretty poor record over the past hundred years, but the scientists, natural or social, have also had mixed reports. The danger has been not that social scientists have been *too* removed from the concerns of power, political or entrepreneurial, but that they have not had enough distance from them, have not exerted themselves forcefully enough to rise above the supposed common sense of their epoch, and have consoled themselves with the vacuous and the insignificant: hence, on the part of the natural sciences, the effort devoted to weapons of mass destruction and the failure, till very late in the day, to predict the impact of mankind on the environment, distortions amply reproduced by the social scientists, including those in International Relations. Here, above all, the social scientists have often failed to display independence and intellectual enterprise. For all, politicians and academics, natural scientists and social scientists, the least that can be said is that the record of the past hundred years has not been a very good one and that the enormous suffering visited on humanity can teach us the better to address the questions we face. Many of the forces that will shape the next century, and the next millennium, and which will shape the agenda of politicians and social scientists alike, have already been unleashed: they had better take stock of them now. Perhaps it would not be too unrealistic to hope that a better job can be done in the next century than was made of it in the last.

Notes

1 Introduction: The Pertinence of the 'International'

1. The belief in a single paradigm as 'normal' and desirable received confirmation from Thomas Kuhn's *The Structure of Scientific Revolutions* (London: University of Chicago, 1962). The contrary argument, that diversity is desirable, was made in Paul Feyerabend's *Against Method* (London: NLB, 1975).
2. This 'international' context for the spread of nationalism is recognised by a variety of theories, whether the political theory of Elie Kedourie (*Nationalism*, London: Hutchinson, 1960) or the sociological approach of Ernest Gellner (*Nations and Nationalism*, Oxford: Basil Blackwell, 1983).
3. Robin Blackburn, *The Overthrow of Colonial Slavery, 1776-1848* (London: Verso, 1988).
4. Ulrich Albrecht, *Internationale Politik* (Munich: Oldenbourg, 1986) ch. 9, 'Das Demokratieproblem in der internationalen Politik'.
5. For surveys of this see Howard Williams, *International Relations in Political Theory* (Milton Keynes: Open University Press, 1992); Torbjorn Knutsen, *A History of International Relations Theory* (Manchester: Manchester University Press, 1992); Terry Nardin and David Mapel (eds) *Traditions of International Ethics* (Cambridge: Cambridge University Press, 1992); Martin Wight, *International Theory: The Three Traditions* (Leicester University Press, 1991).
6. For general histories and surveys of IR see, amongst others, Margot Light and A.J.R. Groom (eds) *International Relations: A Handbook of Current Theory* (London: Frances Pinter, 1985; 2nd edn forthcoming 1994); Steve Smith (ed.) *International Relations: British and American Perspectives* (Oxford: Basil Blackwell, 1985); Hugh Dyer and Leon Mangassarian (eds) *The Study of International Relations: The State of the Art* (London: Macmillan, 1989); Marc Williams (ed.) *International Relations in the Twentieth Century: A Reader* (Basingstoke: Macmillan, 1989); William Olson and A.J.R. Groom *International Relations Then and Now* (London: Routledge, 1992).
7. Woodrow Wilson, 'The coming age of peace' from *The State* (1918) excerpted in Evan Luard (ed.) *Basic Texts in International Relations* (Basingstoke: Macmillan, 1992) pp. 267–71.
8. E.H. Carr, *The Twenty Years Crisis* (London: Macmillan, 1966); Hans Morgenthau, *Politics Among Nations*, 5th edn (New York: Alfred Knopf, 1978); Henry Kissinger, *A World Restored* (Boston: Houghton Mifflin, 1957); Kenneth Waltz, *Man, the State and War* (New York: Columbia University Press, 1954).

9. Hedley Bull, *The Anarchical Society* (Oxford: Oxford University Press, 1977); Fred Northedge, *The International Political System* (London: Faber & Faber, 1976).

10. Alan James, *Sovereign Statehood* (London: Allen & Unwin, 1986) and his counter-attack against recent theoretical developments in IR, 'The realism of realism: The state and the study of international relations', *Review of International Studies*, vol. 15, no. 2, July 1989; Michael Donelan, *Elements of International Political Theory* (Oxford: Clarendon, 1990); James Mayall, *Nationalism and International Society* (Cambridge: Cambridge University Press, 1990); Adam Watson, *The Evolution of International Society* (London: Routledge, 1992).

11. Carl Schmitt, *The Concept of The Political* (New Brunswick, NJ: Rutgers University Press, 1975).

12. Charles Merriam, *Political Power* (New York: McGraw-Hill, 1939); Harold Lasswell, *Who Gets What, When, How* (Cleveland, Ohio: The World Publishing Company, 1958).

13. For a cogent critique of the assumptions of realism see Justin Rosenberg, 'What's the matter with realism?' *Review of International Studies*, vol. 16, no. 3, October 1990.

14. Karl Deutsch, *Nationalism and Social Communication* (New York: Wiley, 1953); James Rosenau (ed.) *Linkage Politics* (New York: Free Press, 1969); Morton Kaplan, *System and Process in International Politics* (New York: Wiley, 1957).

15. This debate is resumed in Klaus Knorr and James Rosenau (eds) *Contending Approaches to International Politics* (Princeton: Princeton University Press, 1969). See also the contemporaneous debate between Rosenau and Northedge in *Millennium*, vol. 5, no. 1, 1976.

16. I am particularly grateful to my colleague Michael Banks for his assessment of this debate: see, for example, his 'The inter-paradigm debate' in Light and Groom (eds) *International Relations*.

17. See in particular the chapter in Light and Groom (eds) *International Relations* by Christopher Hill and Margot Light.

18. Robert Keohane and Joseph Nye (eds) *Transnational Relations and World Politics* (Cambridge, MA: Harvard University Press, 1971).

19. Kenneth Waltz, 'The myth of national interdependence' in Charles Kindelberger (ed.) *The International Corporation* (Cambridge, MA: MIT Press, 1970).

20. Stephen Krasner, *Structural Conflict: The Third World Against Global Liberalism* (Berkeley: University of California Press, 1985).

21. Robert Tucker, *The Inequality of Nations* (London: Martin Robertson, 1977).

22. Kenneth Waltz, *Theory of International Relations* (New York: Random House, 1979).

23. John Burton, *World Society* (Cambridge: Cambridge University Press, 1972). For a critique of Burton see Christopher Hill, 'Implications of the world society perspective for national foreign

policies' in Michael Banks (ed.) *Conflict in World Society: A New Perspective on International Relations* (Brighton: Wheatsheaf, 1984).

24. For an alternative, sociological, approach to foreign policy, see David Gibbs *The Political Economy of Third World Intervention: Mines, Money, and U.S. Policy in the Congo Crisis* (London: University of Chicago Press, 1991).

25. Examples of this interaction between historical sociology and the international include John Hall, *Powers and Liberties* (London: Pelican, 1986) and Michael Mann, *The Sources of Social Power*, vol. 1 (Cambridge: Cambridge University Press, 1988). These issues were explored further at a series of seminars, funded by the Economic and Social Research Council, under the title 'Structural Decline in the West' held at Cambridge between 1988 and 1991. The proceedings of the first of these conferences are in Michael Mann (ed.) *The Rise and Decline of The Nation State* (Oxford: Basil Blackwell, 1990).

26. Two examples: the role of 'imperialism' in shaping and distorting the national economies of third world states; the role of the Cold War in strengthening centralised government in the USA and producing a 'national security state'.

27. For work on this see references in Note 5, above, also Charles Beitz, *Political Theory and International Relations* (Princeton: Princeton University Press, 1979) and 'Sovereignty and morality in international affairs' in David Held (ed.) *Political Theory Today* (Cambridge: Polity Press, 1991); Andrew Linklater, *Men and Citizens in the Theory of International Relations* (London: Macmillan, 1981) and *Beyond Realism and Marxism: Critical Theory and International Relations* (Basingstoke: Macmillan, 1990); John Vincent, *Human Rights and International Relations* (Oxford; Oxford University Press, 1988).

28. This is, amongst other things, the domain of international economy. See in particular Susan Strange, *States and Markets: An Introduction to International Political Economy* (London: Pinter, 1988).

2 Theories in Contention

1. This is a point well made in the stimulating work of Charles Reynolds, *The World of States: An Introduction to Explanation and Theory* (Aldershot: Edward Elgar, 1992).

2. Yosi Lapid, 'The third debate: On the prospects of international theory in a post-positivist era', *International Studies Quarterly*, September 1989. What theory needed was not 'post-positivism' but a return to some good, 'pre-positivist', foundations.

3. For two, among many, examples see Michael Howard, *The Lessons of History* (Oxford: Clarendon, 1991), and Walter Laqueur, *World of Secrets, The Uses and Abuses of Intelligence* (London: Weidenfeld & Nicolson, 1985).

4. In the Anglo-Saxon world in particular empiricism has the status of a

secular religion: intellectual ability is conflated with 'general knowledge' – hence the UK competition for someone who knows as many facts as possible goes under the title 'Brain of Britain'.

5. For two powerful critiques of empiricism see C. Wright Mills, *The Sociological Imagination* (Oxford: Oxford University Press, 1959), and David and Judith Willers, *Systematic Empiricism: Critique of a Pseudoscience* (Hemel Hempstead: Prentice-Hall, 1973).

6. On this see the perceptive essay 'History and International Relations' by Christopher Hill in Steve Smith (eds) *International Relations: British and American Approaches* (Oxford: Basil Blackwell, 1985) and his own *Decision-making in British Foreign Policy* (Cambridge: Cambridge University Press, 1990).

7. For earlier critiques of the 'English school' see Michael Nicholson, 'The enigma of Martin Wight', *Review of International Studies*, 1981, vol. 7, no. 1, 1981; Roy Jones 'The English school of international relations: A case for closure?' *Review of International Studies*, vol. 7, no. 1, 1981.

8. For two overviews see Quentin Skinner (ed.) *The Return of Grand Theory in the Human Sciences* (Cambridge: Cambridge University Press, 1985); Perry Anderson, *A Zone of Engagement* (London: Verso, 1992).

9. In Herbert Butterfield and Martin Wight (eds) *Diplomatic Investigations* (London: Allen & Unwin, 1966). Deference to the historians' definition of the subject is present even in the title of the volume.

10. See Chapter 3, below, pp. 56–8, 61–3.

11. For materials in this debate see the exchange between Fred Northedge and James Rosenau in *Millennium*, vol. 5, no. 1, 1976, and the chapters in Klaus Knorr and James Rosenau (eds) *Contending Approaches to International Politics* (Princeton: Princeton University Press 1969). For an earlier perceptive 'British' critique of US political science, touching on many of the same issues raised in the IR debate, see Bernard Crick, *The American Science of Politics* (London, Routledge & Kegan Paul, 1959).

12. Ekkehart Krippendorff, 'The dominance of American approaches in IR', in Hugh Dyer and Leon Margassaran (eds) *The Study of International Relations: The State of the Art* (London: Macmillan, 1989).

13. James Rosenau, *The Scientific Study of Foreign Policy*, 2nd edn (London: Pinter, 1980); J.P. Singer (ed) *Quantitative International Politics* (New York: Free Press, 1965).

14. For two other rather different critiques of the orthodox view of scientific method see Rom Harré, *The Philosophies of Science* (London: Cambridge University Press, 1972) and Paul Feyerabend, *Against Method* (London, NLB, 1975).

15. For an account see James Dougherty and Robert Pfatzgraff, *Contending Theories of International Relations*, 2nd edn, pp. 347–50 (New York: Harper & Row, 1981). As the authors prudently put it: 'Up to now, statistical techniques have provided no startling results,

and few conclusive ones, useful for the development of a coherent theory of war' (p. 347). The phrase 'up to now' contains, of course, the promise of a breakthrough: more than a decade later none has been reported.

16. Robert Keohane, *After Hegemony: Cooperation and Discord in the World Political Economy* (Princeton: Princeton University Press, 1987).
17. Karl Kautsky, socialist German leader, was the originator of the theory of 'ultra-imperialism', according to which the major powers would reduce their tensions and proceed to collaborate against the rest of the world. Few analyses in the social sciences can have had such an unfortunate short-term fate, since this theory was enunciated in the summer of 1914, as the First World War began. See Karl Kautsky, 'Ultra-imperialism', *New Left Review*, no. 59, January–February 1970.
18. Kenneth Waltz, *Theory of International Politics* (New York: Random House, 1979); significant portions were re-published in Robert Keohane (ed.) *Neo-Realism and its Critics* (New York: Columbia University Press, 1986), which also included a further text by Waltz, 'Reflections on *Theory of International Politics*: A response to my critics'. Subsequent references will give both sources.
19. Waltz, *Theory*, p. 66; Keohane, *Neo-Realism*, p. 53.
20. Waltz, *Theory*, p. 73; Keohane, *Neo-Realism*, p. 62.
21. Goran Therborn, 'The economic theorists of capitalism', *New Left Review*, nos 87–88, September–December 1974, p. 125.
22. Keohane, *Neo-Realism*, p. 329.
23. Waltz, *Theory*, p. 95; Keohane, *Neo-Realism*, p. 90.
24. Waltz, *Theory*, p. 91; Keohane, *Neo-Realism*, p. 85.
25. Waltz, *Theory*, p. 65; Keohane, *Neo-Realism*, p. 52.
26. Keohane, *Neo-Realism*, pp. 323–30.
27. Ibid., p. 323.
28. Ibid., pp. 127–8.
29. For accounts of the emergence of this school see James Der Derian and Michael Shapiro *International/Intertextual Relations: Post Modern Readings of World Politics* (Lexington, MA: D.C. Heath, 1989); Mark Hoffman, 'Restructuring, reconstruction, reinscription and rearticulation: Four voices in critical international theory', *Millennium*, vol. 16, no. 2, 1987.
30. See p. 256, n. 3.
31. One, confused, exception is Richard Ashley in Der Derian and Shapiro, *International/Intertextual Relations*, pp. 317–19. Ashley recognises the existence of these criticisms and then falls back on the advice to listen to marginal groups. Yes, but . . .
32. Der Derian and Shapiro, *International/Intertextual Relations*, pp. ix–x.
33. Among the many critiques of post-modernism see Peter Dews, *Logics of Disintegration* (London: Verso, 1986); Perry Anderson, *In the Tracks of Historical Materialism* (London: Verso, 1983); Ernest

Gellner, *Post-Modernism, Reason and Religion* (London: Routledge, 1992).

34. Robert Walker, *Inside/Outside: International Relations and Political Theory* (Cambridge: Cambridge University Press, 1993).

35. Walker, *Inside/Outside: International Relations and Political Theory*, p. 1.

36. For an illuminating discussion of Weber's views on nationalism and international conflict, and the place of these in his broader work, see Anderson, *A Zone of Engagement*, ch. 9, p. 158.

37. Karl Marx and Friedrich Engels, *The Revolutions of 1848* (London: Penguin, 1973) pp. 70–1.

38. For one illuminating assessment of post-modernism and international affairs see Christopher Norris, *Postmodernism, Intellectuals and the Gulf War* (London: Lawrence & Wishart, 1992).

39. One influential body of literature on the 'new social movements' was that of Ernesto Laclau and Chantal Mouffe, notably their *Hegemony and Social Classes* (London: Verso, 1985). Beyond their own, rather more skilled, deployment of the language and indeed aura of the Parisian debate, it is questionable, with hindsight, whether their analysis had any more purchase on political reality in industrialised democracies than that of the more orthodox Marxist school they claimed to displace. On this see their spirited debate with Norman Geras in *New Left Review*, nos. 163 (May–June 1987), 166 (November–December 1987) and 169 (May–June 1988).

40. See my debate with E.P. Thompson in Robin Blackburn (ed.) *After The Fall* (London: Verso, 1991). Also Paul Hirst 'Peace and political theory', *Economy and Society*, vol. 16, no. 2, May 1987.

3 Necessary Encounter: Historical Materialism and International Relations

1. On the history of independent Marxism see Perry Anderson, *Considerations on Western Marxism* (London: NLB, 1976). For one representative of that tradition see Karl Korsch, *Marxism and Philosophy*, translated and introduced by Fred Halliday (London: NLB, 1970).

2. See Miklos Molnar, *Marx, Engels et la Politique Internationale* (Paris, Gallimard, 1975); Vendulka Kubalkova and Andrew Cruickshank, *Marxism and International Relations* (Oxford: Oxford University Press, 1986); Tony Thorndike, 'Marxism and International Relations' in Trevor Taylor (ed.) *Approaches and Theory in International Relations* (London: Longman, 1978).

3. Stephen Gill (ed.) *Gramsci, Historical Materialism and International Relations* (Cambridge: Cambridge University Press, 1992); Robert Cox, 'Social forces, states and world orders: Beyond international

relations theory', *Millennium*, vol. 10, no 2, summer 1981. Cox's work, a breakthrough in theoretical terms, relied rather too heavily on an extrapolation from the doomed campaign for a New International Economic Order.

4. Andrew Linklater, *Beyond Realism and Marxism: Critical Theory and International Relations* (London: Macmillan, 1990).

5. Martin Wight in *International Theory: The Three Traditions*, edited by Gabriele Wight and Brian Porter (Leicester: Leicester University Press) has four mentions of Marx, three of which turn out to be repeating his view on force as the midwife of history (pp. 107, 214, 222). At no point does he assess the case for including Marx as a theorist of one of his three categories 'revolutionism'. Morgenthau's *Politics Among Nations*, 5th edn (New York: Alfred A. Knopf, 1978) is no better: all he does is to devote two pages to what he terms the 'devil' theory of imperialism: none of this comes from Marx, whose works he fails to mention at all, and the rest is a simplification of Lenin.

6. For a spirited critique of the orthodox approach see Bill Warren, *Imperialism: Pioneer of Capitalism* (London: Verso, 1981).

7. On this see the very perceptive interpretation by Erica Benner, *Marx and Engels on Nationalism and National Identity: A Reappraisal* (Oxford: Oxford University Press, 1994).

8. Valentino Gerratana, 'Marx and Darwin', *New Left Review*, no. 82, November–December 1973.

9. In his otherwise judicious *The World of States*, Charles Reynolds summarises Marx's theory as 'man is what he eats' (pp. 5, 29): this German pun (*man ist was er isst*) is in fact the view of Feuerbach, whom Marx rejected.

10. Karl Marx and Friedrich Engels, *The German Ideology* (London: Lawrence & Wishart, 1965) pp. 46–7.

11. Ralph Miliband, *The State in Capitalist Society* (London: Weidenfeld & Nicolson, 1969).

12. See, for example, the readings that formed the basis for the innovative Open University course on world politics, in Richard Little and Michael Smith (eds) *Perspectives on World Politics*, 2nd edn (London: Routledge, 1991).

13. Karl Marx, *Capital*, vol. 1, (London: Penguin Books in association with *New Left Review*, 1976) pp. 929–30.

14. On Cox see Note 3, and the discussion by Linklater in *Beyond Realism and Marxism*. On Habermas: Ian Craib, *Modern Social Theory* (Brighton: Harvester/Wheatsheaf, 1984), and Anthony Giddens 'Jurgen Habermas' in Quentin Skinner (ed.) *The Return of Grand Theory in the Human Sciences* (Cambridge: Cambridge University Press, 1985).

15. Susan Strange, *States and Markets* (London, Pinter, 1988); Johann Galtung, 'A structural theory of imperialism' in Michael Smith *et al.* (eds) *Perspectives on World Politics*.

16. On this see, above all, Bill Warren *Imperialism: Pioneer of*

Capitalism, and Nigel Harris, *The End of the Third World* (London; Penguin, 1985).

17. For an illuminating interpretation see Georg Lukacs, *Lenin: A Study in the Unity of his Thought* (London: NLB, 1970), ch. 4.

18. For the original statement see Immanuel Wallerstein, *The Modern World System* (London: Academic, 1974). See *Historical Capitalism* (London: Verso, 1983) for a more succinct statement of his view.

19. Peter Worsley, 'One World or Three: A Critique of the World System of Immanuel Wallerstein' *Socialist Register*, 1980; Ernesto Laclau, *Politics and Ideology in Marxist Theory* (London: NLB, 1977); Theda Skocpol, 'Wallerstein's world capitalist system: A theoretical and historical critique', *American Journal of Sociology*, vol. 82, no. 5, 1977.

20. E.P. Thompson, Fred Halliday and Rudolf Bahro, *Exterminism and Cold War* (London: NLB, 1982).

21. Kees van der Pijl, *The Making of an Atlantic Ruling Class* (London: Verso, 1984). Another influential body of work in parallel here is that of the French 'regulation' school of Alan Lipiers and Michel Aglietta. For a powerful critique of this school see Alice Amsden 'Third World Industrialisation: "Global Fordism" or a New Model', *New Left Review*, no. 182, July–August 1990).

22. Eric Wolf, *Europe and The People Without History* (Berkeley: University of California Press, 1982).

23. Perry Anderson, *Lineages of the Absolutist State* (London: NLB/ Verso, 1974).

24. *The Age of Revolutions 1789–1848* (London: Weidenfeld & Nicolson, 1962); *The Age of Capital 1848–1875* (London: Weidenfeld & Nicolson, 1975); *The Age of Imperialism 1875–1914* (London: Weidenfeld & Nicolson, 1987).

25. For the best surveys see Molnar, *Marx, Engels et la Politique Internationale*; on war see Bernard Semmel (ed.) *Marxism and the Science of War* (Oxford: Oxford University Press, 1981); on nations and nationalism, see Benner, *Marx and Engels on Nationalism and National Identity*.

26. Derek Sayer, *The Violence of Abstraction* (Oxford: Blackwell, 1987) for a non-reductionist interpretation of Marx.

27. It is this argument which, in addition to forming the central theme of the works of Wolf, Anderson and Hobsbawm mentioned above, forms the basis of Justin Rosenberg's analysis of the origins and development of the international system: *The Empire of Civil Society: A Critique of The Realist Theory of International Relations* (London: Verso, 1994). I am extremely grateful to Justin Rosenberg for the many helpful suggestions he has made on the material in this chapter.

28. Eric Hobsbawm, 'Marx and History', *New Left Review*, no. 143, January–February 1984.

29. The question of the impact of the Vietnam War on IR, and specifically on the writing produced in the USA, might appear to be unanswerable, since its main apparent consequence was to render

some subjects, such as the study of revolutions and social conflict, less attractive. One answer is, however, that the impact is to be found in the interest in 'interdependence', since the conflict in South-East Asia was seen to be provoking major conflict within the USA.

30. Tom Bottomore, *Classes in Modern Society* (London: Allen & Unwin, 1965). For one application to IR see Cox 'Social forces, states and world orders'.

31. One obvious example of this interaction is the oil industry, where, for a century or more, major corporations have influenced and utilised states, in producer and consumer countries, to further their interests: Simon Bromley, *American Hegemony and World Oil* (Cambridge: Cambridge University Press, 1991). For an outstanding account of the interaction of US banks and the US state see Jeffery Frieden, *Banking on The World* (New York: Harper and Row, 1987). For another revealing study of US foreign policy in terms of the influence of business see David Gibbs, *The Political Economy of Third World Intervention*.

32. This is discussed at greater length in Chapter 6.

33. For one illuminating example of the application of Marxist method to a major historical event see Ernest Mandel, *The Meaning of World War II* (London: Verso, 1986).

34. Arno Mayer, *Politics and Diplomacy of Peace-Making: Containment and Counter-Revolution at Versailles, 1918–1919* (New York: Knopf, 1967).

35. See Rosenberg, *The Empire of Civil Society*, ch. 5.

36. Julian Lider, *Correlation of Forces: An Analysis of Marxist-Leninist Concepts* (Aldershot: Gower, 1988); Margot Light, *The Soviet Theory of International Relations* (Brighton: Wheatsheaf, 1988).

4 State and Society in International Relations

1. The argument for a diversity of paradigms is energetically made in Paul Feyerabend, *Against Method* (London: Verso, 1975). Feyerabend's anarchist theory that any paradigm 'goes' is implausible, but his demonstration of the benefits of paradigm competition, and of the many 'non-scientific' factors that go into scientific development, and into the acceptance of paradigms, is convincing.

2. One notable discussion of this is Stanley Hoffmann's 'An American social science: International relations', *Daedalus*, vol. 106, no. 3, October 1977. Hoffman avoids the tendency of some others who have criticised the manner in which a certain North American orthodoxy has dominated International Relations: namely, to pose the question in national terms as that of an 'American' approach. What both the orthodox exponents of International Relations, and their nationalist critics, obscure is that there is immense diversity within the US literature, and that it is the denial of this diversity that constitutes the real problem with the orthodox US presentation.

3. On incommensurability, see T.S. Kuhn, *The Structure of Scientific Revolutions* (Chicago: University of Chicago, 1970) pp. 148ff.

4. Ralph Miliband, *The State in Capitalist Society* (London: Weidenfeld & Nicolson, 1969) is the classic analysis of this question. For an overview of subsequent debates see Bob Jessup, *The Capitalist State* (Oxford: Martin Robertson, 1982).

5. Peter Evans, Dietrich Rueschemeyer and Theda Skocpol (eds) *Bringing the State Back In* (Cambridge: Cambridge University Press, 1985). Among other contributions see John Hall and John Ikenberry, *The State* (Milton Keynes: Open University Press, 1989); John Hall, *Powers and Liberties* (Harmondsworth: Penguin, 1986); John Hall (ed.) *States in History* (Oxford: Basil Blackwell, 1986) and his entry 'State' in Joel Krieger (ed.) *The Oxford Companion to Politics of the World* (Oxford: Oxford University Press, 1993); Michael Banks and Martin Shaw (eds) *State and Society in International Relations* (London: Harvester/Wheatsheaf, 1991); and Anthony Giddens, *The Nation State and Violence* (Cambridge: Cambridge University Press, 1985). Giddens, p. 17, distinguishes the two meanings of the state but does not see this as posing a major problem. A recent discussion of some implications of Giddens' work for international relations is found in Linklater, *Beyond Realism and Marxism*, *passim*.

6. Yale Ferguson and Richard Mansbach, *The Elusive Quest: Theory and International Politics* (Columbia, SC: University of South Carolina Press, 1988) ch. 5: 'The state as an obstacle to international theory'; Ferguson and Mansbach, *The State, Conceptual Chaos, and the Future of International Relations Theory* (London: Lynne Reiner, 1989); Ferguson and Mansbach, 'Between celebration and despair: Constructive suggestions for future international theory', *International Studies Quarterly*, vol. 35, no. 4, December 1991. The 'constructive suggestions' turn out to be general ideas – to be historically aware, etc. – little more than a random list of injunctions.

7. Hedley Bull, *The Anarchical Society* (London: Macmillan, 1977) p. 8; Kenneth Waltz, *Man, The State and War* (New York: Columbia University Press, 1954) pp. 172–8.

8. F.S. Northedge, *The International Political System* (London: Faber & Faber, 1976) p. 15. A more recent statement of this classical position can be found in Alan James, *Sovereign Statehood* (London: Allen & Unwin, 1986). James presents the concept of the state as straightforward, using it to comprise 'territory, people and a government' (p. 13).

9. This is the argument of Cornelia Navari in her introduction to *The Condition of States* (Milton Keynes: Open University Press, 1991) pp. 11–15. Her awareness of the different meanings of state is not replicated in the chapters of her other contributors.

10. Theda Skocpol, *States and Social Revolutions* (Cambridge: Cambridge University Press, 1979) p. 29.

11. Louis Althusser, 'Ideology and ideological state apparatuses' in *Lenin and Philosophy* (London: New Left, 1971).

12. Fred Block, 'Beyond relative autonomy: State managers as historical subjects', *Socialist Register*, 1980.
13. Robert Brenner, 'The "Autonomy" of the State', Isaac Deutscher Memorial Lecture, London School of Economics, 21 November 1986.
14. Any concept of 'international society' presupposes a concept of domestic society. On this see Chapter 5.
15. Paul Cammack 'Bringing the State Back In?', *British Journal of Political Science*, vol. 19, April 1989.
16. The long-run implications of foreign policy analysis are such as to challenge the prevailing totality concept of the state: but much of the literature has been within a behavioural framework that ignores the relevance of sociological writing on the state, or has become restricted by a fetishism of decision-making as an end in itself.
17. Charles Tilly, 'War making and state making as organised crime' in Evans *et al.* (eds) *Bringing the State Back In*, and Charles Tilly (ed.) *The Formation of National States in Europe* (Princeton, NJ: Princeton University Press, 1975). For a masterful exposition of the role of violence in constituting modern states see J.B. Barrington Moore, *The Social Origins of Dictatorship and Democracy* (London: Allen Lane, 1966).
18. Goran Therborn, *What Does the Ruling Class do When it Rules?* (London: New Left, 1978) provides an illuminating survey of the relationship of external factors to the functioning of state apparatuses.
19. Felix Gilbert (ed.) *The Historical Essays of Otto Hintze* (New York: Oxford University Press, 1975) chs 4 to 8, provides detailed historical analysis of the relationship between individual state formation and the international competition between states in modern European history. For an illuminating study of the impact of international political factors on state economic policies see Gautam Sen, *The Military Origins of Industrialisation and International Trade Rivalry* (London: Frances Pinter, 1984). Karl Polanyi's *The Great Transformation: The Political and Economic Origins of Our Time* (Boston: Beacon Press, 1957) provides an overview of nineteenth- and twentieth-century history in similar vein.
20. Michael Mann, *The Sources of Social Power*, vol. 1 (Cambridge: Cambridge University Press, 1976); 'The autonomous power of the state: Its origins, mechanisms and results' in John Hall (ed.) *States in History* (Oxford, Blackwell, 1986); Mann, *States, War and Capitalism* (Oxford: Basil Blackwell, 1988), especially Chapter 1.
21. Skocpol, *States and Social Revolutions*, ch. 1.
22. A pioneering survey of the relative international accesses of hegemonic and dominated classes is that of Carolyn Vogler, *The Nation State* (Aldershot: Gower, 1985).
23. Goran Therborn, 'The rule of capital and the rise of democracy', *New Left Review*, no. 103, May–June 1977. As Therborn points out, the principle of 'one person – one vote' was not effective in either the US or the UK until the 1960s.
24. The briefest glance at standard International Relations textbooks can

show how little the implications, theoretical and empirical, of revolutions have been taken into account, with the partial exceptions of discussion of intervention and 'subversion'. For a comparable neglect of the international dimension within most conventional sociological literature on revolution see Stan Taylor, *Social Science and Revolutions* (London: Macmillan, 1984).

25. Raymond Aron, *Peace and War* (London: Weidenfeld & Nicolson, 1966) pp. 373–81.
26. See Martin Wight, *Power Politics* (Harmondsworth: Pelican, 1979) p. 92. In an illuminated footnote, Wight suggests that for the majority of the years between 1942 and 1960 international relations have been 'revolutionary' rather than 'normal'. The implications of this have not, however, been conventionally recognised.
27. Immanuel Wallerstein, *The Modern World System* (London, Academic Press, 1974) and Eric Wolf, *Europe and the People Without History* (Berkeley, CA: University of California Press, 1982).

5 International Theory as Homogeneity

1. For an early discussion of 'homogeneity', see Raymond Aron, *Peace and War* (London: Weidenfeld & Nicolson 1966), pp. 373–81.
2. Alexander Gerschenkron, *Economic Backwardness in Historical Perspective* (Cambridge: Harvard University Press, 1962).
3. See, for example, Leslie Sklair, *Sociology of the Global System* (Hemel Hempstead: Harvester/Wheatsheaf, 1991); and essays by Featherstone, Urry, Robertson and Apparudai in Michael Featherstone (ed.) *Global Culture: Nationalism*, Globalization and Modernity, special issue of *Theory, Culture and Society* (London, Sage, 1990).
4. 'The ends of Cold War' in Robin Blackburn (ed.) *After the Fall* (London: Verso, 1991) pp. 78–99.
5. See, among others, James Mayall, 'International society and international theory' in Michael Donelan (ed.) *The Reason of States* (London: Allen & Unwin, 1978) pp. 122–141; and Hedley Bull and Adam Watson, *The Expansion of International Society* (London: Oxford University Press, 1984).
6. Hedley Bull, *The Anarchical Society: A Study of Order in World Politics* (Basingstoke: Macmillan, 1977) p. 13. Emphasis in the original.
7. Ibid., p. 41, and indeed all of chapter 2.
8. Martin Wight, *International Theory: The Three Traditions*, edited by Gabriele Wight and Brian Porter (Leicester: Leicester University Press; London: The Royal Institute of International Affairs) ch. 3.
9. On the development in English usage of the term 'society', see Raymond Williams, *Keywords* (London: Fontana, 1976).
10. For an account of the term in classical and modern thinking see David

Frisby and Derek Sayer, *Society* (Chichester: Ellis Horwood, London: Tavistock, 1986).

11. An interesting further example of this élitist usage is found in early twentieth-century Russian political vocabulary, where the word *obshchestvo* tended to mean 'educated urban and landowning noble society'. 'The term described those members of the population who, by virtue of education, wealth or public service had an implied right to participate in politics but were thwarted by the state' (David McLaren Macdonald, *United Government and Foreign Policy in Russia, 1900–1914*, London: Harvard University Press, 1992, p. 222, note 5).

12. Martin Wight, *Power Politics* (Harmondsworth: Pelican, 1979) p. 105.

13. On these three interpretations of the concept of hegemony see Brian Turner, Paul Abercrombie and Stephen Hill, *The Dominant Ideology Thesis* (London: Allen & Unwin, 1981). On Gramsci's theory of hegemony, a rather more robust and specific one than its recent occurrence within International Relations literature would suggest, see: Antonio Gramsci, *Selections from the Prison Notebooks*, edited and trans. by Quintin Hoare and Geoffrey Nowell Smith (London: Lawrence & Wishart, 1971); John Cammett, *Antonio Gramsci and the Origins of Italian Communism* (Stanford, CA: Stanford University Press, 1967) ch. 10; and Perry Anderson, 'The antinomies of Antonio Gramsci', *New Left Review*, no. 100, November–December 1976, pp. 5–78.

14. Immanuel Wallerstein, *The Modern World System* (London: Academic Press, 1979); Eric Wolf, *Europe and the People Without History* (Berkeley, CA: University of California Press, 1982); and Eric Hobsbawm, *The Age of Empire* (London: Weidenfeld & Nicolson, 1987).

15. I am particularly grateful to Justin Rosenberg for his many insights on this matter: see his, 'What's the matter with realism?', *Review of International Studies*, vol. 16, no. 4, October 1990, pp. 285–303.

16. Robert O. Keohane and Joseph Nye, *Power and Interdependence* (Boston: Little, Brown, 1977); John Burton, *World Society* and Susan Strange, *States and Markets* (London, Pinter, 1988).

17. Evan Luard, *International Society* (Basingstoke: Macmillan, 1990).

18. Sklair, *Sociology of the Global System*.

19. Featherstone (ed.), *Global Culture*.

20. For a historical overview of the enduring sociological concern with international formation of individual societies see the essay by Bryan Turner, 'The two faces of sociology: Global or national?' in Michael Featherstone (ed.) *Global Culture*.

21. See Chapter 2, pp. 30–1.

22. For an excellent discussion see Joseph Camilleri and Jim Falk, *The End of Sovereignty?* (Aldershot: Edward Elgar, 1992).

23. For critiques of theories of an increasingly 'transnational' economy, see David Gordon, 'The global economy: New edifice or crumbling?' *New Left Review*, no. 168, March–April 1988, pp. 24–64; and Paul

Hirst and Graeme Thompson, 'The problem of "Globalisation" ', *Economy and Society*, vol. 21, no. 4, November 1992, pp. 357–96.

24. As quoted in Adam Watson, *The Evolution of International Society* (London: Routledge, 1992) pp. 206–8. Watson (p. 8) also quotes Gibbon as claiming that 'a philosopher may be permitted to consider Europe as one great republic'. Despite his affiliation to the English school, Watson seems little concerned with the distinction between 'systems' and 'societies' of states. On the eighteenth-century background, and its implications for ideas of a common set of values, see Felix Gilbert 'The "new diplomacy" of the eighteenth century', *World Politics* (1951) pp. 4–5.

25. For a general overview of the implications of Burke's theories for international relations see John Vincent, 'Edmund Burke and the theory of international relations', *Review of International Studies*, vol. 10, no. 3, July 1984, pp. 205–18, and Hans-Gerd Schumann, *Edmund Burke's Anschauungen von Gleichgewicht in Staat und Staatensystem* (Meisenheim: Glan, 1964). For discussion of his later writing on France, with extended excerpts and some commentary, see Conor Cruise O'Brien, *The Great Melody: A Thematic Biography and Commented Anthology of Edmund Burke* (London: Sinclair-Stevenson, 1992) pp. 542–69. He argues that, while Burke was wrong to see the post-1794 regime as revolutionary, he was right in foreseeing Napoleon's pursuit of 'honor, glory and riches' through expansion (p. 555). A discussion of Burke's theory that closely parallels the one here is to be found in Jennifer Welsh's 'Edmund Burke and the Commonwealth of Europe', paper presented to annual conference of British International Studies Association, December 1992.

26. For an interpretation of Burke as in some measure a radical, see Conor Cruise O'Brien, *Introduction to Reflections on the Revolution in France* (Harmondsworth: Penguin, 1968).

27. Burke, *Reflections*, pp. 125–6, 262–5 and 376–7. All other quotations are from *The Works and Correspondence of Edmund Burke*, vol. 5 (London: Francis and John Rivington, 1852).

28. Burke, *Works and Correspondence*, pp. 305–6.

29. Ibid., pp. 320–1.

30. Ibid., pp. 307–9.

31. Ibid., p. 259.

32. Ibid., p. 313.

33. Ibid., p. 322.

34. On this similarity between Marx and other contemporaries see my 'Bringing the economic back in: The case of nationalism', *Economy and Society*, vol. 21, no. 4, November 1992.

35. Quotations from Saint-Simon and discussion in Emile Durkheim, *Socialism and Saint-Simon*, edited by Alvin Gouldner (London: Routledge & Kegan Paul, 1959) pp. 170–5.

36. *Manifesto of the Communist Party* in Karl Marx, *The Revolutions of*

1848: Political Writings, ed. David Fernbach, vol. 1 (Harmondsworth: Penguin Books in association with *New Left Review*, 1973) p. 71.

37. On the changing focus in Marx's work see Teodor Shanin (ed.) *Late Marx and the Russian Road* (London: Routledge, 1983).

38. See Tom Kemp, *Imperialism* (London: Dennis Dobson, 1967); and Bill Warren, *Imperialism: Pioneer of Capitalism* (London: Verso, 1980); Michael Löwy, *The Politics of Combined and Uneven Development* (London: Verso, 1981).

39. Francis Fukuyama, 'The end of history', *The National Enquirer*, Summer 1989; and *The End of History and the Last Man* (London: Hamish Hamilton, 1992).

40. Fukuyama, *End of History*, p. 76.

41. Ibid., pp. xiv–xv.

42. Michael Doyle, 'Liberalism and world politics', *American Political Science Review*, vol. 80, no. 4, December 1986, pp. 115–69.

43. *Manifesto*, p. 71.

44. It may, at first sight, appear unfair to include Ireland in this category, since, in contrast to the fascist countries, it allowed political pluralism and a measure of constitutional liberty from independence in 1922. In certain respects however, particularly under the Fianna Fáil Governments of the 1930s and 1940s, it was engaged in a mild version of semi-peripheral escape: ideological repression through censorship and clerical control of education, economic delinking through import substitution and trade controls, all of this topped off with nationalist cant about Hibernian exceptionalism, in the economy and in the eyes of God.

45. For a brief analysis of the Portuguese case, see my 'Whatever happened to the Portuguese Revolution?', *New Statesman*, 15 April 1992. The argument here is that to see the Portuguese Revolution of 1974–5 as having been 'betrayed' or 'lost' misses the intentions of the majority of those who organised and supported it, which was precisely to fulfil the uncompleted agenda of the 1910 liberal constitutional revolution, to integrate with the rest of Europe and cast off the anachronistic burden of the African colonies.

46. Such comparisons were much less evident in the more insulated political environment of the United Kingdom, where nationalist appeals to British uniqueness, especially on issues of constitutional reform, still seemed to carry the day. One striking exception was the front page headline on the low educational standards in Britain: 'Bottom of the Class – Only Brazil, Mozambique and the old Soviet Union have WORSE schools', *The Daily Mirror*, 13 March 1992.

47. For one attempt to theorise precisely such a process see G. John Ikenberry and Charles A. Kupchan, 'Socialization and hegemonic power', *International Organization*, vol. 44, no. 3, Summer 1990, pp. 283–315.

6 'The Sixth Great Power': Revolutions and the International System

1. See Harry Eckstein, *Internal War* (New York: Free Press, 1964), and James Rosenau, 'Internal War as an International Event' in Rosenau (ed.) note 9 below.
2. This is a core tenet of realism and neo-realism, despite concessions by many realists that the exclusion of internal factors is merely an analytic convenience. Waltz's argument is clearly spelt out in *Theory of International Politics*, ch. 4: I have discussed this assumption and the shifts in argument involved in Chapter 2, above. Examples of conventional IR suppression of the question of the international dimensions of revolution are legion. For example, Jack Plano and Roy Olton's *The International Relations Dictionary*, 4th edn (Santa Barbara: Longman, 1988) has no discussion of the general inter-relationship of the two subjects: an (unindexed)item on revolution and war discusses only internal aspects. IR literature is replete with discussion of alliances, yet rarely is it made clear that (*a*) many alliances have as their original purpose the suppression of revolution within member states and (*b*) that one of the main reasons for the collapse or ending of alliances is that revolutions occur within some of the constituents: the fates of SEATO, CENTO and the Warsaw Pact should make this latter point evident enough – victims, respectively, of the Vietnamese, Iranian and Eastern European upheavals. Indeed CENTO fell victim to revolution twice over: its initial form, the Baghdad Pact, had to be abandoned in favour of CENTO after the Iraqi Revolution of 1958.
3. See for example the overview of the sociological literature in Stan Taylor, *Social Science and Revolutions* (London: Macmillan, 1984).
4. Jack Goldstone, Ted Robert Gurr and Farrokh Moshiri (eds) *Revolutions of the Late Twentieth Century* (Boulder and Oxford: Westview, 1991) p. 41. See also Jack Goldstone, *Revolution and Rebellion in the Early Modern World* (Berkeley and Oxford: California University Press, 1991; Jack Goldstone (ed.) *Revolutions: Theoretical, Comparative and Historical Studies* (London: Harcourt, Brace, Jovanovitch, 1986). For extensive discussion of, and by, Goldstone see *Contention: Debates in Society, Culture, and Science* Winter 1993, no. 5, particularly the article by John Foran, 'Revolutionising theory/Theorising revolutions', which assesses Goldstone's *Revolution and Rebellion*. Foran (p. 73) poses the intriguing question of how far demographic growth can be treated as an independent (by which he means externally determined) variable, and how far it is the result of different, national, processes.
5. Fred Northedge, *The International Political System* (London, Faber & Faber, 1976), pp. 28–30; Waltz, *Theory of International Politics*, pp. 127–8. Despite non-conformity on other matters James Der Derian comes to similar conclusions: *On Diplomacy: The Revolutionary State*

in International Society: A Genealogy of Western Estrangement (Oxford: Basil Blackwell, 1989) p. 198.

6. *Revolution and World Order* (Oxford: Clarendon Press, 1993), pp. 8–11, 40–1, 75–8, 155–7, 242–3, 307–10.

7. I have developed this argument in my *The Making of the Second Cold War* (London: Verso, 1983). Some writers on strategic studies, including Alexander George, Raymond Garthoff and Michael Mandelbaum, have discussed this interrelationship, but it has, in the main, failed to find sufficient place in analyses of the post-war arms race and strategic competition. For example, Garthoff's *Reflections on the Cuban Missile Crisis* (Washington, Brookings Institution, 1987) makes mention of Soviet fears of a US invasion of Cuba but greatly understates the importance of this, eminently rational, concern in the Soviet decision to station missiles on the island. That this was a possibility is confirmed by Pierre Salinger, at that time Kennedy's press secretary: see 'Kennedy and Cuba: The pressure to invade was fierce', *International Herald Tribune*, 6 February 1989. In conventional British academic studies of the nuclear arms race the impact of third world revolutions rates hardly a mention.

8. The chronology of funding and publication of US works on internal wars and their international dimensions tells its own story: a rush of interest, motivated by concern in the wake of the Cuban revolution, in the early 1960s, followed by a taut silence once the difficulties of the Vietnam War became evident. The impact, explicit and tacit, of the Vietnam War on the academic study of International Relations has yet to be analysed.

9. Henry Kissinger, *A World Restored* (Gloucester, MA: Peter Smith, 1973); Richard Rosecrance, *Action and Reaction in International Politics* (Boston: Little Brown, 1963); Martin Wight, *Power Politics* (London: Penguin, 1966), ch. 7; James Rosenau (ed.) *International Aspects of Civil Strife* (Princeton: Princeton University Press, 1964); Kim Kyong-won, *Revolutions and the International System* (London: University of London Press, 1970); and Peter Calvert, *Revolution and International Politics* (London: Frances Pinter, 1984).

10. The hypostatisation of 'terrorism' such that it becomes a term covering a far wider range of actions than the use of terror itself, in academic writing on IR has been one of the the the discipline's more sloppy chapters. Terrorism, in the sensational sense in which it has normally been used, is a subaltern feature of international relations. For historical, and some ethical, perspective see Walter Lacqueur, *Terrorism*, 2nd edn (London: Weidenfeld & Nicolson, 1989); Conor Gearty, *Terror*, (London: Faber & Faber, 1991); Fred Halliday, 'Terrorism in historical perspective', *Arab Studies Quarterly*, vol. 9, no. 2 (Spring 1987).

11. R.R. Palmer, 'The world revolution of the West', *Political Science Quarterly*, vol. 69, no. 1, March 1954; R.R. Palmer, *The Age of the Democratic Revolution, 1760–1800*, 2 vols, (Princeton: Princeton University Press, 1959 and 1964); George Rudé, *Revolutionary*

Europe 1783–1815 (London: Fontana, 1964); Jacques Godechot, *La Grande Nation* (Paris: Aubier, 1956); Eric Hobsbawm, *The Age of Revolution: Europe 1789–1948* (London: Weidenfeld & Nicolson, 1962); E.H. Carr, *The Bolshevik Revolution*, vol. 3 (London: Penguin, 1973); Marcel Liebman, *Leninism under Lenin* (London: Merlin Press, 1975), part 4; Isaac Deutscher, *Marxism, Wars and Revolution* (London: Verso, 1984), and his biographies of Stalin and Trotsky; Neil Harding, *Lenin's Political Thought*, vol. 2 (London: Macmillan, 1981).

12. These points are well brought out in Jack Goldstone, 'Theories of revolution: The third generation', *World Politics*, April 1980.

13. Theda Skocpol, *States and Social Revolutions* (Cambridge: Cambridge University Press, 1979) p. 4.

14. *Der Neuzeitliche Revolutionsbegriff, Entstehung und Entwicklung* (Weimar: Hermann Bohlaus Nachfolger, 1955). A section was translated in Heinz Lubacs, *Revolution* (London: Macmillan, 1968).

15. A classic article that covers some of the same ground as Griewank is A.T. Hatto, ' "Revolution": An enquiry into the usefulness of an historical term', *Mind*, October 1949.

16. Wight, *Power Politics*, p. 92.

17. On the revolutions of the 1640s, see Geoffrey Parker and Lesley Smith (eds) *The General Crisis of the Seventeenth Century* (London: Routledge & Kegan Paul, 1978).

18. See Palmer, 'World revolution', and *Democratic revolution*.

19. Of the eight US presidents between 1945 and 1988 no less than six gave their names to security doctrines designed to contain communist and other radical challenges in the third world: Truman, Eisenhower, Kennedy, Nixon, Carter, Reagan. Lyndon Johnson may have had no doctrine to his name, but he certainly had a practice, in Vietnam and in the Dominican Republic. Only Gerald Ford, a stopgap who occupied the White House for two years after the resignation of Richard Nixon in 1974, was an exception. See Fred Halliday, *Cold War, Third World* (London: Radius/Hutchinson, 1989) ch. 3 for further discussion.

20. I have gone further into the relation between East–West conflict and third world revolution in my *The Making of the Second Cold War* (London: Verso, 1983) and in *Cold War, Third World*. An interesting, if belated, recognition of the linkage is to be found in the Pentagon report, *Discriminate Deterrence* (Washington: Department of Defense, 1989).

21. For example, Andrew Scott, *The Revolution in Statecraft: Informal Penetration* (New York: Random House, 1965). Der Derian, *On Diplomacy* has a similar discussion.

22. An example of such an argument with regard to the Iranian Revolution is to be found in the conclusions to James Bill, *The Eagle and the Lion* (New Haven and London: Yale University Press, 1988): Bill proposes twelve ways in which US policy in such revolutionary

situations can be improved, to reduce conflict with the revolutionary state. These are, in the main, counsels of perfection.

23. Fred Halliday, 'Iranian foreign policy since 1979: Internationalism and nationalism in the Islamic Revolution', in Juan Cole and Nikki Keddie (eds) *Shi'ism and Social Protest* (New Haven and London: Yale University Press, 1986).

24. Raymond Aron, *Peace and War* (London: Weidenfeld & Nicolson, 1966) pp. 373–81. As discussed in Chapter 5, this presumption of homogeneity in internal political and social arrangements is distinct from that found in the English school concept 'international society': the latter is concerned only with homogeneity of international values and practices.

25. Rosenau's concept of 'fused linkage' captures this interrelationship well. On Waltz's refusal to accept this as a legitimate part of IR theory, see Note 2 above.

26. Kim Kyong-won, *Revolution and International System* (New York: New York University Press, 1970).

27. On the contrasting powers of 'dominant ideology' and 'common culture' theses, see Nicholas Abercrombie, Stephen Hill and Brian Turner, *The Dominant Ideology Thesis* (London: Unwin Hyman, 1980). These writers do not discuss how international factors, ideological and more material, can contribute to the formation, strengthening and weakening of specific ideologies, dominant or subordinate, within any one society, but it is not difficult to see how their argument can be extended to show how important such external factors, confirmatory and challenging, can act upon a specific society. The force of example alone plays an important part. One has only to chart the global spread of such phenomena as universal suffrage or respect for human rights, or of religious trends, be these in the Reformation or contemporary Islamic societies, to see how external forces can shape internal ideological systems.

28. Recent contributions to the field include John Hall, *Power and Liberties* (London: Penguin, 1986) and Michael Mann, *States, War and Capitalism* (Oxford: Basil Blackwell, 1988).

29. For historical materialist analyses of international dimensions of revolution, see: Giovanni Arrighi, Terence Hopkins and Immanuel Wallerstein, *Anti Systemic Movements* (London: Verso, 1989); Michael Lowy, *The Politics of Combined and Uneven Development: The Theory of Permanent Revolution* (London: Verso, 1981); Jan Pieterse, *Empire and Emancipation, Power and Liberation on a World Scale* (London: Pluto, 1990); Franz Schurmann, *The Logic of World Power: An Inquiry into the Origins, Currents and Contradictions of World Politics* (New York: Pantheon, 1974).

30. This is one of the main arguments of Paul Kennedy's *Preparing for the Twenty-first Century* (London: Harper Collins, 1993).

7 Hidden from International Relations: Women and the International Arena

1. Among many other contributions to individual branches of the social sciences see, for development studies, Ester Boserup, *Women and Economic Development* (London: Allen & Unwin, 1970), perhaps the first major irruption of feminism into the social sciences, and Kate Young, Carol Wolkowitz and Rosalyn McCullagh (eds) *Of Marriage and the Market* (London: CSE, 1981); for political theory, Anne Phillips, *Engendering Democracy* (Cambridge: Polity, 1991) and Carole Pateman, *The Sexual Contract* (Cambridge: Polity 1988); for anthropology, Henrietta Moore, *Feminism and Anthropology* (Cambridge: Polity, 1988); for history, Sheila Rowbotham, see Note 3, below.
2. Among the rare exceptions of relevant discussion of international relations literature are Georgina Ashworth, 'The UN Women's Conference and international linkages in the women's movement' in Peter Willets (ed.) *Pressure Groups in The Global System* (London: Frances Pinter, 1982), and Ellen Bonepath (ed.) *Women, Power and Policy* (New York and Oxford: Pergamon, 1982) part 4.
3. Sheila Rowbotham, *Hidden From History: Three Hundred Years of Women's Oppression and the Fight Against It* (London: Pluto, 1973).
4. For discussion of this issue see Edward Crapol (ed.) *Women and American Foreign Policy* (Westport, CT: Greenwood, 1987). In the mid-1980s a Women's Foreign Policy Council was established by a group of US women, including Bella Abzug and Mim Kelber, calling for the location of a critical mass of women in senior foreign policy and defence positions.
5. Quoted in Anna Davin, 'Imperialism and motherhood', *History Workshop Journal*, no. 5, spring 1978, p. 29.
6. On the Sandinistas, see Maxine Molyneux, 'The politics of abortion in Nicaragua: Revolutionary pragmatism – or feminism in the realm of necessity?', *Feminist Review*, no. 29, spring 1988, p. 123. On Saddam see 'Saddam Hussein awards medals to women, says their role more important than men's', *BBC Summary of World Broadcasts*, Part 4, 7 March 1992, ME/1323/A/4–7.
7. Without claiming that this attitude was universal, or constituted the inner truth of hegemonic expansion in the post-war epoch, it is worth recording the fictional rendering of the US mission as conveyed in Norman Mailer's account of the CIA in the Cold War, *Harlot's Ghost* (London: Abacus, 1992) pp. 734–5. Ruminating on his colleague Sherman's visits to the brothels of Montevideo the narrator speculates: 'He saw himself, good yeoman legionnaire of the American Empire, as owning the females in the countries through which he travelled . . . Or was I, all regional differences to the side, close to describing myself as well?
   Even as I was buying my hour from one girl that night, and a second

women for a second hour, and feeling freer with these strangers than in all my twenty-five years . . . maybe the taproot where my greed was stored was pouring out at last into the American Century, and I, too, was out there copulating for the flag. Greed having transmuted itself into a more noble emotion, I felt a glow of inner power as if I were finally attached to the great wheeling scheme of things.'

8. On Machiavelli, Hanna Fenickel Pitkin, *Fortune is a Woman: Gender and Politics in the Thought of Niccolo Machiavelli*, (Berkeley: University of California Press, 1984). On Western theory more generally, Susan Moeller Okin, *Women in Western Political Thought* (Princeton: Princeton University Press, 1979); Diana Coole, *Women in Political Theory* (Brighton: Wheatsheaf, 1988).

9. 'Letters on a Regicide Peace', Letter I, in *The Works and Correspondence of Edmund Burke*, vol. 5, p. 257.

10. The classic, and very funny, account of this is Carol Cohn, 'Sex and death in the rational world of defense intellectuals', *Signs*, vol. 12, no. 4, summer 1987. The voyeurism suggested by Pentagon videos of cruise missiles hitting their targets in the Kuwait war may not have escaped viewers.

11. For general work on political theory and gender see Anne Phillips *Engendering Democracy* (Cambridge, Polity, 1991) and Carol Pateman, *The Sexual Contract* (Cambridge: Polity, 1988); and Okin and Coole, note 7. For a critical overview of feminist-IR writing see Marysia Zalewski, 'Feminist theory and international relations' in *From Cold War to Collapse: Theory and World Politics in the 1980s* (Cambridge: Cambridge University Press, 1993). On international political theory see the chapter by J. Ann Tickner in Rebecca Grant and Kathleen Newland *Gender and International Relations* (Milton Keynes: Open University Press, 1991) and her *Gender in International Relations* (Oxford: Columbia University Press, 1992).

12. On this see the reports Dame Anne Warburton, *EC Investigative Mission into the Treatment of Muslim Women in the Former Yugoslavia, Report to the EC Foreign Ministers*, February 1993; Amnesty International, *Bosnia-Herzegovina: Rape and Sexual Abuse by Armed Forces*, January 1993.

13. On the Red Army see the symptomatic exchange between Stalin and his Yugoslav interlocutors on the subject in Milovan Djilas, *Conversations With Stalin* (London: Penguin, 1962) p. 87–8. Later (p. 132) we learn that Marshal Zhukov had been dismissed from his post as commander of the Soviet forces for stealing jewellery in occupied Berlin: 'You know, Comrade Stalin cannot stand immorality', one of his advisers confides in the author.

14. For an overview of literature on this see Ruth Pearson, 'Latin American women and the new international division of labour: a reassessment', *Bulletin of Latin American Research*, vol. 5, no. 2, 1986, and, for an earlier analysis, Diane Elson and Ruth Pearson, 'The subordination of women and the internationalisation of factory production' in Kate Young, Carol Wolkowitz and Rosalyn

McCullagh, *Of Marriage and the Market: Women's Subordination in International Perspective* (London, CSE, 1981).

15. Haleh Afshar and Carolynne Dews (eds) *Women and Adjustment Policies in the Third World* (London: Macmillan, 1992); Jeanne Vickers, *Women and the World Economic Crisis* (London: Zed, 1991).

16. Maxine Molyneux, 'Marxism, feminism and the demise of the Soviet model' in Grant and Newland (eds) *Gender and International Relations* and her 'The "women question" in the age of perestroika', *New Left Review*, 183, September–October 1990; Peggy Watson 'The new masculinism in Eastern Europe', *New Left Review*, no. 198, March–April 1993.

17. She was one of the originators of the theory of 'proletarian internationalism'. Dominique Desanti, *Flora Tristan: Vie, Oeuvre Mêlées* (Paris: Union generale d'editions, 1973).

18. For discussion of these issues see Sharon Macdonald, Pat Holden and Shirley Ardener (eds) *Images of Women in Peace and War* (London: Macmillan, 1987), especially the essay by Ruth Pearson who develops the distinction between a feminist critique based upon ideas of motherhood and one deriving from women's separation from the means of warfare. An excellent discussion of issues involved is Micaela di Leonardo, 'Morals, mothers and militarism: Anti-militarism and feminist theory', *Feminist Studies*, vol. 11, no. 3, Fall 1985.

19. See Anne Wiltsher, *Most Dangerous Women: Feminist Peace Campaigners of the Great War* (London: Pandora, 1985) and Lela Costin 'Feminism, pacifism, internationalism and the 1915 International Congress of Women' in Judith Stiehm (ed.) *Women and Men's War* (Oxford: Pergamon, 1983). A fascinating study of the relationship between the suffragette movement, the trades unions and the Irish independence movement on the eve of the First World War is given in George Dangerfield, *The Strange Death of Liberal England* (New York: Capricorn, 1961). Dangerfield's thesis is that the combination of these three opposition forces was threatening to overthrow the British state, and that the challenge was only deflected by the outbreak of war.

20. Stiehm (ed.), *Women and Men's War*; Jean Bethke Elshtain, *Women and War* (New York: Basic, 1987). Elshtain's earlier work has been subject to considerable debate as in Judith Stacey, 'The new conservative feminism', *Feminist Studies*, autumn 1983.

21. Judith Stiehm, *Bring Me Men and Women: Mandated Change at the US Air Force Academy* (Berkeley, CA: University of California Press, 1972); Cynthia Enloe, *Does Khaki Become You? The Militarisation of Women's Lives* (London: Pluto Press, 1983); Wendy Chapkis (ed.) *Loaded Questions: Women in the Military*, (Amsterdam: Transnational Institute, 1981).

22. On US military use of women in the Gulf War and elsewhere see, *inter alia*, Helen Vozelinker, 'Women in the military: deceptive feminist gain', *In These Times*, 17–23 April 1991. Discussing the case

of Captain Linda Bray, who led a troop of soldiers in Panama, she writes:'I would like a woman who kills a battering spouse to get as much publicity and praise as did Capt. Bray and the women who served in the Gulf'.

23. On the UN Decade for Women see Carolyn Stephenson in Stiehm (ed.) *Women and Men's War*. The classic study of women and development remains Ester Boserup, *Women's Role in Economic Development*. Also, Gita Sen and Caren Grown, *Development, Crises and Alternative Visions: Third World Women's Perspectives* (New York: Monthly Review, 1987).

24. On women and the EEC see Catherine Hoskyns, 'Women, European law and transnational politics', *International Journal of the Sociology of Law*, vol. 14, no. 3/4, winter 1986, and 'The community of women', *Marxism Today*, January 1987.

25. *BBC Summary of World Broadcasts*, Part 4, 31 January 1989, ME/ 0372 A/5.

26. Jeffrey Robinson, *The End of the American Century; Hidden Agendas of The Cold War* (London: Hutchinson, 1992) pp. 290–1.

27. For a comprehensive overview, see Kumari Jayawardena, *Feminism and Nationalism in the Third World* (London: Zed, 1986). For critical assessments see Jan Pettiman, *Living in the Margins: Racism, Sexism and Feminism in Australia* (Sydney: Allen & Unwin, 1992) and Deniz Kandiyoti, 'Identity and its Discontents: Women and the nation', *Millennium*, vol. 20, no. 3, 1991; Nira Yuval Davis and Floya Anthias (eds) *Woman, Nation, State* (London: Macmillan, 1989) and Deniz Kandiyoti, *Women, Islam and the State* (London: Macmillan, 1991).

28. Norberto Bobbio, *Liberalism and Democracy* (London: Verso, 1990) pp. 68–72.

29. Virginia Woolf, *A Room of One's Own. Three Guineas* (Oxford: Oxford University Press, 1992) p. 313. The discussion of woman and war in Woolf contrasts with the very different picture contained in a work of literature produced in the very same year, Brecht's *Mother Courage and Her Children* (London: Methuen Drama, 1990): in the latter, the mother is not against war as such, since it enables her to make money, and she indeed puts her commercial preoccupations, epitomised in her cart, above her supposedly maternal ones, embodied in her children, or any general 'womanly' commitment to peace. At one point, when there are rumours of peace, Mother Courage says: 'Peace'll wring my neck. I went and took Chaplain's advice, laid in fresh stocks only t'other day. And now they're going to demobilise and I'll be left sitting on me wares' (p. 63); her response to the death of her daughter is to go on with her profiteering business (p. 87). Both works were written in 1938, in the shadow of the oncoming world war and contain uncanny resonances of the classic IR work of E.H. Carr, *The Twenty Years' Crisis*, written at the same time.

30. J.P. Nettl, *Rosa Luxemburg*, abridged edn. (Oxford: Oxford University Press, 1969) pp. 500–19; and Horace B. Davis (ed.) *The*

National Question: Selected Writings by Rosa Luxemburg (New York: Monthly Review, 1976).

31. These issues of women's rights and nationalist 'authenticity' have been posed especially sharply in countries where religion constitutes the national position on women: Ireland, Algeria and Iran have all been cases of this. A searing critique of 'reverse ethnocentricity' and the use of national-religious ideology to subordinate women in Iran is given by Azar Tabari, 'The women's movement in Iran: A hopeful prognosis', *Feminist Studies*, vol. 12, no. 2, Summer 1986. Similar issues with regard to Iran are posed by Kate Millett, *Going to Iran* (New York: Coward, McCann and Geohegan, 1982). For a debate on 'feminist orientalism', see Mai Ghoussoub, 'Feminism – or the eternal masculine – in the Arab world', *New Left Review*, no. 161, January–February 1981, and the articles in *New Left Review*, no. 170, July–August 1988.

32. See, for example, two *Focus* briefings by Amnesty International, 'Women and human rights', March 1990, 'Against their will: Rape and sexual abuse in custody', February 1992. The work of the Change network and of its organiser Georgina Ashworth, was also important in affecting non-governmental and state activity.

33. *International Herald Tribune*, 'Seoul tells Japan: Compensate women', 22 January 1992; 'Of sex and lies: Japanese teacher debunks "comfort women" myths', *IHT*, 29 January 1992; George Hicks 'They won't allow Japan to push the "comfort women" aside', *IHT*, 10 February 1993. Later in 1993 the Japanese Government reached agreement with the Korean Government on the compensation question.

34. 'Rape victim's case stirs Unionist fears', *The Guardian*, 20 February 1992.

35. Georgina Ashworth, 'A Feminist Foreign Policy', talk given to LSE International Relations Department General Seminar, February 1987.

36. See Chapter 5.

37. For one characteristic variant of this see Christopher Coker 'Women and international relations', *The Salisbury Review*, June 1990.

38. Some of those concerned with this issue are also concerned with the question of title: the arguments for 'women and international relations' as against 'gender and international relations' have been well rehearsed, with the former suggesting a marginalisation from the mainstream of the discipline and the latter committing the course to consideration of the constitution of gender beyond an examination of women themselves. In practice, there may be less difference in the course and research programmes of these two titles than at first sight appears. A programme entitled 'Women and International Relations' perhaps promises a less ambitious programme than a course claiming to encompass the broader range of questions raised by analysing gender, the latter comprising constructions and uses of masculinity and of alternative sexualities within the international sphere.

39. On the feminist critique of post-modernism and with special reference to IR see the trenchant remarks of Marysia Zalewski in 'Feminist theory and international relations', Mike Bowker and Robin Brown (eds) *From Cold War to Collapse: Theory and World Politics in the 1980s* (Cambridge: Cambridge University Press, 1993). More generally, see Sabina Lovibond, 'Feminism and postmodernism', *New Left Review*, no. 178, November–December 1989, 'Feminism and Pragmatism: A reply to Richard Rorty', *New Left Review*, no. 193, May–June 1992, and Kate Soper 'Postmodernism, subjectivity and the question of value', *New Left Review*, no. 186, March–April 1991.

8 Inter-Systemic Conflict: The Case of Cold War

1. J.L. Gaddis, 'The emerging post-revolutionist synthesis on the origins of the cold war', *Diplomatic History*, Vol. 7, 1983.
2. For one overview of the critical literature see Michael Cox, 'Radical theory and the new Cold War' in Mike Bowker and Robin Brown (eds) *From Cold War to Collapse: Theory and World Politics in the 1980s* (Cambridge: Cambridge University Press, 1993). Cox has many pertinent things to say about the writings of radical writers on the Cold War, but he misrepresents two issues with regard to my own writing: first, while I argued that the historical responsibility of East and West was distinct, my work was precisely an attempt to look at the dynamic relationship between the two blocs and to see how each had contributed; secondly, he appears to accept, in an uncritical way, claims about Soviet expansionism in the third world. Most importantly, Cox seems to think that in the end the Cold War ended through mutual accommodation, thus missing the rather large historical fact that one side capitulated and its socio-political system collapsed. His own, largely implicit, theory bears traces of a residual Trotskyism ('they are only two gangs of capitalists anyway'), evident in his earlier work (see note 8). In these writings, still under the influence of a 'state capitalist' Trotskyist approach, Cox advances many of the arguments with which he was later to belabour other writings, including the thesis that only socialist renewal in East and West could bring peace to the continent. Most pertinently, however, he argues that the Soviet Union presented no challenge to the West or the West to the Soviet Union.
3. For earlier discussion of this literature see my *The Making of the Second Cold War* (London, Verson, 1983), ch. 2, and 'Vigilantism in international relations: Kubalkova, Cruickshank and Marxist theory', *Review of International Studies*, vol. 13, no. 3, 1987.
4. Thus in his textbook of realist theory, *The Anarchical Society*, Hedley Bull treats East–West conflict in the post-war period as illustration and confirmation of this broader argument. Many others –

Morgenthau, Waltz, etc. – did likewise. For realists, there was not a conceptual problem.

5. As discussed in Chapter 6, the argument that the conflict between revolutionary and status quo powers was in some sense avoidable is found, *inter alia*, with regard to the French revolution in Kim Kyong-won, *Revolution and International System* (New York: New York University Press, 1970), and with regard to Iran in James Bill, *The Eagle and the Lion*.

6. As quoted in Cox, 'Radical theory and the new Cold War', p. 44. For an attempt to engage with Chomsky on these issues see my discussion with him in Bill Bourne, Udi Eichler and David Herman (eds) *Writers and Politics* (Nottingham: Russell Press, 1987).

7. Mary Kaldor, *The Disintegrating West* (London: Penguin, 1978) and *The Imaginary War: Understanding East–West Conflict* (Oxford: Basil Blackwell, 1990); Alan Wolfe, *The Rise and Fall of The 'Soviet Threat'* (Washington: Institute for Policy Studies, 1979).

8. 'Western capitalism and the Cold War System' in Martin Shaw (ed.) *War, State and Society* (London: Macmillan, 1984); 'The Cold War as a System', *Critique*, no. 17, 1986.

9. E.P. Thompson, Fred Halliday and Rudolf Bahro, *Exterminism and Cold War* (London: Verso, 1982).

10. For one recognition of this inter-systemic dimension see Oyrind Osterud, 'Intersystemic rivalry and international order: Understanding the end of the Cold War' in Pierre Allan and Kjell Goldmann (eds) *The End of The Cold War* (London: Martinus Nijhoff, 1992).

11. 'The sources of Soviet conduct', *Foreign Affairs*, July 1947.

12. In Evan Luard (ed.) *Basic Texts in International Relations* (Macmillan, 1992) pp. 478–9.

13. Two classic discussions of heterogeneity within mainstream IR literature are Richard Rosecrance, *Action and Reaction in International Politics* (Boston: Little, Brown, 1963) and Raymond Aron, *Peace and War* (London: Weidenfeld & Nicolson, 1966).

14. Vendulka Kubalkova and Albert A. Cruickshank, 'The new Cold War' in 'Critical international relations studies', *Review of International Studies*, vol. 12, no. 3, July 1986, and Fred Haliday, 'Vigilantism in International Relations: Kubalkova, Cruikshank and Marxist Theory' *Review of International Studies* vol. 13, no. 2, April 1987.

15. Carl Schmitt, *The Concept of The Political* (New Brunswick: Rutgers University Press, 1976); Paul Hirst, 'Carl Schmitt's decisionism', *Telos*, no. 72, summer 1987.

16. A powerful historical account of the universalising drive of capitalism can be found in Eric Hobsbawm, *The Age of Empire* (London: Weidenfeld & Nicolson, 1987). What is striking is that this generally accepted historical thesis, and one eloquently stated in the *Communist Manifesto*, should have had so little impact on much left-wing writing on Cold War in the 1980s: assertions that capitalism *did*

have a tendency both to prevail over alternatives to it, and to establish global hegemony, was deemed to play into the hands of Soviet policy; instead we had the debatable symmetry of the internalists.

17. For accounts of the subjugation of the GDR, see the diary of Kohl's political adviser Horst Teltschik, *329 Tage: Innenansichten der Wiedervereinigung* (Berlin: Siedler Verlag, 1991) and Ulrich Albrecht, *Die Abwicklung der DDR* (Opladen: Westdeutscher Verlag, 1992).

18. The Soviet term 'correlation of forces', a supposedly more dynamic and materialist alternative to the 'balance of power' was never taken seriously in the West and was abandoned in the 1980s in the USSR: in fact, it has proved its validity, precisely because it did take socio-economic and ideological factors in international competition into account and did see the possibility of a decisive shift in favour of one bloc. That it mistook which bloc would benefit from a shift in the correlation was perhaps a secondary oversight. For a lucid analysis of the concept see Margot Light, *The Soviet Theory of International Relations* (Brighton: Wheatsheaf, 1988); and Julian Lider, *Correlation of Forces: An Analysis of Marxist-Leninist Concepts* (Aldershot: Gower, 1988).

19. Chapter 6.

20. Giovanni Arrighi, Terence Hopkins and Immanuel Wallerstein, *Anti-Systemic Movements* (London: Verso, 1989).

21. Roger Owen, *The Middle East in the World Economy 1800–1914*, 2nd edn (London: I.B. Tauris, 1993).

22. For applications of these ideas to the collapse of the Soviet bloc see also my 'The ends of Cold War', *New Left Review*, no. 180, March–April 1990.

9 A Singular Collapse: The Soviet Union and Inter-State Competition

1. It is striking that the *end* of the Cold War provoked rather more theoretical reflection than did the Cold War itself. See Pierre Allan and Kjell Goldmann (eds) *The End of The Cold War* (London: Martinus Nijhoff, 1992); J.L. Gaddis, 'International relations theory and the end of the Cold War', *International Security*, vol. 17, no. 3, 1992–3; Lynn Eden, 'The end of U.S. Cold War history? A review essay', *International Security*, vol. 18, no. 2, 1993. See also my 'The ends of Cold War', *New Left Review*, no. 180, March–April 1990; George Schopflin, 'Why communism collapsed', *International Affairs*, January 1990; Gale Stokes, 'The lessons of 1989', *Problems of Communism*, vol. XL, no. 5, September–October 1991; Daniel Deudney and John Ikenberry 'Soviet Reform and the end of the Cold War: Explaining large-scale historical change', *Review of International Studies*, vol. 17, no. 3, July 1991.

2. For the argument as to why, on economic grounds, the state socialist model could not work, despite initial successes and a margin for reform, see Wlodzimierz Brus and Kazimierz Laski, *From Marx to Market* (Oxford: Clarendon Press, 1989), and Daniel Deudney and John Ikenberry 'Soviet Reform'.

3. Theda Skocpol, *States and Social Revolutions* (Cambridge: Cambridge University Press, 1979); Ellen Kay Trimberger, *Revolution From Above* (New Brunswick, NJ: Transaction, 1978).

4. Moshe Lewin, *The Gorbachev Phenomenon* (London: Radius, 1988) is a lucid overview of the social and economic preconditions for the breakdown of the Brezhnevite order in the 1980s.

5. Much has been made of the concept 'mixed economy' in the context of both systems in the 1980s, yet, on more precise examination, two kinds of mixed economy are indicated – a 'socialist' and a 'capitalist' variant, e.g. a Yugoslavia and a Sweden. A clear distinction still operated between those where the state played the dominant role, with or without sectoral markets in some areas of production, and those where the market, in both production and capital, prevailed, with or without a significant state role in terms of ownership, employment, fiscal regulation, policy coordination.

6. On the failure of the Yugoslav and Hungarian reforms see Brus and Laski, *From Marx to Market*.

7. Gorbachev's declarations up to the end of 1987 at least endorsed the traditional view that socialism had superior potential to capitalism. As late as the autumn of 1989 he seems to have believed that Eastern European countries would maintain socialism even after the Soviet tanks had withdrawn (conversation with Georgi Shakhnazarov, Gorbachev adviser, Moscow, 10 June 1993).

8. Arno Mayer, *Why Did the Heavens Not Darken?* (London: Verso 1990) ch. 1, in which the 'general crisis' of the twentieth century is depicted.

9. Immanuel Wallerstein, *Historical Capitalism* (London: Verso, 1986) for a cogent survey of this process.

10. See note 1 for further discussions of this theme.

11. Skocpol, *States and Social Revolutions*, remains a classic exposition of this thesis.

12. On the arms race see Fred Halliday, *The Making of the Second Cold War* (London, Verso, 1989) ch. 3.

13. This was conventionally known as the 'arms race theory of arms control'.

14. In the early 1970s Taiwan spent 10 per cent of GNP on military expenditure, Israel 20 per cent: International Institute of Security Studies, *The Military Balance, 1972–1973*, London.

15. US expenditure in 1971 was $120 billions, as against Soviet $94 billions, in 1980 $111 billions as against $107. Total expenditure by the Soviet Union and its allies was only half that of its opponents, NATO and its Far Eastern allies (China, Japan): in 1980 $120 billions for the WTO (Warsaw Treaty Organisation) as against $243

billions. All data from *SIPRI Yearbook* 1981, figures in constant 1978 prices. US expenditure was conventionally understated by a number of accounting devices: one calculation was that the 1980 figure of $127 billions should be adjusted upwards to $223 billions, i.e. from 5.2 per cent to 9.5 per cent of GNP: James Cypher in *Monthly Review*, November 1981.

16. See Brus and Laski, *From Marx to Market.*
17. For a Soviet view of the western embargo see Igor Artemiev 'International economic security' in *International Economic Security: Soviet and British Approaches*, Chatham House Discussion Paper no.7, 1988.
18. Galia Golan, *The Soviet Union and National Liberation Movements in the Third World* (London: Unwin Hyman, 1988); Jerry Hough, *The Struggle For The Third World: Soviet Debate and American Options* (Washington: Brookings Institution, 1986); Fred Halliday, *Cold War, Third World*, ch. 4, for the rethinking of Soviet policy towards the third world.
19. According to OECD DAC figures.
20. On 'stagnation' see Mikhail Gorbachev *Perestroika: New Thinking for Our Country and the World* (London: Collins, 1987) ch. 1.
21. On the NATO–WTO comparison see Note 15, above. The degree of economic integration between the Eastern European Comecon members was far less than that within the EEC: most trade was on a bilateral, Soviet–East European, basis.
22. Hedrick Smith, *The Russians* (London: Sphere Books, 1976) gives a powerful evocation of this attitude in the period prior to the collapse of Soviet confidence.
23. Gorbachev's *Perestroika* is replete with calls for the Soviet economy to rise to 'world standards' i.e. those of the West.
24. On Kohl's calculations in this period see the diary of his political adviser, Horst Teltschik, *329 Tage: Innenansichten der Einigung* (Berlin: Siedler Verlag, 1991).
25. Teltschik, *329 Tage*, pp. 54–6.
26. Seminar by Gerald Mansell, former head of BBC Overseas Broadcasting, LSE, November 1992.

10 International Relations and the 'End of History'

1. For overviews see Mike Bowker and Robin Brown (eds) *From Cold War To Collapse: Theory and World Politics in the 1980s* (Cambridge: Cambridge University Press, 1993); Robin Blackburn (ed.) *After the Fall: The Failure of Communism* (London: Verso, 1991); Michael Hogan (ed.) *The End of The Cold War, its Meaning and Implications* (Cambridge: Cambridge University Press, 1992); Gabriel Partos, *The World That Came in from the Cold* (London: BBC World Service/

Royal Insitute of International Affairs, 1993); Horst Teltschik, *329 Tage: Inneinansichten der Einigung* (Berlin: Seidler Verlag, 1991).

2. As in the term used by Jurgen Habermas, *die Nachholende Revolution*, the 'catching-up' or 'recuperating' revolution: 'What does socialism mean to-day? The revolutions of recuperation and the need for new thinking' in Blackburn (ed.) *After the Fall*. Habermas may have intended some contrast with the previous orthodox communist view of the (socialist) revolution as *uberholend*, 'over-taking', the capitalist west.

3. For one interesting optic see Gale Stokes, 'The lessons of 1989', *Problems of Communism*, vol. 40, no. 5, September–October 1991.

4. Richard Rosecrance, 'A new concert of powers', *Foreign Policy*, vol. 71, no. 2, spring 1992; John Mearscheimer 'Back to the future': Instability in Europe after the Cold War', *International Security*, vol. 15, no. 1, summer 1990.

5. 'Liberalism and world politics', *American Political Science Review* vol. 80, no. 4, December 1986, and the two-part 'Kant, liberal legacies and foreign affairs' in *Philosophy and Public Affairs*, vol. 12, summer 1983, and autumn 1983. For a trenchant critique of ideological misuses of the Doyle argument, but not of the core argument itself, see Benedict Anderson, 'The new world disorder', *New Left Review*, no. 193, May–June 1992.

6. For a perceptive, fictional, location of communism in the broader current of rationalist and messianic thought, Christian and Judaic, see George Steiner, *Proofs and Three Parables* (London: Faber & Faber, 1992).

7. Perry Anderson, *A Zone of Engagement* (London: Verso, 1992), pp. 367–9.

8. On secession see James Mayall, *Nationalism and International Society* (Cambridge: Cambridge University Press, 1990) and Alexis Heraclides, *The Self-Determination of Nationalities in International Politics* (London: Frank Cass, 1991).

9. For a corrective to the prevailing view of nationalism as the dominant ideology of the age see Eric Hobsbawm, *Nations and Nationalism Since 1870* (Cambridge: Cambridge University Press, 1990).

10. See Chapter 11, Note 3, p. 276.

11. For a general overview of the war see Lawrence Freedman and Efraim Karsh, *The Gulf Conflict 1990–1991: Diplomacy and War in the New World Order* (London: Faber & Faber, 1992). On casualties see John Heidenrich, 'The Gulf War; How many Iraqis died?', *Foreign Policy*, no. 90, spring 1993.

12. For an excellent overview of the issues involved, see Joseph Camilleri and Jim Falk, *The End of Sovereignty? The Politics of a Shrinking and Fragmenting World* (Aldershot: Edward Elgar, 1992). On the internationalisation of finance, see Susan Strange, *Casino Capitalism* (Oxford: Basil Blackwell, 1986).

13. *Preparing for the Twenty-First Century* (London: Harper Collins, 1993).

14. I am grateful to Meghnad Desai and other colleagues in the LSE Centre for the Study of Global Governance for stimulating discussions on this issue.
15. On Fukuyama see Perry Anderson, 'The ends of history' in *A Zone of Engagement*; History Workshop, *After the End of History* (London: Collins & Brown, 1992); Gregory Elliott, 'The cards of confusion: Reflections on historical communism and the "end of history" ', *Radical Philosophy*, no. 64, summer 1993.
16. Immanuel Wallerstein, *Historical Capitalism* (London: Verso, 1983, p. 98): 'It is simply not true that capitalism as a historical system has represented progress over the various previous historical systems that it destroyed or transformed'.
17. An example of this is to be found in the otherwise measured assessment by Martin Walker, *The Cold War and the making of the Modern World* (London: Fourth Estate, 1993), ch. 14, 'The Superlosers'. A liberal critic of US policy, Christopher Lasch could write (*International Herald Tribune*, 13 July 1990): 'If the West won the Cold War, the United States can hardly be said to have shared in the fruits of that victory. It would be closer to the truth to say that the Soviet Union and the United States have destroyed each other as major powers.'
18. On the debate with the socialist movement on the significance of Cold War see the contributions by Mike Davis and myself to *Exterminism and Cold War* (London: Verso, 1983), ch. 2 of my *The Making of the Second Cold War*, and the exchanges in Robin Blackburn (ed.) *After the Fall* (London: Verso, 1991).
19. Ch. 23, 'The "Unreality" of realism'.
20. For Fukuyama, humans demand recognition of their worth and revolt, or fight, when they do not get it. This is why they are not just content with economic well-being, which a prosperous dictatorship could provide, but need democracy and a measure of equality as well. He is on to something here: no one can deny that this is a factor in the political activity of humans, at the interpersonal, national and international levels. Yet, as rendered in his book, this invocation of *thymos* is forced. First, even granting that there is a thymotic instinct as he describes it, like other instincts – smiling, eating, touching, etc. – it only takes on a meaning in a social context. Moreover, what constitutes acceptable dignity or recognition varies from historical period to period, and from one society to another: what is tolerable in one place and time is not in another, let alone variations across gender. *Thymos* is a social construct: there can be no meaningful invocation of *thymos* if it does not take account of the socialisation of people into groups and collectivities, and, regrettably, of what one may only term the anti-thymotic, q.v. Dostoevsky.

The apparent authority of the concept of thymos is derived from Fukuyama's reading of Plato's *Republic*, via Allan Bloom, but this part of the operation is thin indeed, reminding the Marxist of nothing so much as the attempt to squeeze a general theory of socialist politics out of some decontextualised lines of Marx, Lenin or Mao. In classical Greek the word *thymos* means rage, or lust (for food or drink) and is a quality associated with animals and spirited horses. Interestingly, in this original meaning it approximates to the Arabic word *thawra*, contemporary Arabic for revolution, but in origin a word denoting the spiritedness of bulls and other animals. In Plato himself it has a more specific meaning akin to self-respect – 'the part that loves honour and winning'. But even Plato's usage does not square with that of Bloom/Fukuyama, as a reading of other commentators indicates, and he is misreading Plato to imply that the soul has 'parts' at all, since all Plato meant by 'parts of the soul' was that people are complex. For different accounts of *thymos* in Plato see R.C. Cross and A.D. Woozley, *Plato's Republic: A Philosophical Commentary* (London: Macmillan, 1964) pp. 120–1; and Julia Annas, *An Introduction to Plato's Republic* (Oxford: Clarendon Press, 1981) pp. 126–8. *Thymos* is identified with the irrational, since it is the seat of anger and rage, akin to spirit or heart, and is something that approximates, though Fukuyama evidently does not feel this is appropriate, to psychoanalytic concepts of the id. The key story that Fukuyama invokes, from Plato, to illustrate the concept itself points in another direction: it concerns Leontius, the son of Aglaion, who, while walking near the walls of Athens, sees some bodies lying under the wall, at first turns away his eyes, and then out of curiosity looks. He is then ashamed and angry with himself, suffering an attack of *thymos*. This is a story anyone can understand, but it hardly illustrates the Fukuyama concept of *thymos*, which is both relational, involving what others think of one, and about recognition, not anger. All of which suggests that whatever the validity of the insights on the role of recognition in politics, the derivation of it amidst a flurry of textual back-up is inconclusive.

21. Giovanni Arrighi, 'World income inequalities and the future of socialism', *New Left Review*, no. 189, September–October 1989.
22. Goran Therborn 'The rule of capitalism and the rise of democracy', *New Left Review*, no. 103, May–June 1977.

11 Conclusion: The Future of International Relations

1. For discussion of ethical issues in the international domain see, *inter alia*: Janna Thompson, *Justice and World Order: A Philosophical Enquiry* (London: Routledge, 1992); Terry Nardin and David Mapel (eds) *Traditions of International Ethics* (Cambridge: Cambridge University Press, 1992); Charles Beitz, *Political Theory and International Relations* (Guildford, Surrey: Princeton University Press, 1979); Mervyn Frost, *Towards a Normative Theory of International Relations* (Cambridge: Cambridge University Press, 1986).
2. Ernest Gellner, *Nations and Nationalism* (Oxford: Blackwell, 1983); Elie Kedourie, *Nationalism* (London: Hutchinson, 1960).

3. For further discussion see Fred Halliday, 'The Gulf War and the study of international relations', *Review of International Studies*, vol. 20, no. 1, January 1994.
4. On the uprising and its aftermath see Kanan Makiya, *Cruelty and Silence* (London: Century Hutchinson, 1993).
5. James Mayall, 'Non-intervention, self-determination and the "new world order" ', *International Affairs*, vol. 67, no. 3, July 1991; Christopher Greenwood, 'Is there a right of humanitarian intervention?' *The World To-day*, vol. 49, no. 2, February 1993; Adam Roberts, 'Humanitarian war: Military intervention and human rights', *International Affairs*, Vol. 69, No. 3, July 1993; Hedley Bull (ed.) *Intervention in World Politics* (Oxford: Clarendon Press, 1984).
6. For the debate in the Arab world see Kevin Dwyer, *Arab Voices* (London: Routledge, 1991) and Anne Mayer, *Islam and Human Rights: Tradition and Politics* (London: Pinter, 1991). Mayer is particularly interesting on the manipulation of the third world critique by interested parties within Islamic states.

Name Index

Subject Index